For Frederic O Hatch

from

Donald Gottwald

Xmas 1948

THE JUDICIAL OPINIONS OF
OLIVER WENDELL HOLMES

★

MR. JUSTICE HOLMES A FEW YEARS AFTER HIS
APPOINTMENT TO THE SUPREME COURT
IN WASHINGTON

THE JUDICIAL OPINIONS OF OLIVER WENDELL HOLMES

———◆▶◆◆◀———

*CONSTITUTIONAL OPINIONS,
SELECTED EXCERPTS AND EPIGRAMS
AS GIVEN IN THE SUPREME JUDICIAL
COURT OF MASSACHUSETTS
(1883–1902)*

★

BY

HARRY C. SHRIVER, A.B., LL.M.
*Member of the Bar of the District of Columbia
and of the Supreme Court of the United States*

WITH A FOREWORD BY
FRANCIS BIDDLE
*Solicitor General of United States and
Formerly Judge of the Circuit Court of Appeals Third Circuit*

DENNIS & CO., INC.
LAW BOOK PUBLISHERS
BUFFALO, N. Y.
1940

Copyright 1940 by
DENNIS & CO., INC.

A MAN'S SPIRITUAL HISTORY IS BEST TOLD IN WHAT HE DOES IN HIS CHOSEN LINE

★

FOREWORD

A good deal more is yet to be written about Mr. Justice Oliver Wendell Holmes. I know of two or three books now in the preliminary stage. Mr. Shriver's collection of Massachusetts decisions, therefore, is a useful step in bringing together typical data and clearing the way for synthesis and for a more creative approach than I have yet found. For the coming lay biographer, in a mass of material which is so chiefly legal, in a background where the figure of a witty and liberal man of the world emerges too readily because of his brilliant talk and writing, must have a sense of the simple and profoundly American sources of his subject's background. These opinions, usually a little longer and less inevitable than those which came down when Holmes was on the United States Supreme Court, show many of his convictions already crystallized. The approach, of course, was the immediate result of his research which had culminated in the "Common Law," published just before he went on the state court, reaching for unity in his own thinking. We find conclusions which occur again and again later. Thus he says in an opinion written in 1900: "I think it pure phantasy to suppose that there is a body of capital of which labor as a whole secures a larger share by that means (a strike). The annual product, subject to an infinitesimal deduction for the luxuries of the few, is directed to consumption by the multitude, and is consumed by the multitude, always" (p. 75). This is a recurring belief which he liked to confirm by examples in his own experience, such as the impossibility, as he once told me, of finding a designer for a piece of jewelry; they were all working for the multitude who bought paste at the five and tens.

Here and there are charming examples of his beautifully accurate wit, of the way he had of touching rather unpromising facts into sudden incandescence. He suggests: "If it is a bad rule, that is no reason for making a bad exception to it" (p. 288). And again: "A boy who is dull at fifteen probably was dull at fourteen" (p. 288). Or, with a polite but none the less satisfying irony: "If a single woman not otherwise distinguished should be minded to prolong the remembrance of her family name by a beautiful monument over her grave, we could not pronounce it unsuitable or improper as a matter of law" (p. 291). The first expresses both his passion to generalize and to simplify, his need, as a philosopher, to find the ultimate behind the confused stream of facts; and then to express the result with lucid casualness, in order, as it were, to avoid making a display of the labor of thinking which had brought it about. The two last are, I think, typical of his warm instinct for everyday reality, which made his opinions glow out of the solid legal frames about them.

—Francis Biddle

August, 1940

PREFACE

The plan and purpose of this present work is to give in a concise and compact form a selection of the judicial opinions of Justice Oliver Wendell Holmes (1841–1935) as handed down by him while on the bench of the Supreme Judicial Court of Massachusetts (1883–1902). This selection is intended not only for professional lawyers, but also for the appreciation of those admirers of Holmes who do not follow the legal profession.

For twenty years prior to his appointment by President Theodore Roosevelt to the United States Supreme Court in 1902, Justice Holmes had served on the Supreme Judicial Court of Massachusetts. His tenure of office as a Massachusetts judge began on January 3, 1883, and ended on December 8, 1902, with the last three years serving as Chief Justice. As a State judge, Justice Holmes wrote about thirteen hundred opinions. The extent and value of his early judicial contribution might well be compared to that of other eminent American jurists, such as Kent, Shaw, Ruffin, and Cooley.

It is not an easy matter for the student of Holmes to have access to his principal opinions. Holmes' State court opinions are scattered throughout forty-nine volumes of the Massachusetts official reports. It is there that we must go in order to obtain a picture of Holmes' contribution to the legal science, his understanding and interpretation of what constitutes the rights and duties between the State and the individual, as well as a broader conception of his social philosophy of the law.

Justice Holmes' decisions have been found to be the expression of a true and great mind, embodying a soul bent upon the task of aiding to adjust the problems of life, the social differences great and small as we find them represented in everyday litigations.

But the work of a lifetime for other men was but the prelude for Holmes. We know by this time that his greatest and most brilliant achievements occurred during the thirty years he spent in Washington as a Justice on the United States Supreme Court. In recent years much has been written upon his work as a United States judge to the exclusion of his earlier judicial career. It is this lacuna in our empirical knowledge of Holmes that the author is trying to correct.

Although Holmes' social ideas are expressed at their best in his United States Supreme Court opinions, the understanding of their interpretation and background will be found to a large degree in his earlier State Court findings as a Massachusetts judge. Moreover, we also find that these earlier opinions of Holmes no less reflect the same profound concept of the law and much of the impressive style and clarity of thought than those found in his federal opinions.

The selection of opinions presented in this work has been gathered from the forty-nine volumes of Massachusetts State Reports (134 Mass. 26 to 182 Mass. 348), and has been made to include the important judicial findings of Justice Holmes, particularly in matters of conflict between the laws of the State and the social interests and rights of the individual.

Part I of this volume contains Holmes' principal opinions bearing on Constitutional Law, with a few opinions of kindred interest such as the rights of eminent domain, taxation, and labor contracts. The opinions selected are given in their entirety. Some citations have been purposely omitted in order to avoid any interruption in the reading. Whenever the facts of the case are not stated within the text of the opinion, they will be found briefly set forth at the beginning of each case.

Part II consists of excerpts and epigrams gathered from Holmes' other State Court opinions. The excerpts and epigrams are presented chiefly because of their lasting value and general interest apart from their legal relation.

Five appendices of complementary interest to Holmes' judicial career are also given at the end of this work to supplement the author's efforts in trying to present that great American jurist to a more extended reading group than the professional lawyers.

The author of this collection wishes to express his appreciation and gratitude to Edward Dumbaugh, Esq., Assistant to the Attorney General of United States, for reading the draft of the manuscript and for his many valuable suggestions and constructive criticism in the final preparation of this work.

H. C. S.

Law Library,
Library of Congress,
Washington, D. C.
April, 1940

CONTENTS

Foreword _____ vii–viii
Preface _____ ix–xi
Contents _____ xii–xvi

Part I

CONSTITUTIONAL OPINIONS

Chapter 1.—Legislative Freedom.   PAGE
  May Cities and Towns Engage in Business? _____ 5
  Power of Legislature to Grant Women Suffrage _____ 6
  Right to Fix Reasonable Water Rates _____ 10
  May an Insurance Broker Be an Agent of the Insured? 19
  Constitutionality of Pensions _____ 23
  Control by the Legislature over Public Works _____ 28
  Use of Election Voting Machines _____ 33
  Right of Legislature to Provide a Remedy Affecting
    Pending Cases _____ 39
  Restoration of Remedy Extinguished by Lapse of Time 44

Chapter 2.—Freedom of Speech.
  May a Policeman Talk Politics? _____ 51
  Speeches on the Boston Common without a Permit __ 54

Chapter 3.—Capital and Labor.
  Withholding Labor's Wages _____ 59
  Right to Picket _____ 62
  Enticing Servants from Their Masters _____ 70
  Boycotts and Strikes to Unionize Shops _____ 73
  Inducements to Violate a Labor Contract _____ 76

Chapter 4.—Bill of Rights.
  May the Form of Indictments Be Changed? _____ 81
  Right of Trial by Jury _____ 83
  Poor Debtors—Imprisonment _____ 85
  Dilatory Tactics and Constitutional Guarantees _____ 89
  Cruel or Unusual Punishment? _____ 95
  Ex Post Facto Laws _____ 99

PAGE

Appointment of Temporary Guardian of Insane Person without Notice _____ 103

CHAPTER 5.—IMPAIRMENT OF OBLIGATION OF CONTRACT.

Foreign Creditor's Rights in Massachusetts _____ 109
Discharge in Insolvency No Bar to Non-Resident Creditor _____ 112
Discharge No Bar to Action on Debt Due a Partnership _____ 117
Foreign Corporation Doing Business in Massachusetts _ 120
Foreign Judgment Creditor's Ancillary Administrator _ 124
Right to Be Second Assistant Engineer in a Fire Department _____ 128

CHAPTER 6.—FULL FAITH AND CREDIT CLAUSE.

Applying the Law of Another State _____ 133
Judgment in Another State without Service of Process _ 136
Effect of Invalid Marriage upon Right of Issue to Inherit _____ 140
Validity of Divorce Obtained in Another State _____ 150

CHAPTER 7.—DUE PROCESS UNDER THE MASSACHUSETTS CONSTITUTION.

Obligations Arising out of the Marriage Status _____ 159
Right of Legislature to Limit Height of Boundary Fences _____ 162
More about Boundary Fences _____ 167
A Railroad Sues a Passenger for His Fare _____ 169
Right of State to Kill Diseased Horses _____ 171
Powers of Board of Aldermen _____ 181
Validity of Ordinance Forbidding Selling in Streets ___ 184
Being Present Where Gaming Instruments Are Found _ 186
Flimsy Exceptions _____ 190
Statute Giving Labor an Additional Remedy _____ 195
Right of City Council to Fix Sewage Charges _____ 196
Assessing Abutters for Betterments _____ 200
Rights of a Non-Resident Alien _____ 207
Payment for Public Works _____ 212
A Statute Is Held Unconstitutional _____ 217
What Is Gambling? _____ 220

[xiii]

	PAGE
Mortgagee's Right of Redemption—Class Legislation	222
More Betterment Assessments	224
Validity of a Sewer Assessment	234

CHAPTER 8.—DUE PROCESS UNDER THE FEDERAL CONSTITUTION.

Right of Legislature to Establish Land Court	241
Liability of Foreign Corporation in Cross-Action	254
Holding Act of a Neighboring State Unconstitutional	258

CHAPTER 9.—MISCELLANEOUS CONSTITUTIONAL CASES.

What Is a Taking of Property under the Constitution?	265
Limiting Height of Buildings near the State House	269
Is the Practice of Medicine a Business?	274
Is Injury to a Business an Appropriation of Property?	278

PART II

EXCERPTS AND EPIGRAMS

1. Appeal for Enhancing Punishment	285
2. Estoppel *In Pais* Like Nebuchadnezzar's Image	285
3. Decisions More Important Than Simple Test	285
4. Effect of Dislike of Litigation	285
5. Disturbing a Rule of Property	285
6. Acquittal from a False Charge by Honest Means	285
7. Licensee's Risk	286
8. General Maxims Used as Excuse for Analysis	286
9. Construing Declarations	286
10. Lack of Technical Accuracy	286
11. Legislation Often Tentative	287
12. Good Intentions No Excuse for Slander	287
13. Giving Known Language Different Meaning	287
14. Risks from Known Causes	287
15. Establishing Jurisdiction	288
16. Bad Rule No Reason for Bad Exception	288
17. Law Tending to Consistency of Theory	288
18. Living on an Estate	288
19. Values Anticipations of Future	288
20. Boy Dull at Fifteen	288
21. Guarding Pleadings against Perverse Ingenuity	288
22. Occasional Jolt	289
23. A Libel and Categorical Certainty	289
24. Defendant's Recalcitrance	289
25. Ready-Made Generalizations	289

		PAGE
26.	Shifting One's Own Misfortunes	290
27.	Trespasser Not an Outlaw	290
28.	Ignorance of Men Enough Uncertainty	290
29.	Justification for a Libel	290
30.	Costumes Worn by Dancing Women	290
31.	Defeating a Man's Gain	291
32.	Civil Proceedings Not Scientific Investigations	291
33.	Idiomatic Interpretation	291
34.	Technicalities in Legal Distinctions	291
35.	Monument over Grave	291
36.	Literal Sense of Words	292
37.	Discretion vs. Authority	292
38.	Libel	292
39.	Standard of Care	294
40.	Standard of Good Faith in Sales	295
41.	Public vs. Private Interest	295
42.	Act of the Sovereign Power	296
43.	Public Funds for Band Concert	296
44.	A Corporation Is a Fiction	297
45.	Pitfalls in the Use of a Formula	297
46.	What Is Fraud	297
47.	Duty Regarding Trap-Doors	298
48.	Importing a Rule of Construction in Will Cases	298
49.	Collateral Issues—Dealings with Cheats	299
50.	Judicial Review	299
51.	Crossing Railway Tracks When Train Is Approaching	299
52.	Assent Is a Matter of Overt Acts	299
53.	Promotion of a Lottery	300
54.	Assent and Undisclosed State of Mind	300
55.	Immunity of Sovereign from Suit	300
56.	Inferences and Presumptions	300
57.	Agreed Facts Not Like Contracts	301
58.	Cannon Fired on Boston Common	301
59.	Is Stone Porch a Portico or Bay Window?	302
60.	Use of One's Land	303
61.	Reasonable Man vs. Private Taste	304
62.	Infringement of Trade-Marks	305
63.	Following the Precedents	305
64.	Libel and Privileged Communications	305
65.	Liability for Servant's Torts	306
66.	School Land Used for Town Way	307
67.	Barbarous Isolation of States	307
68.	Standards of Conduct Laid Down by Judges	307
69.	Property Value When Street Discontinued	307
70.	Public Monopoly	308
71.	Early Law Is Matter of Antiquarianism	308

		PAGE
72.	Balance of Interests	308
73.	Presumptions of Fact Major Premises of Inferences	309
74.	Statute of Frauds—Instrument of Fraud	309
75.	Horse Car Cannot Be Handled Like a Rapier	309
76.	Sacramental Words and Statutory Power	310
77.	Legislation and Paramount Principles	310
78.	Bad Faith—Assumption of Risk	310
79.	Presumptions of Fact Are for the Jury	311
80.	Law Aims to Prevent External Results Not to Punish Sins	312
81.	Policy and Custom Draw Line between Opposing Interests	312
82.	Contact of Decisions Clustering around Opposite Poles	313
83.	Every Dog Entitled to One Worry	313
84.	Abnormal Meaning of Words	314
85.	Trade-Mark—Waltham Watch	314
86.	Line between the Lawful and Unlawful	315
87.	Fair Cash Value	315
88.	Meaning of Words	315
89.	Advantages of Widow without Troubles of Wife	316
90.	Growth of the Law and Judicial Legislation	316
91.	Liability and Immunity	317
92.	Decision Could Be Made Either Way	318
93.	No Fiction of Identity between Mother and Child	318
94.	Conflicting Social Desires	318
95.	Liability for Unforeseen Wrongs	319
96.	Domicil	320

PART III

APPENDIX I:—Judges of the Massachusetts Supreme Judicial Court Contemporary with Justice Holmes ___ 323

APPENDIX II:—Number of Opinions Written by Holmes 324

APPENDIX III:—Number of Dissenting *Opinions* of the Individual Judges of the Massachusetts Supreme Judicial Court ___ 325

APPENDIX IV:—Number of Dissenting *Votes* of the Individual Judges of the Massachusetts Supreme Judicial Court ___ 326

APPENDIX V:—Chronological List of Cases in Which Justice Holmes Wrote an Opinion ___ 327

INDEX TO CASES ___ 357

PART I

CONSTITUTIONAL OPINIONS

CHAPTER 1
LEGISLATIVE FREEDOM

The asterisks which recur throughout the opinions in Part I refer to citations of decisions which have been omitted.

★

COLBURN, J.   WILLIAM ALLEN, J.   FIELD, J.   MORTON, C. J.   DEVENS, J.   CHARLES ALLEN, J.   HOLMES, J.

SUPREME JUDICIAL COURT
1882–1885

MAY CITIES AND TOWNS ENGAGE IN BUSINESS?

Opinion of the Justices
155 Mass. 598, 607 (1892)

[The Massachusetts House of Representatives requested the opinion of the Justices of the Supreme Judicial Court as to the constitutionality of a proposed bill to enable cities and towns to purchase, sell, and distribute coal and wood as fuel. Chief Justice Field, and Justices Allen, Knowlton, Morton and Lathrop answered in the negative. Barker said, yes "if the necessities of the people can be met only in that way." Holmes' opinion follows.]

I am of opinion that when money is taken to enable a public body to offer to the public without discrimination an article of general necessity, the purpose is no less public when that article is wood or coal than when it is water, or gas, or electricity, or education, to say nothing of cases like the support of paupers or the taking of land for railroads or public markets.

I see no ground for denying the power of the Legislature to enact the laws mentioned in the questions proposed. The need or expediency of such legislation is not for us to consider.

POWER OF LEGISLATURE TO GRANT WOMAN SUFFRAGE

Opinion of the Justices
160 Mass. 586, 593 (1894)

[The Massachusetts House of Representatives requested the opinion of the Justices of the Supreme Judicial Court upon the following questions:

1. Is it constitutional, in an act granting to women the right to vote in town and city elections, to provide that such act shall take effect throughout the Commonwealth upon its acceptance by a majority vote of the voters of the whole Commonwealth?

2. Is it constitutional to provide in such an act that it shall take effect in a city or town upon its acceptance by a majority vote of the voters of such city or town?

3. Is it constitutional, in an act granting to women the right to vote in town and city elections, to provide that such an act shall take effect throughout the Commonwealth upon its acceptance by a majority vote of the voters of the whole Commonwealth, including women specially authorized to register and to vote on this question alone?]

If the questions proposed to the justices came before us as a court and I found myself unable to agree with my brethren, I should defer to their opinion without any intimation of dissent. But the understanding always has been that questions like the present are addressed to us as individuals and require an individual answer.

It is assumed in the questions that the Legislature

persons deeming themselves aggrieved by the price charged for water by any such company may, in the year eighteen hundred and ninety-eight and every fifth year thereafter, apply by petition to the Supreme Judicial Court, asking to have the rate fixed at a reasonable sum, measured by the standard above specified; and two or more judges of said court, after hearing the parties, shall establish such maximum rates as said court shall deem proper; and said maximum rates shall be binding upon said water company until the same shall be revised or altered by said court pursuant to this act."

When we first read this sentence the impression of some of us was that it was an attempt to make out of this court a commission for the taking of one step in fixing a legislative rule of future conduct, irrespective of any present relation between the parties concerned, and that it was no more competent for the Legislature to impose or for us to accept such a duty than if the proposition were to transfer to us the whole lawmaking power. See *Smith* v. *Strother,* 68 Cal. 194. But upon further reflection it seems to a majority of the court that the act can be sustained. If we can do so without perverting the meaning of the act, we are bound to construe it in such a way that it will be consistent with the Constitution, and we think that this can be done without any wresting of the sense, even if we should doubt, which we do not intimate that we do, whether the Legislature had the limit of its power distinctly in mind.

The statute goes upon the footing that every taker of water from the companies in question has a right to be furnished with water at a reasonable rate. No one questions the power of the Legislature to require these water companies to furnish water to the takers at reasonable rates. (*Attorney General* v. *Old Colony Railroad,* 160 Mass. 62, 86, 87; *Spring Valley Water Works* v. *Schottler,* 110 U. S. 347, 354; *Budd* v. *New York,* 143 U. S. 517, 537, 549, 552), and this statute does require the companies to do so, and thereby gives to water takers a corresponding right, or declares that they have it. It is with the relations between actual water takers and the companies that the statute calls on this court to deal. It does not undertake merely to make of the court a commission to determine what rule shall govern people who are not yet in relation to each other, and who may elect to enter or not to enter into relations as they may or may not like the rule which we law down: it calls on us to fix the extent of actually existing rights. With regard to such rights judicial determinations are not confined to the past. If it legitimately might be left to this court to decide whether a bill for water furnished was reasonable, and, if not, to cut it down to a reasonable sum, it equally may be left to the court to enjoin a company from charging more than a reasonable sum in the immediate future.

But it has been regarded as competent for a court to pass on the reasonableness of a rate even when established by the Legislature, to the extent of declaring it unreasonably low. * * * *A fortiori,* when the rate is established by the company and it has undertaken to charge the plaintiff a sum which he alleges to be unreasonable, and the Legislature in terms has referred him to this court, this court has "jurisdiction to inquire into that matter and to award to the [plaintiff] any amount exacted from him in excess of a reasonable rate." *Reagan* v. *Farmers' Loan and Trust Co.* 154 U. S. 362, 397.

It is true that in *Reagan* v. *Farmers' Loan and Trust Co.* it was said, also, that "it is not the function of the courts to establish a schedule of rates," 154 U. S. 400; and to that proposition we fully agree. But it will be observed that the proposition is laid down in connection with the statement that "the challenge in this case is of the tariff as a whole, and not of any particular rate upon any single class of goods." Probably to prepare a new schedule, or to rearrange the old one, would have gone beyond the scope of the rights immediately affected or threatened in the case before the court, into the realm of abstract law making for the future, and so beyond the power of the court; and, if it had not been beyond the court's power, still very possibly it might have been refused in the court's discretion, the court leaving it to the proper body to undertake that task. But it is implied that if the challenge had been of a single rate threatened to be charged for a service demanded, the court might have determined the question between the parties for the immediate future, as it is stated three pages earlier that the court would determine it with regard to a charge for past services. When you are prepared to say that a given charge is too high or too low, it hardly would be consistent to say that you had not power or ability to say what is a proper charge.

It is true that the phrase "shall establish such maximum rates as said court shall deem proper," and the following provision that such "maximum rates shall be binding upon said water company until the same shall be revised or altered by said court," etc., suggest that the Legislature had in mind the establishment of a rate to be charged to all parties for the use of water for domestic purposes, and not merely a rate to be charged the petitioner. It may be that the former was the main object which the Legislature had in mind. But although we cannot doubt that the meaning of the words last quoted is that the rate shall be binding as a general rate, even that is not said distinctly, and we feel bound to assume in support of the act that the Legislature is dealing primarily with the rights of the party aggrieved before the court, and only secondarily adopts in advance the rate thus fixed between the parties as a general rate for all. If this is so, the question whether such a legislative consequence can be attached to the decision is not before us. Even if it should fail, the failure would not necessarily affect the constitutionality of sending "persons deeming themselves aggrieved" to this court to get their rights settled. But as it is not likely that a rate thus established for a given moment after full investigation would be departed from upon the application of a second person similarly circumstanced, it may be questioned whether there is anything to prevent the Legislature from sanctioning without further hearing a rate which once has been declared judicially to be reasonable. It is to be remarked in this connection that the decisions which we have cited for the proposition that the Legislature may require rates to be reasonable, establish the further proposition that the Legislature may fix what the rates shall be, subject only to judicial inquiry whether they are so unreasonably low as to deprive the company of its property without due compensation.

It will be understood from the reasoning on which we sustain the act that the court would not regard itself as warranted or called on to undertake the fixing of rates except so far as they concern interests actually and legitimately before the court.

The liberty to apply to this court is confined to the year 1898 and every fifth year thereafter, so that seemingly it is contemplated that the rate when fixed will remain unchanged for five years. This is another indication that the Legislature had its attention directed to the establishment of a general rate. But supposing a party aggrieved should obtain an injunction, obviously the decree would be drawn so as to bind the defendant for a reasonable time, or, if it were drawn in the common form, subject to review on a change of circumstances, the court would not be likely to grant leave to file a bill of review until a reasonable time had elapsed, and if the Legislature should say that in these cases five years was a reasonable time, we could not say that it was wrong. It is true that the party aggrieved is not given an injunction in terms by the act, and this is another peculiarity in the procedure, looking as it does to a decree affecting the future. Of course it is assumed, and no doubt rightly, that a company would not venture to disregard the decree. But if a company should prove recalcitrant, in case such disregard should not be construed as *ipso facto* a contempt, undoubtedly the decree could be enforced by injunction.

There is still one more peculiarity in the statutory proceedings which adds a little to the difficulty of the question before us. We have construed the statute to deal primarily with existing rights and grievances. But the proceedings are given to "the selectmen of a town, or any persons deeming themselves aggrieved." So far as the alternative mention of the selectmen should be used as an argument that the primary purport of the act was not to deal with present rights, we should answer that it does not appear that the towns within the ten mile radius do not all of them take water in their corporate capacity, and if it was assumed by the Legislature that they did, as they probably do, the argument would lose its force. It may be that the Legislature thought of the selectmen rather as representing the whole body of water takers in the town. Whether they could be made compulsory agents to represent private interests in that way it is not necessary to inquire. We may add that we understand the demurrer to be intended to raise the single question of constitutionality, and therefore we do not consider whether the petition in strictness ought not to show that the town or whoever may be represented by the petitioning selectmen is a water taker, and, in short, disclose enough to make out a present grievance. If there is any defect of form, which we do not intimate, probably it could be amended.

One question remains. The fixing of a reasonable rate is not left at large to the court. The rate is to be "a reasonable sum, measured by the price ordinarily charged for a similar service in the other cities and towns within said metropolitan district." Of course it is argued that this is an attempt to let one company fix a price for another. To a certain extent the standard runs in a circle, since the price charged by water companies in the other towns within ten miles of Boston also may come before this court for revision. But leaving that consideration on one side, it is evident that the Legislature regarded the cities and towns referred to as constituting a class; and while a mere accumulation of instances is not evidence of what is reasonable, the general practice in the class to which a case belongs stands on a different footing, and if the circumstances are sufficiently similar may be instructive. See *McMahon* v.

McHale, ante, 320; *Veginan* v. *Morse,* 160 Mass. 143, 148.

As has been said, the cases establish the power of the Legislature to fix rates, subject to the qualification that they shall not be unreasonably low. It cannot be assumed on demurrer, as against the implied opinion of the Legislature, that the circumstances are not similar, or that all the prices in the ten mile circuit will be unreasonable. If in the opinion of the court at any time they should be so, no doubt in that event it would be bound to disregard the standard of comparison set for it by the act. The governing requirement is that the price should be reasonable. But, especially in view of the fact that companies furnishing the standard have before them the possibility of a petition like the present, such a possibility is not to be feared.

It is suggested that the duty to be done by the court sitting with two justices, under this statute, calls for an investigation of details and the consideration of matters of administration which cannot properly be required of the Supreme Judicial Court. If an extended investigation of accounts or an examination of minute details is necessary in the hearing upon this petition, it will be in the power of the court to appoint a master, in accordance with the practice of the court in equity, to hear the parties and report the facts. The statute authorizes a novel proceeding not known to the common law. It does not say whether it shall be deemed a proceeding at law or a proceeding in equity. In some particulars it is more nearly analogous to suits in equity than to suits at law. It is a judicial investigation in aid of a legislative regulation. In actions at law, when accounts are involved, an auditor may be appointed. The Legislature must be presumed to have intended that the court should have the assistance of a master when needed in hearing such matters as have always been heard by masters under the equity practice of the court.

Demurrer overruled.

MAY AN INSURANCE BROKER BE AN AGENT OF THE INSURED?

Commonwealth v. *Nutting*
175 Mass. 154 (1900)

[Nutting was indicted under a Massachusetts statute (St. 1894, c. 522, secs. 87, 98) and found guilty of negotiating and transacting unlawful insurance with a foreign insurance company not admitted to do business in that Commonwealth. Chief Justice Holmes upheld the statute and the case was later affirmed by the United States Supreme Court, see 183 U. S. 553.]

The defendant is indicted for acting in the negotiation and transaction of unlawful insurance by negotiating in Boston with foreign insurers not admitted to do insurance business in this Commonwealth, and procuring a policy of insurance upon a vessel in Boston, to be issued by them. The agreed facts sustain the indictment subject to certain questions which are brought before us by exceptions to a ruling that the facts warranted the jury in finding the defendant guilty, and to the refusal of several requests which need not be mentioned in detail.

The foundation of the defendant's argument is the decision in *Allgeyer* v. *Louisiana,* 165 U. S. 578. That was a proceeding by the State to recover a penalty for violating a State law intended to prevent dealing with any marine insurance company that had not complied with the law. The defendants were the parties insured. The policy, an open one, was issued outside the State, and the only act done within the State was the mailing of a letter describing certain cotton to which the defendants desired the policy to attach. But the court intimate[d] somewhat broadly that a State legislature cannot make it unlawful for a man to make a contract of insurance outside the State, although he resides and is present in the State at the time when the contract is made. It now is contended that, if this is so, it cannot be unlawful for another man to obey a request to get such insurance, if made by the one who wants it, and that the contract in the present case was made outside the Commonwealth, on principles which cannot be affected by St. 1894, c. 522, sec. 3. It might be argued further that at the least this was not unlawful insurance, and so that this particular indictment fails, whether the defendant had done a punishable act or not.

We bow to the decision, and even to the intimations of the case cited, without criticism. But that case expressly leaves intact the settled power of the State to impose such conditions as it pleases upon the doing of any business by foreign insurance companies within its borders. Although the reasoning of many of the cases turns on the fact that such companies are corporations, we apprehend that the power is not dependent upon that fact, but is an unsurrendered portion of the State's general right to legislate. See 165 U. S. 591; *Leavenworth* v. *Booth,* 15 Kans. 627, 634. One main object in imposing such conditions in this Commonwealth is to secure people against fraudulent or worthless contracts, and, in case of litigation, to save them from having to go abroad. See *Lamb* v. *Lamb,* 6 Biss. 420, 422. We assume, until it is decided otherwise, that the power to enforce these objects will be regarded as too important and substantial to be defeated by a device, even though the device apart from its purpose would only embody a common law right. We are of opinion, therefore, that notwithstanding the right of McKie, if so minded, to apply from Boston to the London Lloyds for insurance, the Legislature has power to prohibit the agents of the Lloyds as well as the Lloyds themselves from soliciting business in Boston, and to make that prohibition effectual by providing that it shall not be escaped by an agreement making the solicitors the agents of the insured in the transaction. In other words, while the Legislature cannot impair the freedom of McKie to elect with whom he will contract, it can prevent the foreign insurers from sheltering themselves under his freedom in order to solicit contracts which otherwise he would not have thought of making. It may prohibit not only agents of the insurers, but also brokers, from soliciting or intermeddling in such insurance, and for the same reasons. What we have said goes very little if any further than what is laid down in similar terms in *Hooper* v. *California,* 155 U. S. 648, 657, 658, and the authority of that case is saved in terms in *Allgeyer* v. *Louisiana,* and is recognized again in *Orient Ins. Co.* v. *Daggs,* 172 U. S. 557, 566. See further *Pierce* v. *People,* 106 Ill. 11.

What the Legislature can do it has done by St. 1894, c. 522. By sec. 3, "it shall be unlawful . . . for any person as insurance agent or insurance broker to make, negotiate, solicit, or in any manner aid in the transaction of" insurance upon any property or interests in this Commonwealth or with any resident thereof, except as authorized by the act. By sec. 98, "any person . . . who shall act in any manner in the negotiation or transaction of unlawful insurance with a foreign insurance company not admitted to do business in this Commonwealth or who as principal or agent shall violate any provision of this act in regard to the negotiation or effecting of contracts of insurance" is subjected to a penalty.

Whether the description of the insurance in the indictment as unlawful be rejected as surplusage, or whether the insurance be held to be unlawful within the meaning of the act and indictment because transacted through a broker acting unlawfully, an offence under the statute is set forth and the defendant properly was convicted. It is unnecessary to consider whether the same result could be reached in another way. Possibly, for the reasons given above, it would be within the power of the Legislature to enact that the insurance broker should be regarded as the agent of the insurers, whatever the agreement of the parties, and in that way reach the result that any contract made through him when he and the insured were here would be made in this State and thus would be subject to our laws. Possibly it might be argued that such was the effect of our statute, although, if so, it fails to state it as clearly as could be wished. See sec. 3, end, 87, 90.

Exceptions overruled.

CONSTITUTIONALITY OF PENSIONS

Opinion of the Justices
175 Mass. 599 (1900)

[The Massachusetts Senate requested the opinion of the Supreme Judicial Court upon the following questions: (1) Has the General Court the right to appropriate money to pay to the widow, heirs or legal representatives of a person who died while holding an office, the salary of which is payable from the treasury of the Commonwealth or from the treasury of a county, city or town, the salary, for any period of time after such decease, to which such person would have been entitled if living and continuing to hold such office? (2) Has the General Court the right to authorize a county, city or town to appropriate money to pay to the widow, heirs or legal representatives of a person who died while holding an office, the salary of which is payable from the treasury of such county, city or town, the salary, for any period of time after such decease, to which such person would have been entitled if living and continuing to hold such office? This opinion was signed by all the justices. The language seems to be that of Chief Justice Holmes.]

The questions, as we understand them, both assume that there was no provision of law in existence before the death of the officer by which the money in question would be payable as supposed. If such a provision should be enacted with regard to the widow, heirs, or legal representatives of a living officer, it naturally would be regarded as pledging the faith of the State to the officer himself, and thus as constituting part of the consideration for his future service. We understand the questions to refer to payments which technically are pure gratuities. We also understand them to refer to payments of money raised by taxation in the ordinary way.

In general the power to pay gratuities to individuals is denied to the Legislature by the Constitution. Ordinarily a gift of money to an individual would be an appropriation of public funds to private uses which could not be justified by law. *Mead* v. *Acton,* 139 Mass. 341. * * * We deem this proposition so plain that we de not delay to enforce it, but it is not a proposition which disposes of the question before us. For it is hardly less clear that when a public purpose can be carried out or helped by spending public money, the power of the Legislature is not curtailed or destroyed by the fact that the money is paid to private persons who had no previous claim to it of any kind.

We need not illustrate by cases where the payment is made on the footing that there would have been an obligation had not one party been the sovereign power and where the public advantage is in the manifestation that the sovereign power is just. We will take a case which is in the strictest sense a gift. A conspicuous example which occurs to every one is the granting of military pensions after a war. The soldiers have been paid all to which they are entitled, yet the State may grant them a partial or total support for disabilities contracted in service. Such a gift may be intended primarily for an object which is no more private than is a memorial hall. *Kingman* v. *Brockton,* 153 Mass. 255, 256. It may be meant to bring home to all minds by visible facts that now, as of old, the courage of the battlefield is honored, and that if a man will risk his life for his country, his country afterwards will not necessarily hold him to the letter of his generous bond and deem him fully paid at thirteen dollars a month.

In the language of the Supreme Court of the United States, the "power to grant pensions is not controverted, nor can it well be, as it was exercised by the States and by the Continental Congress during the war of the Revolution; and the exercise of the power is coeval with the organization of the government under the present constitution, and has been continued without interruption or question to the present time." *United States* v. *Hall,* 98 U. S. 343, 346. * * *

If the power of Congress is unquestioned, that of the State legislatures under their broader authority is still less questionable, subject to some inquiry as to what would be legitimate occasions for exercising it, for which we need not stop. On January 16, 1781, it was resolved that there be allowed and paid to the non-commissioned officers and soldiers "who were engaged to serve during the war on or before the second day of December last, the sum of twenty-four dollars in silver or gold equivalent thereto as a gratuity . . . as a testimony of the sense this Commonwealth entertains of their faithful services." Resolves, 1780, January session, c. 9. See c. 39 and c. 240. There were many special resolves of the same kind. So far as we have seen expressions of opinion by the courts of other States, they agree with what we have quoted from the Supreme Court of the United States, and with what is to be inferred from the practice of our own Legislature within four months of the time when the Constitution had come into force. * * *

If further justification for the power to grant military pensions be needed, Article 6 of the Bill of Rights recognizes that advantages distinct from those of the community may be conferred upon the consideration of services rendered to the public. And although in *Brown* v. *Russell,* 166 Mass. 14, 22, 23, it was intimated as the prevailing view of the court that, so far as these words were applicable to the filling of public offices, they must be taken to refer to services to be rendered, that conclusion was drawn from the dependence of the advantages upon the office, not from a general construction of the words. That the words include past as well as future services is shown by the authorities and facts to which we have referred, and perhaps is indicated by the mention of rewards and immunities in Chapter 5, section 2, of the second part of the Constitution.

The power to give rewards after the event for conspicuous public service, if it exists at all, cannot be limited to military service. If a man has deserved greatly of the Commonwealth by civil services, the public advantage of recognizing his merit may stand on ground as strong as that for rewarding a general. We cannot foresee the possibilities of genius or distinguished worth and settle in advance the tariff at which its action shall be paid.

It will be plain from what we have said that in our opinion the public welfare alone must be the ground, as it is the only legal justification, for this kind of payment. And it follows that our answer to the first of the two questions before us is that the General Court has the right to appropriate money for the purposes supposed in a case where it fairly can be thought that the public good will be served by the grant of such an unstipulated reward, but that it has not that right where the only public advantage is such as may be incident and collateral to the relief of a private citizen. To a great extent the distinction must be left to the conscience of the Legislature. Whether a judicial remedy could be found if a clear case should arise of an unconstitutional appropriation, it happily is unnecessary to inquire.

We make no different answer to the second question, and have not found it necessary to consider distinctions between what the Legislature can do, as representing the sovereign power, and what it can authorize counties, cities, or towns to do; we assume that if the General Court should confer such a power in any case it would so far specify the object and occasion as to adjudicate that they were sufficient to warrant an expenditure for the public good. The ground of decision in *Mead* v. *Acton,* 139 Mass. 341, which certainly went very far, was not a distinction between the direct and indirect action of the Legislature, but was that, because the war had been over so long, it was manifest that the public welfare could not be promoted by the payment of the proposed bounties, and therefore a statute attempting to authorize such a payment by any one attempted to divert public funds to private uses and was void. Possibly other reasons could have been invoked. Some of the language used in that case and in *Kingman* v. *Brockton,* 153 Mass. 255, may need qualification. It goes beyond the point which the court was called upon to decide.

CONTROL BY THE LEGISLATURE OVER PUBLIC WORKS

Browne v. *Turner*
176 Mass. 9 (1900)

[The plaintiffs filed a bill in equity to restrain the Boston Transit Commission from constructing a tunnel from Boston to East Boston and to prevent the city treasurer from issuing bonds of the city to cover the cost of construction. It was contended that to carry out the proposed construction would result in taking the property of the city without reasonable compensation or due process of law, and that it called for an unwarranted exercise of the taxing power. Holmes' opinion upholding the constitutionality of the statute authorizing the construction and the issuing of bonds follows.]

This bill purports to be brought under St. 1898, c. 490, amending Pub. Sts. c. 27, sec. 129. As we are of opinion that it fails to make out a case, and as all parties are anxious for a decision upon the merits, we have not considered whether the plaintiffs bring themselves within the purview of the act. The decree will be the same that it would be if we were against them on the preliminary point, and therefore there seems to be no objection to stating the grounds of substantive law, which seem to us to support the result.

The point of the bill may be stated in a few words. The Boston Transit Commission proposes to obey St. 1897, c. 500, sec. 17, by constructing a tunnel from a point on or near Hanover Street in Boston proper to a point at or near Maverick Square in East Boston, and by executing a lease of the tunnel, when completed, to the Boston Elevated Railway Company, for twenty-five years from the date of that act, at the rental specified in the same section. The treasurer of the city proposes to obey sec. 18 of the act by selling bonds and applying the proceeds to the payment of the cost of the tunnel. The plaintiffs seek an injunction on the ground that the requirements of these sections are unconstitutional, as calling for an unwarranted exercise of the power of taxation, as taking the property of the city without reasonable compensation or due process of law when the lease is executed, and as impairing the obligation of a contract already made by the subway commissioners with the West End Street Railway.

In view of the decisions as to the subway, it does not appear to us to need further argument to show that the contemplated tunnel, even if permanently confined to street railway travel, is a public work for a public use, for building which the Legislature can require the city to pay. *Prince* v. *Crocker,* 166 Mass. 347, 361. *Mahoney* v. *Boston,* 171 Mass. 427, 429. Local precedent is more important than abstract theory in determining this question, at least so far as the State Constitution is concerned; and if it be true, as it may be, that the difference between uses which are public within the requirements of the Constitution and those which are not is one of degree, that is no novelty, and it is enough that this use has been determined to fall on the right side of the line. Apart from the distinctions suggested between the subway and the tunnel, which do not impress us, it is said that, because of the direction to let the tunnel, and because of the difference between the rental under the statute and that which would have been received under the contract which we have mentioned, the real object of the statute is to throw upon the city the burden of constructing part of its roadbed for a private corporation and to give it a lease on easier terms. We cannot accept the suggestion. It does not appear that the statute will have either effect. But if it will, so long as it is possible we are bound to assume that the Legislature did its duty, meant what it said, and regarded the work as a public work really needed by the public, as it may be. The purpose of the act on its face is to create a lawful public improvement.

The lease comes up in another aspect, however. It is said that the compensation to the city is inadequate, and that the lease will be a taking of the city's property for a private corporation without paying for it. *Mount Hope Cemetery* v. *Boston,* 158 Mass. 509. With regard to the former proposition, if the Legislature has the same power that it has with regard to other roads, the matter of compensation is wholly within its power. * * * Commonly, when a city or town is required to build a road or bridge within its limits, no compensation is provided for beyond the local benefit of having it there. With regard to the latter branch of the objection, we are of opinion that the case is not like *Mount Hope Cemetery* v. *Boston,* or that supposed of an act requiring a transfer of the city hall to a railroad company for a station. This is not a transfer, but only a temporary and *quasi* experimental lease for a not unreasonable time. The property of the city in the tunnel, assuming it to have a property, is not of a half private sort, as in case of a cemetery, but is merely the control of a public agency. There is no element of the *Mount Hope Cemetery* case about the matter.

* * * As was said at the argument, if the tunnel is to be built it is to be used, and naturally will not be used by the city directly. If the Legislature could authorize it to be let on terms to be agreed upon, as was held in *Prince* v. *Crocker,* it could require it to be let upon terms which the Legislature thought just, to a corporation selected by itself engaged in a public work like that for which the tunnel is to be used. In fact, when once the power to require the tunnel to be built is conceded, the rest follows, in the situation now existing in Boston. Assuming that the city is not to go into the transportation business further than it has gone, the use of the tunnel by the corporation which manages the consolidated street railways of the city is the alternative, and such use is not to be expected without a lease.

The contract the obligation of which it is said will be impaired is the former lease of the subway executed by the transit commissioners under Sts. 1893, c. 478; 1894, c. 548; 1895, c. 440; and 1896, c. 492. This lease was to the West End Street Railway Company, to whose rights the Elevated Railway Company has succeeded, but was a different rental from the present. The lease declares the word "subway" as used therein to include all the subways, tunnels, etc., which the commission has constructed or may construct under the aforesaid acts. As to future tunnels, of course, this is not a lease but only a contract to let them if they are built under the said acts. The Statute of 1894, c. 548, sec. 26, was to the effect that the commission "may construct a tunnel . . . from a point on or near Scollay Square in the city of Boston, . . . to a point on or near Maverick Square." Such a contract is not impaired in any way by a repeal of so much of the act as gives the commission authority to build, and it may be that, if it were necessary, we should say that a tunnel with a different terminus built in form under another and later act is not within the words of the lease,—that, in the words of *Browne* v. *Turner,* 174 Mass. 150, 160, the contemplated tunnel is "a substitute for the tunnel authorized by St. 1894." We prefer, however, to put our decision on more substantial grounds. The railroad company does not object to the change, as was the case in *Walla Walla* v. *Walla Walla Water Co.* 172 U. S. 1. The city has no greater interest in the lease than it has in the tunnel. Its interest in the lease is as much public property and as subject to legislative control as its interest in the tunnel. No part of the proceeds go[es] to its private uses, (St. 1894, c. 548, sec. 38; *Mahoney* v. *Boston,* 171 Mass. 427, 430,) and if any part did go to such uses it is hard to see how, as against itself, the city, by making a contract to let public property held by it subject to the control of the Legislature, could cut down this control. The control is not subject to the chance of the city's contracting, but the contract is subject to the power of the Legislature over the subject matter. * * * We assume, for purposes of discussion, without deciding, that the contract as to future tunnels was within the authority given by St. 1895, c. 440, sec. 6; St. 1896, c. 492.

Bill dismissed.

USE OF ELECTION VOTING MACHINES

Opinion of the Justices
178 Mass. 605 (1901)

[The Massachusetts House of Representatives requested the opinion of the Supreme Judicial Court on the following question: Has the General Court (the legislature) the right to authorize the use of voting and counting machines at elections by the people of national, State, district, county, city or town officers? Chief Justice Holmes, and Justices Knowlton and Lathrop concurred in the opinion below. Loring concurred in a separate opinion. Morton, Barker and Hammond dissented.]

The ground for doubt as to the power of the General Court under the Constitution of the Commonwealth is to be found in the requirement that representatives "shall be chosen by written votes," Part 2, c. 1, sec. 3, art. 3, and in the implication of the provision for sorting and counting the votes for governor, c. 2, sec. 1, art. 3, and for senator, c. 1, sec. 2, art. 2. To these may be added the requirement that certain militia officers shall be elected by written vote, c. 2, sec. 1, art. 10, and articles 16 and 17 of the Amendments, one or both of which might be held to adopt the method of voting for governor for the election of certain other officers. Whether the first mentioned requirement, as to representation, has been repealed by art. 21 of the Amendments, giving the Legislature power to prescribe the "manner of ascertaining" the election of representatives, it is unnecessary to consider, although it may be well to bear that Amendment in mind in weighing the arguments which we shall adduce. Apart from these provisions, no doubt, the general power of the Legislature would extend to authorizing the use of a voting machine. See for example Amendments, art. 19.

With regard to votes for representatives in Congress it is provided by c. 154 of the Statutes of the United States for 1899, that they may be by "voting machine the use of which has been duly authorized by the State law," so that the elections of national officers require no separate consideration.

We assume that the voting machines which the Honorable House has in mind vary in their mode of recording votes, that all of them dispense with the use of a separate piece of paper for each vote, that some of them register a large number of successive votes by successive punches upon one strip of paper, in separate lines for separate candidates, with the names, if necessary, against the lines, and that some of them abandon the use of paper altogether in recording, each vote being marked by the partial revolution of a cog-wheel or other similar device, and the total number being shown by some easily adapted index. If necessary, however, in this class of machines the names of the candidates may appear in writing attached to the point where the voter registers his vote, in such manner as to indicate that his turning a particular key or pressing a particular knob expresses a vote for the name written above.

The question whether such a machine satisfies whatever requirements or implications there may be in the Constitution of the Commonwealth, depends upon how far we are to follow the line of argument started by Chief Justice Parker in *Henshaw* v. *Foster,* 9 Pick. 312. In that case it was pointed out, with regard to this very matter, that, as the Chief Justice puts it, "words competent to the then existing state of the community, and at the same time capable of being expanded to embrace more extensive relations, should not be restrained to their more obvious and immediate sense, if, consistently with the general object of the authors and the true principles of the compact, they can be extended to other relations and circumstances which an improved state of society may produce." (p. 317.)

To state in our own way the mode of approaching the question, it is not so important to consider what picture the framers of the Constitution had in their minds, as what benefits they sought to secure, or evils to prevent,—what they were thinking against in their affirmative requirement of writing, and what they would have prohibited if they had put the clause in a negative form. The answer, or a part of it, is given by Chief Justice Parker in the case already cited: "The practice had been to elect many town officers by hand vote, and probably in some instances representatives had been so chosen. It became necessary therefore to prescribe that the choice should be made by ballot; but even the word *ballot* itself is ambiguous, and therefore it was required that representatives shall be elected *by written votes."* No doubt the picture in the minds of those who used the words was that of a piece of paper with the names of the candidates voted for written upon it in manuscript, but the thing which they meant to stop was oral or hand voting, and the benefits which they meant to secure were the greater certainty and permanence of a material record of each voter's act and the relative privacy incident to doing that act in silence. They did not require the signature of the voter, or any means of identifying his vote as his after it had been cast. It was settled by *Henshaw* v. *Foster* that they did not require manuscript. In our opinion they did not require a separate piece of paper for each voter. That is to say, by requiring writing they did not prevent the Legislature from authorizing several voters to use a single ballot if the voters all signed it, or in some way sufficiently indicated that a single paper expressed the act and choice of each. It seems to us that the object and even the words of the Constitution in requiring "written votes" are satisfied when the voter makes a change in a material object, for instance, by causing a wheel to revolve a fixed distance, if the material object changed is so connected with or related to a written or printed name purporting to be the name of a candidate for office, that, by the understanding of all, the making of the change expresses a vote for the candidate whose name is thus connected with the device.

So far we have been considering the requirement of written votes alone, and have assumed that all other constitutional conditions are complied with. But it remains to consider whether the result is changed by the provisions as to sorting and counting votes where those provisions apply. These seem to us to raise less difficulty. The provisions do not express a constitutional end; they express merely assumptions that sorting and counting will be necessary if you have written votes, as they would have been necessary a hundred years ago. It would not be true to say that the framers of the Constitution chose the risk of errors incident to sorting and counting in preference to the risk of errors of a different class incident to some different way of finding out the result. They never thought of any other way. Probably the only distinctions which occurred to them concerned different modes of sorting and counting.

It is theoretically possible to exclude by a mechanical device every chance of error in the sorting and counting of votes. Whether that is accomplished by existing machines is a matter about which we have no adequate information, and is a question of fact which it would not fall within our province to determine. We assume that the Legislature before authorizing the use of a machine would satisfy itself that the voter would be sufficiently apprised of what to do in order to vote for his candidate, that the machine really would carry out and express the intent which it purported to be ready to express, that it was of such mechanical perfection as to exclude the possibility of internal error, and that sufficient arrangements were made to prevent external fraud. Under such circumstances, the sorting and counting of the votes shrink by atrophy to a mere survival, but there is nothing contrary to the Constitution in that. If it be deemed technically necessary that the possibility at least of sorting and counting should remain, it does remain. Whether in the form of successive punches in a line upon paper, or in the marked revolutions of a wheel appropriated to a given candidate, material changes abide which signify by predetermined language the number of votes cast, exactly to the same extent that it would be signified by slips of paper bearing characters in printer's ink. The votes could be counted as cast, if it were necessary. They can be counted afterwards as well. The fact that the index of machinery has cut down the chance of personal error to a minimum surely is not an objection sanctioned by the Constitution.

The views which we express coincide with the opinion of a majority of the judges of the Supreme Court of Rhode Island in regard to the McTammany machine, *In re Voting Machine,* 19 R. I. 729, and with some other discussion of the subject which we have seen.

It is proper to add that we have considered only the answer to the general question. What provisions should be made in the exceptional case of challenged votes, etc., is a question of detail, easily dealt with by special arrangements.

RIGHT OF LEGISLATURE TO PROVIDE A REMEDY AFFECTING A PENDING CASE

Danforth v. Groton Water Co.
178 Mass. 472 (1901)

These are petitions to the Superior Court for a jury to assess damages for the taking of water rights. The respondent filed motions to dismiss on the ground that the petitioners had not applied first to the county commissioners. The Superior Court dismissed the petitions, and on report its action was sustained by this court. 176 Mass. 118. The decision was rendered on May 17, 1900. On May 3 had been passed c. 299 of the statutes of that year, but it escaped every one's attention until after the rescript had gone. A rehearing subsequently was granted by agreement of all concerned, on the single question of the effect of that act upon this case.

The water was actually withdrawn in November, 1897, and was taken not later than that date. By the respondent's charter, the right of the petitioners to apply for the assessment of damages was limited to one year from the taking. Therefore as the law stood just before the enactment of St. 1900, c. 299, the petitioners had lost their chance of recovery from the respondent, because it then was too late to file new applications, and, as the previous decision in this case has shown, the petitions on file could not be entertained.

The statute provides that no such petition as the present "now or hereafter pending in the superior court . . . shall be dismissed for want of jurisdiction in said court solely on the ground that no previous application for the assessment of such damages had been made to a board of county commissioners." These words seem to us plainly to apply to the present petitions. It is true that the petitions had been ordered to be dismissed, but the orders were made subject to a report to this court, as we have said, and the cases were still pending in the Superior Court. There can be no doubt of the intent of the statute, and the only question is whether it is constitutional with regard to those who, like the respondent, at the time of its passage had a good defense. There certainly is a strong argument that as against parties in the respondent's position the act cannot be sustained.

In *Campbell* v. *Holt,* 115 U. S. 620, in which it was held by majority of the court that a repeal of the statute of limitations as to debts already barred violated no rights of the debtor under the fourteenth amendment, Mr. Justice Miller speaks as if the constitutional right relied on were a right to defeat a just debt. But the constitutional right asserted was the same that would be set up if the Legislature should order one citizen to pay a sum of money to another with whom he had been in no previous relations of any kind. Such a repeal requires the property of one person to be given to another when there was no previous enforceable legal obligation to give it. Whether the freedom of the defendant from liability is due to a technicality or to his having had no dealings with the other party, he is equally free, and it would seem logical to say that if the Constitution protects him in one case it protects him in all. With regard to cases like *Campbell* v. *Holt,* under the State Constitution the later intimations of this court have been that such a repeal would have no effect. * * *

Nevertheless in this case, as in others, the prevailing judgment of the profession has revolted at the attempt to place immunities which exist only by reason of some slight technical defect on absolutely the same footing as those which stand on fundamental grounds. Perhaps the reasoning of the cases has not always been as sound as the instinct which directed the decisions. It may be that sometimes it would have been as well not to attempt to make out that the judgment of the court was consistent with constitutional rules, if such rules were to be taken to have the exactness of mathematics. It may be that it would have been better to say definitely that constitutional rules, like those of the common law, end in a penumbra where the Legislature has a certain freedom in fixing the line, as has been recognized with regard to the police power. *Camfield* v. *United States,* 167 U. S. 518, 523, 524. But however that may be, multitudes of cases have recognized the power of the Legislature to call a liability into being where there was none before, if the circumstances were such as to appeal with some strength to the prevailing views of justice, and if the obstacle in the way of the creation seemed small.

In some such cases there has been at an earlier time an enforceable obligation, in others there never has been one, but in both classes the courts have laid hold of a distinction between the remedy and the substantive right, or have said that "a party has no vested right in a defense based upon an informality not affecting his substantial equities," Cooley, Const. Lim. (6th ed.)

454, or that "there is no such thing as a vested right to do wrong," *Foster* v. *Essex Bank,* 16 Mass. 245, 273, or have called it curing an irregularity, *Thomson* v. *Lee County,* 3 Wall. 327, 331, * * * or have dwelt upon the equities, meaning the moral worth of the claim that was preserved, or by one device or another have prevented a written constitution from interfering with the power to make small repairs which a legislature naturally would possess.

In a case which would seem almost stronger than that of a debt barred by the statute of limitations it was held that services of an unlicensed physician which could not be recovered for when rendered were made a good cause of action by a repeal of the statute which created the bar. *Hewitt* v. *Wilcox,* 1 Met. 154. So in case of a usurious contract after a repeal of the usury law. *Ewell* v. *Daggs,* 108 U. S. 143.

The constitutional difficulties in the way of the present statute are as small as they well can be. Its effect in saving the petitioners from being barred by the statute of limitations in the respondent's charter is only secondary and accidental. All that it does directly which is open to question is to enact that parties having a case in court shall not be turned out for neglect of what under the circumstances was a naked and useless form. The case is stronger for the petitioners than *Campbell* v. *Holt* or *Hewitt* v. *Wilcox*. The respondent had incurred a legal obligation to them which, although not contractual, was voluntary and legal, and which was entitled to the highest protection of the law, as it sprang from the exercise of eminent domain. The petitioners were enforcing the obligation in good faith. There is no especially striking equity in favor of defeating them because of a mistake of procedure, and as the Legislature now has said that they shall not be defeated, we have not much hesitation in yielding to the current of decisions and in accepting its mandate as authoritative in this case.

Motions overruled.

RESTORATION OF REMEDY
EXTINGUISHED BY LAPSE OF TIME

Dunbar v. *Boston and Providence R. R. Corp.*
181 Mass. 383 (1902)

This is a petition for the assessment of damages to land of the petitioner on Dartmouth Street in Boston caused by raising the grade of that street under the terminal company act. St. 1896, c. 516. The petition was filed under sec. 23 of the act, and therefore we may assume that the claim was subject to the limitation of one year imposed by that section, although no land of the petitioner was taken. The section contains a general provision giving a jury to parties who have suffered damage to be compensated under the act, and the limitation no doubt was intended to be coextensive with the grant. Upon this construction it is admitted that the petition was not filed within the year, and indeed the opposite view was not much pressed on any ground. The answer relied upon is that on May 23, 1899, "the time within which any party suffering damages whose land is not taken may file his petition in the Superior Court for damages accruing from a change of grade occasioned by the location and construction of any railroad by any railroad company other than the terminal company" under the above sec. 23 was extended to January 1, 1900. St. 1899, c. 386. The respondent contends that this statute is unconstitutional and brings that question here by exceptions. It argues no other point.

The statute assailed is of general operation, and if valid applies as well to the petitioner, who had unquestioned notice of the change of grade by the actual completion of the work before the year expired, as to possible cases of persons who might have found their remedy gone before they knew that anything affecting their rights had been done. In such a case, apart from the authorities, it is impossible not to feel the greatest difficulty in sustaining the act. The nature of the difficulty is indicated in *Danforth* v. *Groton Water Co.* 178 Mass. 472. However much you may disguise or palliate the change by saying that the statute deals only with the remedy, or that a party has no vested right to a merely technical defense, or by adopting any other cloudy phrase that keeps the light from the fact, such legislation does enact that the property of a person previously free from legal liability shall be given to another who before the statute had no legal claim. It is not merely as it was put by the counsel for the respondent, following the cases, that the defense is as valuable and as much entitled to protection as the claim, if that be true, but the effect of the statute by enabling the barred claim to be collected is to allow property of the respondent to be appropriated which before was free. *Woodward* v. *Central Vermont Railway,* 180 Mass. 599. It is true that the property is not identified until it is seized on execution, but when it is identified by seizure it is taken as truly as land would be if it were allowed to be recovered in a real action notwithstanding the lapse of twenty years.

In the present case there is not the excuse apparent that the statute cured an earlier injustice, as might be the case where a petitioner had had no actual notice of the loss of any rights until he was too late. It cannot be said in more general terms that a statute of limitations as such embodies an arbitrary or merely technical rule. Prescription and limitation are based on one of the deepest principles of human nature, the working of association with what one actually enjoys for a long time, whatever one's defects of title may be, and of dissociation from that of which one is deprived, whatever may be one's rights. The mind like any other organism gradually shapes itself to what surrounds it, and resents disturbance in the form which its life has assumed. In cases like the present, when the period of limitations is short, no doubt other but also important elements are predominant,—the desirableness for business reasons of getting a quasi public transaction finished,—but whatever the details, the principle involved is as worthy of respect as any known to the law.

Nevertheless in *Danforth* v. *Groton Water Co.* 178 Mass. 472, it was held that a statute was constitutional which removed the bar of an earlier statute under circumstances where, according to the language of the later act and the cases, the lapse of time had destroyed the jurisdiction of the court. S. C. 176 Mass. 118. *Riley* v. *Lowell,* 117 Mass. 76. *Cambridge* v. *County Commissioners,* 117 Mass. 79, 83. So, whatever may be said of the reasoning by which the decision was reached, it was held in *Campbell* v. *Holt,* 115 U. S. 620, that the fourteenth amendment does not prevent the removal of the bar from a personal debt. Without repeating what we have said so recently, it is enough to say that the constitutional provisions allow a certain limited degree of latitude in dealing with cases where remedies have been extinguished by lapse of time when the seeming infraction of right is not very great and when justice requires relief. It is unnecessary to go so far as *Campbell* v. *Holt*. But in a case of this kind, where the original time allowed after actual notice was very short and may have seemed to the Legislature inadequate, where the extension was granted within little more than two months of the time when it could have been granted without question and not improbably before the transaction as a whole had been finished, where the plaintiff's claim is held to be barred only by a somewhat doubtful inference, and where in short we cannot say that the Legislature with its larger view of the facts may not have been satisfied that substantial justice required its action, we are not prepared to pronounce the statute unconstitutional in the face of the most authoritative decisions. We regard this case as distinguishable from a wholesale attempt to relieve from the effect of open and adverse possession of land for twenty years, and even as distinguishable from the similar attempt with regard to debts upheld in *Campbell* v. *Holt*. As yet it is not necessary for us to choose between that decision and the weighty intimations to the contrary in this court and elsewhere.

It is suggested that this is class legislation because the terminal company is excepted from the act. The statute applies to all companies concerned except the one named, so that if any part of it were open to that criticism it would seem to be the portion which makes the exception, not that which lays down the rule. *Holden* v. *James,* 11 Mass. 396. But we have no facts before us which show that the terminal company was not excepted on constitutional grounds.

Exceptions overruled.

CHAPTER 2

FREEDOM OF SPEECH

MAY A POLICEMAN TALK POLITICS?

McAuliffe v. New Bedford
155 Mass. 216 (1892)

This is a petition for mandamus to restore the petitioner to the office of policeman in New Bedford. He was removed by the mayor upon a written complaint, after a hearing, the mayor finding that he was guilty of violating Rule 31 of the police regulations of that city. The part of the rule which the petitioner seems certainly to have violated is as follows: "No member of the department shall be allowed to solicit money or any aid, on any pretence, for any political purpose whatever." There was also evidence that he had been a member of a political committee, which likewise was prohibited. Both parties agree that the city had accepted chapter 319 of the Acts of 1890, by virtue of sec. 1 of which the members of the police force held office "during good behavior and until removed by the mayor, . . . for cause deemed by him sufficient, after due hearing." It is argued by the petitioner that the mayor's finding did not warrant the removal, that the part of the rule violated was invalid as invading the petitioner's right to express his political opinions, and that a breach of it was not a cause sufficient under the statute.

One answer to this argument, assuming that the statute does not make the mayor the final judge of what cause is sufficient, and that we have a right to consider it, (*Ham* v. *Boston Board of Police,* 142 Mass. 90, 95, and *Osgood* v. *Nelson,* L. R. 5 H. L. 636, 649,) is that there is nothing in the Constitution or the statute to prevent the city from attaching obedience to this rule as a condition to the office of policemen, and making it part of the good conduct required. The petitioner may have a constitutional right to talk politics, but he has no constitutional right to be a policeman. There are few employments for hire in which the servant does not agree to suspend his constitutional right of free speech, as well as of idleness, by the implied terms of his contract. The servant cannot complain, as he takes the employment on the terms which are offered him. On the same principle, the city may impose any reasonable condition upon holding offices within its control. This condition seems to us reasonable, if that be a question open to revision here.

The petitioner also argues that he has not had due hearing. The first ground for this argument is some testimony reported that the mayor said that he did not care about the evidence; he knew what McAuliffe had been doing; he knew all about it. A sufficient answer to this is that the fact is not found by the judge who tried the case, and, if necessary to support his findings, we should have to assume that he did not believe the evidence. Next it is said that the charges against the petitioner were not stated specifically, and that when specifications were called for they were refused. The judge was well warranted in finding that the mayor did all that justice required. The complaint was tolerably full, although, no doubt, under some circumstances further specifications properly ought to be demanded. The petitioner attended on notice at the first day appointed for a hearing, and asked for no specifications, and offered no evidence. There was evidence that he said to the mayor at the hearing, "I admit I am guilty; what's the penalty?" and also said to the mayor, at another interview, that, if he was going to be removed, he would like to know it so that he could resign. At an adjourned hearing before the mayor, the petitioner attended with counsel, and his counsel asked for specifications. The mayor refused the request, whereupon the petitioner refused to proceed, and the mayor declared the hearing closed. Under the circumstances, we cannot say that he was wrong. The next suggestion, that no notice was given to the petitioner that a proceeding to remove him from his office was intended, does not require much answer. The petitioner had notice of the proceedings, and must be taken to have known their possible consequences. According to the evidence, he used language to the mayor expressly contemplating those consequences. Finally, it is said that the case should first have been investigated before the committee on police, as provided by Rule 24 of the police regulations. But since the passage of the Act of 1890, if not before, we have no doubt of the power of the mayor to hear all cases on the removal of a police officer in the first instance himself.

Petition dismissed.

SPEECHES ON THE BOSTON COMMON WITHOUT A PERMIT

Commonwealth v. *Davis*
162 Mass. 510 (1895)

[The defendant, Davis, was tried and convicted of violating a Boston city ordinance which provided that, "No person shall . . . make any address" on the Common without a permit from the mayor. Davis contended that the ordinance was unconstitutional. Judge Holmes upheld the statute in the opinion below. More than two years later this case was affirmed by the United States Supreme Court, see 167 U. S. 43.]

The only question raised by these exceptions which was not decided in the former case of *Commonwealth* v. *Davis*, 140 Mass. 485, is one concerning the construction of the present ordinance. That such an ordinance is constitutional is implied by the former decision, and does not appear to us open to doubt. To say that it is unconstitutional means that, even if the Legislature has purported to authorize it, the attempt was vain. The argument to that effect involves the same kind of fallacy that was dealt with in *McAuliffe* v. *New Bedford*, 155 Mass. 216. It assumes that the ordinance is directed against free speech generally, (as in *Des Plaines* v. *Poyer*, 123 Ill. 348, the ordinance held void was directed against public picnics and open-air dances generally), whereas in fact it is directed toward the modes in which Boston Common may be used. There is no evidence before us to show that the power of the Legislature over the Common is less than its power over any other park dedicated to the use of the public, or over public streets the legal title to which is in a city or town. *Lincoln* v. *Boston,* 148 Mass. 578, 580. As representative of the public, it may and does exercise control over the use which the public may make of such places, and it may, and does, delegate more or less of such control to the city or town immediately concerned. For the Legislature absolutely or conditionally to forbid public speaking in a highway or public park is no more an infringement of the rights of a member of the public than for the owner of a private house to forbid it in his house. When no proprietary right interferes, the Legislature may end the right of the public to enter upon the public place by putting an end to the dedication to public uses. So it may take the lesser step of limiting the public use to certain purposes. See Dillon, Mun. Corp. (4th ed.) secs. 393, 407, 651, 656, 666; *Brooklyn Park Commissioners* v. *Armstrong,* 45 N. Y. 234, 243, 244.

If the Legislature had power under the Constitution to pass a law in the form of the present ordinance, there is no doubt that it could authorize the city of Boston to pass the ordinance, and it is settled by the former decision that it has done so. As matter of history we suppose there is no doubt that the town, and after it the city, has always regulated the use of the Common except so far as restrained by statute.* It is settled also that the prohibition in such an ordinance,

---

* In addition to St. 1854, c. 448, sec. 35, which appears in the opinion in *Commonwealth* v. *Davis,* 140 Mass. 485, the government in the present case called the attention of the court to sec. 39 of the same statute, which confers upon the city council the care and management of the public buildings and of all the property of the city.

which would be binding if absolute, is not made invalid by the fact that it may be removed in a particular case by a license from a city officer, or a less numerous body than the one which enacts the prohibition. *Commonwealth* v. *Ellis,* 158 Mass. 555, 557, and cases cited. It is argued that the ordinance really is directed especially against free preaching of the Gospel in public places, as certain Western ordinances seemingly general have been held to be directed against the Chinese. But we have no reason to believe, and do not believe, that this ordinance was passed for any other than its ostensible purpose, namely, as a proper regulation of the use of public grounds.

It follows that, as we said at the outset, the only question open is the construction of the present ordinance. We are of opinion that the words, "No person shall . . . make any public address," in the Revised Ordinances of 1892, c. 43, sec. 66, have as broad a meaning as the words "No person shall . . . deliver a sermon, lecture, address, or discourse," in the Revised Ordinances of 1883, c. 37, sec. 11, under which *Commonwealth* v. *Davis,* 140 Mass. 485, was decided. See Rev. Ord. 1885, c. 42, sec. 11. Whether lecture, political discourse, or sermon, a speech on the Common addressed to all persons who choose to draw near and listen is a public address, and the omission of the superfluous words in the last revision is only a matter of style and the abridgment properly sought for in codification.

Exceptions overruled.

CHAPTER 3
CAPITAL AND LABOR

WITHHOLDING LABOR'S WAGES

Commonwealth v. *Perry*
155 Mass. 117, 123 (1891)

[Perry, an employer, was indicted under the Massachusetts statute of 1891, c. 125, for withholding part of Fielding's wages. Fielding was employed by Perry as a weaver. The statute made it unlawful to, "impose and exact a fine," or withhold part of the wages of a worker for imperfect work. A majority of the court held the statute unconstitutional because it violated fundamental rights by impairing the obligation of contracts. Holmes dissented.]

I have the misfortune to disagree with my brethren. I have submitted my views to them at length, and, considering the importance of the question, feel bound to make public a brief statement, notwithstanding the respect and deference I feel for the judgment of those with whom I disagree.

In the first place, if the statute is unconstitutional, as construed by the majority, I think it should be construed more narrowly and literally, so as to save it. Taking it literally, it is not infringed, and there is no withholding of wages, when the employer only promises to pay a reasonable price for imperfect work, or a price less than the price paid for perfect work, and does pay that price in fact. But I agree that the act should be construed more broadly, and should be taken to prohibit palpable evasions, because I am of opinion that even so construed it is constitutional, so far as any argument goes which I have heard. The prohibition, if any, must be found in the words of the Constitution, either expressed or implied upon a fair and historical construction. What words of the United States or State Constitution are relied on? The statute cannot be said to impair the obligation of contracts made after it went into effect. *Lehigh Water Co. v. Easton,* 121 U. S. 388, 391. So far as has been pointed out to me, I do not see that it interferes with the right of acquiring, possessing, and protecting property any more than the laws against usury or gaming. In truth, I do not think that that clause of the Bill of Rights has any application. It might be urged, perhaps, that the power to make reasonable laws impliedly prohibits the making of unreasonable ones, and that this law is unreasonable. If I assume that this construction of the Constitution is correct, and that, speaking as a political economist, I should agree in condemning the law, still I should not be willing or think myself authorized to overturn legislation on that ground, unless I thought that an honest difference of opinion was impossible, or pretty nearly so.

But if the statute did no more than to abolish in certain cases contracts for a *quantum meruit,* and recoupment for defective quality not amounting to a failure of consideration, I suppose that it only would put an end to what are, relatively speaking, innovations in the common law, and I know of nothing to hinder it. This, however, is not all. I do not confine myself to technical considerations. I suppose that this act was passed because the operatives, or some of them, thought that they were often cheated out of a part of their wages under a false pretense that the work done by them was imperfect, and persuaded the Legislature that their view was true. If their view was true, I cannot doubt that the Legislature had the right to deprive the employers of an honest tool which they were using for a dishonest purpose, and I cannot pronounce the legislation void, as based on a false assumption, since I know nothing about the matter one way or the other. The statute, however construed, leaves the employers their remedy for imperfect work by action. I doubt if we are at liberty to consider the objection that this remedy is practically worthless; but if we are, then the same objection is equally true, although for different reasons, if the workmen are left to their remedy against their employers for wages wrongfully withheld. My view seems to me to be favored by *Hancock* v. *Yaden,* 121 Ind. 366, and Slaughterhouse Cases, 16 Wall. 36, 80, 81.

RIGHT TO PICKET

Vegelahn v. Guntner and Others
167 Mass. 92, 104 (1896)

[The defendants were enjoined against maintaining a patrol before the plaintiff's premises, from interfering with his business, and from intimidating by threats, express or implied, of physical harm to body or property of anyone seeking employment with the plaintiff. Chief Justice Field and Justice Holmes dissented, in separate opinions, holding that the patrol was legal in the absence of force and threats of physical injury to persons or property. Holmes' dissent follows.]

In a case like the present, it seems to me that, whatever the true result may be, it will be of advantage to sound thinking to have the less popular view of the law stated, and therefore, although when I have been unable to bring my brethren to share my convictions my almost invariable practice is to defer to them in silence, I depart from that practice in this case, notwithstanding my unwillingness to do so in support of an already rendered judgment of my own.

In the first place, a word or two should be said as to the meaning of the report. I assume that my brethren construe it as I meant it to be construed, and that, if they were not prepared to do so, they would give an opportunity to the defendants to have it amended in accordance with what I state my meaning to be. There was no proof of any threat or danger of a patrol exceeding two men, and as of course an injunction is not granted except with reference to what there is reason to expect in its absence, the question on that point is whether a patrol of two men should be enjoined. Again, the defendants are enjoined by the final decree from intimidating by threats, express or implied, of physical harm to body or property, any person who may be desirous of entering into the employment of the plaintiff so far as to prevent him from entering the same. In order to test the correctness of the refusal to go further, it must be assumed that the defendants obey the express prohibition of the decree. If they do not, they fall within the injunction as it now stands, and are liable to summary punishment. The important difference between the preliminary and the final injunction is that the former goes further, and forbids the defendants to interfere with the plaintiff's business "by any scheme . . . organized for the purpose of . . . preventing any person or persons who now are or may hereafter be . . . desirous of entering the [plaintiff's employment] from entering it." I quote only a part, and the part which seems to me most objectionable. This includes refusal of social intercourse, and even organized persuasion or argument, although free from any threat of violence, either express or implied. And this is with reference to persons who have a legal right to contract or not to contract with the plaintiff, as they may see fit. Interference with existing contracts is forbidden by the final decree. I wish to insist a little that the only point of difference which involves a difference of principle between the final decree and the preliminary injunction which it is proposed to restore, is what I have mentioned, in order that it may be seen exactly what we are to discuss. It appears to me that the judgment of the majority turns in part on the assumption that the patrol necessarily carries with it a threat of bodily harm. That assumption I think unwarranted, for the reasons which I have given. Furthermore, it cannot be said, I think, that two men walking together up and down a sidewalk and speaking to those who enter a certain shop do necessarily and always thereby convey a threat of force. I do not think it possible to discriminate, and to say that two workmen, or even two representatives of an organization of workmen, do,—especially when they are, and are known to be, under the injunction of this court not to do so. . . . I may add, that I think the more intelligent workingmen believe as fully as I do that they no more can be permitted to usurp the State's prerogative of force than can their opponents in their controversies. But if I am wrong, then the decree as it stands reaches the patrol, since it applies to all threats of force. With this I pass to the real difference between the interlocutory and the final decree.

I agree, whatever may be the law in the case of a single defendant, *Rice* v. *Albee,* 164 Mass. 88, that when a plaintiff proves that several persons have combined and conspired to injure his business, and have done acts producing that effect, he shows temporal damage and a cause of action, unless the facts disclose, or the defendants prove, some ground of excuse or justification. And I take it to be settled, and rightly settled, that doing that damage by combined persuasion is actionable, as well as doing it by falsehood or by force. *Walker* v. *Cronin,* 107 Mass. 55. * * *

Nevertheless, in numberless instances the law warrants the intentional infliction of temporal damage because it regards it as justified. It is on the question of what shall amount to a justification, and more especially on the nature of the considerations which really determine or ought to determine the answer to that question, that judicial reasoning seems to me often to be inadequate. The true grounds of decision are considerations of policy and of social advantage, and it is vain to suppose that solutions can be attained merely by logic and the general propositions of law which nobody disputes. Propositions as to public policy rarely are unanimously accepted, and still more rarely, if ever, are capable of unanswerable proof. They require a special training to enable anyone even to form an intelligent opinion about them. In the early stages of law, at least, they generally are acted on rather as inarticulate instincts than as definite ideas for which a rational defence is ready.

To illustrate what I have said in the last paragraph, it has been the law for centuries that a man may set up a business in a country town too small to support more than one, although he expects and intends thereby to ruin some one already there, and succeeds in his intent. In such a case he is not held to act "unlawfully and without justifiable cause," as was alleged in *Walker* v. *Cronin* and *Rice* v. *Albee*. The reason, of course, is that the doctrine generally has been accepted that free competition is worth more to society than it costs, and that on this ground the infliction of the damage is privileged. *Commonwealth* v. *Hunt,* 4 Met. 111, 134. Yet even this proposition nowadays is disputed by a considerable body of persons, including many whose intelligence is not to be denied, little as we may agree with them.

I have chosen this illustration partly with reference to what I have to say next. It shows without the need of further authority that the policy of allowing free competition justifies the intentional inflicting of temporal damage, including the damage of interference with a man's business, by some means, when the damage is done not for its own sake, but as an instrumentality in reaching the end of victory in the battle of trade. In such a case it cannot matter whether the plaintiff is the only rival of the defendant, and so is aimed at specifically, or is one of a class all of whom are hit. The only debatable ground is the nature of the means by which such damage may be inflicted. We all agree that it cannot be done by force or threats of force. We all agree, I presume, that it may be done by persuasion to leave a rival's shop and come to the defendant's. It may be done by the refusal or withdrawal of various pecuniary advantages which, apart from this consequence, are within the defendant's lawful control. It may be done by the withdrawal, or threat to withdraw, such advantages from third persons who have a right to deal or not to deal with the plaintiff, as a means of inducing them not to deal with him either as customers or servants. * * * *Bowen* v. *Matheson,* 14 Allen, 499. * * * *Mogul Steamship Co.* v. *McGregor* [1892] A. C. 25.

I pause here to remark that the word "threats" often is used as if, when it appeared that threats had been made, it appeared that unlawful conduct had begun. But it depends on what you threaten. As a general rule, even if subject to some exceptions, what you may do in a certain event you may threaten to do, that is, give warning of your intention to do in that event, and thus allow the other person the chance of avoiding the consequences. So as to "compulsion," it depends on how you "compel." *Commonwealth* v. *Hunt,* 4 Met. 111, 133. So as to "annoyance" or "intimidation."

Connor v. *Kent, Curran* v. *Treleaven,* 17 Cos C. C. 354, 367, 368, 370. In *Sherry* v. *Perkins,* 147 Mass. 212, it was found as a fact that the display of banners which were enjoined was part of a scheme to prevent workmen from entering or remaining in the plaintiff's employment, "by threats and intimidation." The context showed that the words as there used meant threats of personal violence, and intimidation by causing fear of it.

I have seen the suggestion made that the conflict between employers and employed is not competition. But I venture to assume that none of my brethren would rely on that suggestion. If the policy on which our law is founded is too narrowly expressed in the term free competition, we may substitute free struggle for life. Certainly the policy is not limited to struggles between persons of the same class competing for the same end. It applies to all conflicts of temporal interests.

So far, I suppose, we are agreed. But there is a notion which latterly has been insisted on a good deal, that a combination of persons to do what any one of them lawfully might do by himself will make the otherwise lawful conduct unlawful. It would be rash to say that some as yet unformulated truth may not be hidden under this proposition. But in the general form in which it has been presented and accepted by many courts, I think it plainly untrue, both on authority and on principle. * * * There was combination of the most flagrant and dominant kind in *Bowen* v. *Matheson* and in the *Mogul Steamship Company's Case,* and combination was essential to the success achieved. But it is not necessary to cite cases; it is plain from the slightest consideration of practical affairs, or the most superficial reading of industrial history, that free competition means combination, and that the organization of the world, now going on so fast, means an ever increasing might and scope of combination. It seems to me futile to set our faces against this tendency. Whether beneficial on the whole, as I think it, or detrimental, it is inevitable, unless the fundamental axioms of society, and even the fundamental conditions of life, are to be changed.

One of the eternal conflicts out of which life is made up is that between the effort of every man to get the most he can for his services, and that of society, disguised under the name of capital, to get his services for the least possible return. Combination on the one side is patent and powerful. Combination on the other is the necessary and desirable counterpart, if the battle is to be carried on in a fair and equal way. I am unable to reconcile *Temperton* v. *Russell,* [1893] 1 Q. B. 715, and the cases which follow it, with the *Mogul Steamship Company Case.* But *Temperton* v. *Russell* is not a binding authority here, and therefore I do not think it necessary to discuss it.

If it be true that workingmen may combine with a view, among other things, to getting as much as they can for their labor, just as capital may combine with a view to getting the greatest possible return, it must be true that when combined they have the same liberty that combined capital has to support their interests by argument, persuasion, and the bestowal or refusal of those advantages which they otherwise lawfully control. I can remember when many people thought that, apart from violence or breach of contract, strikes were wicked, as organized refusals to work. I suppose that intelligent economists and legislators have given up that notion today. I feel pretty confident that they equally will abandon the idea that an organized refusal by workmen of social intercourse with a man who shall enter their antagonist's employ is wrong, if it is dissociated from any threat of violence, and is made for the sole object of prevailing if possible in a contest with their employer about the rate of wages. The fact, that the immediate object of the act by which the benefit to themselves is to be gained is to injure their antagonist, does not necessarily make it unlawful, any more than when a great house lowers the price of certain goods for the purpose, and with the effect, of driving a smaller antagonist from the business. Indeed, the question seems to me to have been decided as long ago as 1842 by the good sense of Chief Justice Shaw, in *Commonwealth* v. *Hunt,* 4 Met. 111. I repeat at the end, as I said at the beginning, that this is the point of difference in principle, and the only one, between the interlocutory and the final decree. * * *

The general question of the propriety of dealing with this kind of case by injunction I say nothing about, because I understand that the defendants have no objection to the final decree if it goes no further, and that both parties wish a decision upon the matters which I have discussed.

ENTICING SERVANTS FROM THEIR MASTERS

May v. *Wood*
172 Mass. 11, 14 (1898)

[Margaret May sued William Wood and another for conspiring to induce Mary Wood to break the contract of employment with her. The contract provided that the plaintiff should continue to reside with Mary Wood, that she should receive $4.00 as a weekly compensation, and a legacy of $700, upon Mary Wood's death. A majority of the court held that, "when the cause of action is alleged to be that the defendants by false and malicious statements induced a master to discharge his servant, it is essential that the statements made should be substantially set out in the declaration, in order that the court may see whether any such effect as is alleged can reasonably be attributed to the statements." Holmes dissented. Knowlton and Morton concurred with him.]

I cannot agree with the decision of the majority, and as the law in cases of this sort is somewhat unsettled, I think it may be useful that I should state my views. I regard it as settled in this Commonwealth, and as rightly settled, whether it be consistent with some dicta in *Allen* v. *Flood,* [1898] A. C. 1, or not, that an action will lie for depriving a man of custom, that is, of possible contracts, as well when the result is effected by persuasion as when it is accomplished by fraud or force, if the harm is inflicted simply from malevolence and without some justifiable cause, such as competition in trade. *Walker* v. *Cronin,* 107 Mass. 555, 566

* * * I think that it does not matter what motive to abstain from dealing is given to the possible customer, whether it be fear or simply prejudice, if the motive be effectual, or whether it be produced by falsehood, or without it by malevolently intended advice. I think it plain that the fact that the conduct of the possible customer in abstaining from dealing is lawful does not affect the liability of the person who induced him to do so, although this person is remoter from the damage complained of. I think this a principle which not only is obviously sound, but is established by the cases first cited above, by the recognition of loss of custom as an element in damages, * * * and by the doctrine that a man who utters a slander may be liable for the privileged repetition of it, if reasonably to be expected, when he would not be liable unless he actually intended it, if the repetition were itself a wrong. * * *

A fortiori, under similar conditions and limitations, an action will lie for inducing the breach of an actual contract. *Walker* v. *Cronin,* 107 Mass. 555. *Tasker* v. *Stanley,* 153 Mass. 148. As in the former case, the ground of liability is not false statements, but the intentional causing of temporal damage, without justifiable cause, by any means contemplated as effectual, and proving so in the event. One of the means alleged in the present declaration, namely, inducing Mary A. Wood to believe that the plaintiff was a dangerous person and unfit associate, might have been accomplished without uttering a falsehood, and might have been alleged as the only means without impairing the count.

I cannot make it plainer than it is upon simply reading the declaration that this is an action of the kind just supposed. It is not an action for slander with special damages, but it is an action for malevolently and without justifiable cause inducing a third person to break a contract. That is the gist of the action, and falsehood or slander is material only as one out of many possible and two alleged means of bringing about the wrong. It is one degree more remote than where the slander itself is the thing complained of, and by all analogy when referred to need not be set out specifically as when slander is the gist. See the form of declaration held good on demurrer in *Lumley* v. *Gye,* 2 El. & Bl. 216; * * *

Of *Rice* v. *Albee,* 164 Mass. 88, I will only say that, whether the decision be right or wrong, the reasoning always has seemed to me inadequate, but that, however that may be, in that case the action was for preventing the making of a contract, not for causing the breach of one already made. I do not understand that it was intended to overrule previous decisions, or to dissent from cases like *Lumley* v. *Gye,* 2 El. & Bl. 216, which previously had been approved by the court.

I deal only with the ground which I understand to be relied on in the judgment of the court. I suppose that nothing else is open on the special demurrer, (*Parker* v. *Huntington,* 2 Gray, 124, 126, 128), but I will add that the declaration, although informal, plainly means that the defendants not only conspired to do, but did, the acts by reason of which, as it is alleged, Wood was induced to break her contract with the plaintiff. If the defendants wanted a more formal allegation, they should have specified the defect in their demurrer. *Windran* v. *French,* 151 Mass. 547.

BOYCOTTS AND STRIKES TO UNIONIZE SHOPS

Plant v. Woods
176 Mass. 492, 504 (1900)

[The defendants, members of a labor union, attempted to persuade employers to have their employees who belonged to a rival union, join the defendants' organization. It was found, that in order to carry out their purpose, the defendants had threatened strikes and boycotts. But no acts of personal violence or physical injury to property were committed. An injunction was granted, and Mr. Justice Hammond, speaking for the court, said that the defendants' threat, "was coercive in its effect upon the will." Chief Justice Holmes dissented.]

When a question has been decided by the court, I think it proper, as a general rule, that a dissenting judge, however strong his convictions may be, should thereafter accept the law from the majority and leave the remedy to the Legislature, if that body sees fit to interfere. If the decision in the present case simply had relied upon *Vegelahn* v. *Guntner,* 167 Mass. 92, I should have hesitated to say anything, although I might have stated that my personal opinion had not been weakened by the substantial agreement with my views to be found in the judgments of the majority of the House of Lords in *Allen* v. *Flood,* [1898] A. C. 1. But much to my satisfaction, if I may say so, the court has seen fit to adopt the mode of approaching the question which I believe to be the correct one, and to open an issue which otherwise I might have thought closed. The difference between my brethren and me now seems to be a difference of degree, and the line of reasoning followed makes it proper for me to explain where the difference lies.

I agree that the conduct of the defendants is actionable unless justified. *May* v. *Wood,* 172 Mass. 11, 14, and cases cited. I agree that the presence or absence of justification may depend upon the object of their conduct, that is, upon the motive with which they acted. *Vegelahn* v. *Guntner,* 167 Mass. 92, 105, 106. I agree, for instance, that if a boycott or a strike is intended to override the jurisdiction of the courts by the action of a private association, it may be illegal. *Weston* v. *Barnicoat,* 175 Mass. 454. On the other hand, I infer that a majority of my brethren would admit that a boycott or strike intended to raise wages directly might be lawful, if it did not embrace in its scheme or intent violence, breach of contract, or other conduct unlawful on grounds independent of the mere fact that the action of the defendants was combined. A sensible workingman would not contend that the courts should sanction a combination for the purpose of inflicting or threatening violence or the infraction of admitted rights. To come directly to the point, the issue is narrowed to the question whether, assuming that some purposes would be a justification, the purpose in this case of the threatened boycotts and strikes was such as to justify the threats. That purpose was not directly concerned with wages. It was one degree more remote. The immediate object and motive was to strengthen the defendants' society as a preliminary and means to enable it to make a better fight on questions of wages or other matters of clashing interests. I differ from my brethren in thinking that the threats were as lawful for this preliminary purpose as for the final one to which strengthening the union was a means. I think that unity of organization is necessary to make the contest of labor effectual, and that societies of laborers lawfully may employ in their preparation the means which they might use in the final contest.

Although this is not the place for extended economic discussion, and although the law may not always reach ultimate economic conceptions, I think it well to add that I cherish no illusions as to the meaning and effect of strikes. While I think the strike a lawful instrument in the universal struggle of life, I think it pure phantasy to suppose that there is a body of capital of which labor as a whole secures a larger share by that means. The annual product, subject to an infinitesimal deduction for the luxuries of the few, is directed to consumption by the multitude, and is consumed by the multitude, always. Organization and strikes may get a larger share for the members of an organization, but, if they do, they get it at the expense of the less organized and less powerful portion of the laboring mass. They do not create something out of nothing. It is only by divesting our minds of questions of ownership and other machinery of distribution, and by looking solely at the question of consumption,—asking ourselves what is the annual product, who consumes it, and what changes would or could we make,—that we can keep in the world of realities. But, subject to the qualifications which I have expressed, I think it lawful for a body of workmen to try by combination to get more than they now are getting, although they do it at the expense of their fellows, and to that end to strengthen their union by the boycott and the strike.

INDUCEMENT TO VIOLATE A LABOR CONTRACT

Moran v. Dunphy
177 Mass. 485 (1901)

[Dunphy was sued for inducing one Cowan to discharge the plaintiff from his employ. The plaintiff contended that by reason of "certain slanderous charges made by the defendant to said Cowan against his character," he was discharged. The defendant demurred contending that the plaintiff "did not state what the slanderous charges consisted of. . . ." Chief Justice Holmes' opinion follows.]

The first count of the declaration in this case substantially follows the form held bad in *May v. Wood,* 172 Mass. 11, and *Rice v. Albee,* 164 Mass. 88, and the plaintiff's argument is directed to getting those cases overruled. It appears in the reports that the later decision did not command the assent of all of us, and it is quite possible at least that if the question came up now for the first time the majority might be found to be on the side which did not prevail. *Van Horn v. Van Horn,* 27 Vroom. 318, 319. But it is not desirable that decisions should oscillate with changes in the bench, and we accept what was decided as the law. Still we deem it proper to call attention to the fact that the cases cited go only to a point of pleading. What they decide, so far as they bear on the present case, is merely that the substance of false statements by which a defendant is alleged to have induced a third person to break or end his contract must be set out. That we accept. But in view of the series of decisions by this court, * * * we cannot admit a doubt that maliciously and without justifiable cause to induce a third person to end his employment of the plaintiff, whether the inducement be false slanders or successful persuasion, is an actionable tort. See also *Angle* v. *Chicago, St. Paul, Minneapolis & Omaha Railway,* 151 U. S. 1, 13.

We apprehend that there no longer is any difficulty in recognizing that a right to be protected from malicious interference may be incident to a right arising out of a contract, although a contract, so far as performance is concerned, imposes a duty only on the promisor. Again, in the case of a contract of employment, even when the employment is at will, the fact that the employer is free from liability for discharging the plaintiff does not carry with it immunity to the defendant who has controlled the employer's action to the plaintiff's harm. The notion that the employer's immunity must be a non-conductor so far as any remoter liability is concerned, troubled some of the judges in *Allen* v. *Flood,* [1898] A. C. 1, but is disposed of for this Commonwealth by the cases cited. See also *May* v. *Wood,* 172 Mass. 11, 14, 15. So again it may be taken to be settled by *Plant* v. *Woods,* 176 Mass. 492, 501, 502, that motives may determine the question of liability; that while intentional interference of the kind supposed may be privileged if for certain purposes, yet if due only to malevolence it must be answered for. On that point the judges were of one mind. See 177 Mass. 504. Finally, we see no sound distinction between persuading by malevolent advice and accomplishing the same result by falsehood or putting in fear. In all these cases the employer is controlled through motives created by the defendant for the unprivileged purpose. It appears to us not to matter which motive is relied upon. If accomplishing the end by one of them is a wrong to the plaintiff, accomplishing it by either of the others must be equally a wrong.

It follows from what we have said that we are of opinion that both counts of the declaration disclose a good cause of action, although the first on the authority of *May* v. *Wood* must be held insufficient in point of form. The second is not within the authority or reason of that case, 172 Mass. 14, and is in a form similar to the third count which was held good in *Walker* v. *Cronin*. See *Lumley* v. *Gye,* 2 El. & Bl. 216. As to that the demurrer will be overruled. Assuming that the demurrer was intended to be a demurrer to each count as well as to the declaration, it will be sustained as to the first count, but it seems to us that under the circumstances the plaintiff should be given an opportunity to amend.

*Demurrer to first count sustained;
demurrer to second count overruled.*

CHAPTER 4

BILL OF RIGHTS

MAY THE FORM OF INDICTMENTS BE CHANGED?

Commonwealth v. *Freelove*
150 Mass. 66 (1889)

This is an indictment for adultery, to which a motion to quash was filed, on the ground that it does not conclude against the peace of the Commonwealth nor against the statute in such cases made and provided. This motion was overruled, and the defendant alleged exceptions. The Pub. Sts. c. 213, sec. 16, expressly enact that no indictment shall be quashed on this ground, if the omission does not tend to prejudice the defendant. But it was argued that the statute is unconstitutional. We shall not consider how far the Legislature might go in simplifying indictments before encountering Article XII of the Massachusetts Bill of Rights. We admit that there are limits to its power in this direction; that, for instance, it could not authorize the omission of allegations necessary to describe a specific crime. * * * But there is no doubt that it can do a good deal in the way of simplification. * * * We do not think that it needs argument to show that the Legislature may dispense with a purely formal averment which would give the defendant no additional information, and the omission of which would not prejudice him. *Commonwealth* v. *Holley*, 3 Gray, 458. "Technical and formal objections of this nature are not constitutional rights." * * * The defendant was safe in assuming that the proceeding was under the statute, although he was not informed so in terms. * * *

Exceptions overruled.

RIGHT OF TRIAL BY JURY
Crocker v. Cotting
173 Mass. 68 (1899)

[Petition under statute to determine validity and define the nature of any restriction or encumbrance on title to land.]

The purpose of this demurrer is only to test the constitutionality of St. 1889, c. 442, and to ascertain whether this case falls within the act.

The objection to the constitutionality of the act is that it provides for a common law proceeding concerning property, and does not provide for a trial by jury, as required by the fifteenth article of our Declaration of Rights. The answer to this objection is that, in the first place, although it is on the law side of the court, the proceeding is more after the analogies of equity than of the common law, as is shown, among other things, by the fact that it ends in a decree and not in a judgment, (*Gurney* v. *Waldron,* 137 Mass. 376, 378), and, next, that the statute does nothing to deprive a party of his trial by jury in any case where such a trial would be proper. The principal object of the statute is to provide an expeditious way to have documents construed when rights depend upon a doubtful construction. If it were necessary in order to save the act, it would not be difficult to confine its operation to such cases. But supposing the statute to go further, and to apply to cases where there is an issue of fact, the word "issues" in sec. 1 would be enough to indicate, if any indication were necessary, that the provision for a petition to the Supreme Judicial Court is a provision for a trial in that court in such manner as settled practice shows to be proper.

The second ground of demurrer is that easements are not within the act. The language of the statute is: "When the title to land appears of record to be affected by a possible condition, restriction, reservation, stipulation, or agreement, etc., any person having a freehold estate . . . may file a petition in the Supreme Judicial Court for the purpose of determining the validity or defining the nature and extent of such possible condition, or other encumbrance," etc. It cannot be denied that an easement is a "restriction" and "encumbrance" within the possible meaning of the words used in the two branches of the sentence, and we see no sufficient reason for giving those words less than their full meaning. If the new remedy is a good thing in the case of an equitable restriction, it is as useful in the case of an easement at common law. We see no ground for preferring a building scheme to a right of way in the search for enlightenment. Very likely those who drew the act were thinking of their own peculiar troubles, whatever they may have been. But they used general words, which we take in their broad and general sense. In *Chase* v. *Walker,* 167 Mass. 293, a decree was made under this statute concerning the extent of an easement, and neither the court nor the able counsel who argued the case seem to have been disturbed by either of the difficulties raised by the defendant. The easement was created by covenant, but there is no difference between an easement by covenant and one by grant. *Hogan* v. *Barry,* 143 Mass. 538.

Demurrer overruled.

POOR DEBTORS—IMPRISONMENT
Brown's Case
173 Mass. 498 (1899)

This is a petition for a writ of habeas corpus. The petitioner is held by virtue of a mittimus issued under St. 1898, c. 549, and the only question argued is whether that statute is constitutional. The statute provides that proceedings may be had in any police, district, or municipal court of the district in which a judgment debtor resides, by which after notice, proof that the debt is for necessaries furnished to the debtor or his family, and an examination, a decree may be made fixing the time, place, and amount of payments to be made by the debtor, and that failure without good cause to comply with the decree shall be treated as a contempt of court, to be proceeded against as courts of equity are accustomed to proceed.

The first objection taken to the act is that it is operative only in those portions of the Commonwealth which are within the jurisdiction of some police, district, or municipal court, and that a number of towns are outside any such jurisdiction, having only trial justices. It is suggested that for this reason the statute creates special privileges, imposes special burdens, and denies the equal protection of the laws to all. But it is settled that municipal regulations of this sort, based simply on the practical necessities of administration in dealing with a population unequally distributed over the State, do not conflict with the Fourteenth Amendment of the Constitution of the United States. *Missouri* v. *Lewis,* 101 U. S. 22. * * * There is even less pretence for finding any inconsistency with the less specific expressions relied on from the State Constitution. * * *

Next it is objected that the law creates a preferred class of creditors. Why not? Such preferences always have existed;—preferences of specialty creditors over creditors by simple contract in former days;—preference of certain classes of debts in the settlement of bankrupt or insolvent estates, and in administration, at the present time;—special privileges in the way of lien given by statute to laborers and materialmen. We know of nothing to prevent the Legislature making the purchase of the necessaries of life easier by giving special remedies against those who wilfully try to avoid paying for them.

Finally, it is suggested that the statute is contrary to the Twelfth Article of the Massachusetts Declaration of Rights, as depriving defendants of their liberty or estate otherwise than by the judgment of their peers or the law of the land. This seems to a majority of the court even less tenable than the previously mentioned objections. The statute applies only to judgment debtors. A valid judgment is assumed to have been obtained. One was obtained in this case. The petitioner might have had a jury if he had wanted it upon the merits of his case. But after they had been tried, the application of this article of the Declaration of Rights is at an end. It does not apply to the procedure of execution. The statute, if the Legislature had seen fit, might have revived unconditional imprisonment in case of failure to pay the judgment, and we apprehend that it would made no difference whether the statute should treat the seizure of the body as satisfaction of the debt, as at common law, or, after the fashion of equity, as a means of compelling a contumacious debtor to obedience. The statute does not go so far. It gives the debtor the benefit of an examination, and does not subject him even to the chance of imprisonment unless the court is satisfied that the debtor is able to pay. It does not imprison him unless it is satisfied further that he is failing to obey the decree without just cause. Looking at the matter apart from the distinctions of law and equity, it seems to us very plain that, when we have reached the stage of execution, what the statute might do out and out in the first place it may do with such mitigating conditions as the Legislature chooses to grant, and that the presence of such a condition cannot make void what would be good without it. It is a pure mitigation to allow the question to be raised whether the failure to obey the decree or to satisfy the judgment is without just cause. The Legislature very properly intrusted the answering of it to the judge, instead of calling in a second jury. It was not the petitioner's constitutional right to have it asked at all. Still less was it his right, if it was asked, to have it answered by the jury rather than by the judge.

Looking at the matter from a somewhat different point of view, What is to hinder the Legislature from enforcing payment of debts for necessaries by decree instead of by judgment, if so minded, if the trial by jury on the merits of the case is saved? It cannot be pretended that the Legislature cannot bring new subject matter under the operation of the injunction. It may to-morrow authorize the prevention of a libel in that way, and may make the payment of a debt a matter of specific performance, just as the courts, of their own motion, have made the transfer of chattels. Furthermore, what the Legislature may put into the power of a chancery court it may put into the power of a district judge, endowing him to that extent with some of the authority of a chancery court.

When it is suggested that imprisonment for contempt is a punishment which is inflicted without trial by jury, the answer is, in the first place, that a court is not obliged by the Constitution to resort to a jury to find our whether a defendant is obeying or disobeying its decree; *State* v. *Becht,* 23 Minn. 411, 414; and, secondly, that it is splitting hairs over words to call the imprisonment a punishment for the purpose of drawing any conclusion from the name. The imprisonment is a means of compelling a contumacious defendant to obey. He can stop it by obedience. Until he obeys, he must look to the statute, not to the Constitution, for the limit of his liability. * * *

Prisoner remanded.

DILATORY TACTICS AND CONSTITUTIONAL GUARANTEES

Commonwealth v. *Storti*
177 Mass. 339 (1901)

[Luigi Storti was indicted for murder. It appeared that he killed Michele Calucci by striking him over the head with an axe in his bed during the late hours of the morning of November 7, 1899. It was contended by the defendant's counsel that the jury found their verdict in accordance with the second count which was bad under the Massachusetts Constitution, in that "No subject shall be held to answer for any crimes or offence, until the same is fully and plainly, substantially and formally, described to him." Exceptions were also taken to the admission and exclusion of evidence. Further facts are stated in Holmes' opinion which follows.]

This is an indictment for murder upon which the defendant has been found guilty, and the case is here on exceptions and upon an appeal from the overruling of a motion to quash. The indictment is in two counts. It cannot be argued that the first is bad. The second count is in the form provided by St. 1899, c. 409, and is attacked on the ground that it does not satisfy the requirements of Article XII of the Massachusetts Bill of Rights. Without giving any countenance to this suggestion, it is enough to say that the two counts are for the same offence, that any evidence which would justify or require a verdict of guilty on the one equally would justify or require it on the other, and that under such circumstances a general verdict is supported by the first count. Therefore any discussion of constitutional law is unnecessary. * * *

The murder was committed in a sleeping-room in which the defendant and the murdered man were passing the night along with others. A witness for the government having testified that he was called from the opposite room by one Sarni after the murder had been committed and the defendant had fled, and having described what and whom he saw, was asked by the defendant what Sarni said. The exclusion of this evidence was excepted to. The exclusion was right. *Commonwealth* v. *James,* 99 Mass. 438, 441. The statement was pure hearsay. It did not concern a state of mind of the speaker, and therefore did not fall within the exception as to cases of that class. Moreover the state of mind of Sarni was immaterial. The state of mind of the witness at the moment when he was called was equally immaterial. Again, what Sarni said did not explain or qualify the summons in any way in which it was admissible to explain it. The summons needed no explanation, and, although admitted without objection, itself was immaterial except as merely introductory to and explanatory of the fact that the witness went to the room. The evidence amounted to no more than that in consequence of what was said the witness went to the scene of the murder. Finally, Sarni did not even see what happened, as he was asleep at the time. See further *Commonwealth* v. *Chance,* 174 Mass. 245, 251.

The next exception is to the admission of evidence of a quarrel and blows between the defendant and the murdered man in Italy about two years before, followed, three or four months later, by threats on the defendant's part. Subject to the question of its admissibility, with which we shall deal in a moment, there was evidence of statements by the defendant showing a continuous state of hostility ever since. The exception cannot be maintained. * * * One of the statements objected to in this connection was that the witness saw the deceased and the defendant in court when he testified on a former occasion. If we are to take the evidence as meaning that the two were seen by the witness when on trial in Italy for their quarrel, the fact was not put in for the purpose of proving the event of the trial or anything else concerning it which called for a production of the Italian record, if there was one. The fact seems to have been mentioned only in the enumeration of the times that the witness had seen the parties. Even if the record had been put in, this evidence would have been proper to identify the parties.

The admission of statements made by the defendant to the officers who arrested him was excepted to, mainly on the ground that the statements were not voluntary. The judges who tried the case were warranted in finding that the statements were freely made, and whatever latitude we may use in reviewing these findings of fact, we cannot say that they were wrong. *Commonwealth* v. *Bond,* 170 Mass. 41. The first conversation was in the station-house, just after the arrest on the day following the murder. In this nothing of great importance was said. But the defendant in denying his guilt said that he never was in Boston, which of course was evidence against him. In the next, on the following day at the same place, the defendant admitted striking the deceased with an axe. So far no inducements had been held out to him, and the facts that the prisoner was in custody and was questioned by an officer are not conclusive against this evidence. On the train from Hudson, where he was arrested, to Boston, he asked the officer whether Calucci was dead, how much imprisonment they would give the defendant, and whether they would make him die. He said that Calcucci and he were great enemies, and it was only a question of time, that Calucci would kill him if he did not kill Calucci, and so on, with further particulars.

The first full and extended examination was in the Boston station-house, in the presence of three officers, one of whom put questions through an interpreter, and the questions and answers were taken down by a stenographer. The interpreter was a witness at the trial, and swore that he accurately translated all that was said by the officer to the prisoner and all the answers which the prisoner made. The stenographer testified that he accurately took it all down. What seems to be the chief ground of objection to this examination is that according to his own testimony the interpreter said to the prisoner that "what would be against him, that will be brought in court against him, or in favor, as it was." We understand this to mean in imperfect English that whatever was said would be used in court, against the defendant if unfavorable, or for him if favorable. It is hard to find an inducement to make a confession or to say things unfavorable to himself in these words. But, if it be thought that there was an inducement to speak when otherwise he might have remained silent, *Bram* v. *United States,* 168 U. S. 532, 549, 550, it is enough to say that, according to the testimony of the stenographer from his notes, the prisoner was asked if he wished to make any statement of his own free will, answered yes, and then was cautioned simply that everything he said might be used against him in court. This is confirmed by other evidence, and, to say the least, the presiding judges were warranted in taking it as the true account.

An objection was taken to the stenographer's evidence on the ground that it was hearsay, as he merely put down what the interpreter reported. But without seeking for further possible answers, it is enough to repeat that the interpreter testified that he reported correctly. See *Commonwealth* v. *Vose,* 157 Mass. 393. It would be refining too much and not in the direction of accuracy to say that the confessions, although taken down in their English translation, should have been proved in Italian and then translated before the jury. The English was the most accurate evidence attainable at the time of the trial. *Camerlin* v. *Palmer Co.* 10 Allen, 539, 541.

After the judges had found that the confessions were admissible, the defendant asked for a string of rulings, largely platitudes, on the question of admissibility. These were presented too late, and the court was quite right in refusing on that ground to consider them.

The only exception which causes hesitation on our part is to the exclusion of evidence that, at the talk in the Hudson station house, Rooney, one of the officers, said in English to Rosatto, another, who was speaking with the prisoner in Italian, "Tell him it will be better for him if he tells." But it appears that the defendant did not speak or understand English, and not only was there no evidence that such a suggestion was communicated to the prisoner, but all the testimony was that it was not communicated, if such a statement was made. It did not even appear that Rooney spoke in the prisoner's hearing.

A witness for the government was allowed to testify in rebuttal how many bottles of beer he had drunk on the evening of the murder. Evidence having been gone into previously by both sides on the question of his sobriety, there is nothing to show that the court exceeded its discretionary powers. *Commonwealth* v. *Meaney,* 151 Mass. 55.

Decree overruling motion to quash affirmed; exceptions overruled.

CRUEL OR UNUSUAL PUNISHMENT?
Storti v. Commonwealth
178 Mass. 549 (1901)

[The defendant, Storti, was convicted of murder and was sentenced under a Massachusetts statute of 1898. The statute substituted electrocution for hanging as a method of punishment in capital cases. Storti was the first person to be sentenced under the new statute. It was contended in his behalf that the punishment was "cruel or unusual" and that the statute was therefore unconstitutional. Holmes' opinion follows.]

These proceedings are respectively a writ of error and a petition for a writ of habeas corpus. Both are intended to raise the same issue, that the punishment, death by electricity, to which the said Storti has been sentenced, under St. 1898, c. 326, sec. 6, is "cruel or unusual" within articles 26 of the Massachusetts Declaration of Rights. Upon the writ of error, the plaintiff in error insisting that the assignment was of error in fact, evidence was heard, the plaintiff in error being brought into court by habeas corpus to be present at the hearing, and the presiding justice found that the assignment was not true. The independent petition for habeas corpus was reserved by agreement of parties for hearing by the full court at the same time with the writ of error.

In the view which we take of the case it is unnecessary to consider any question of procedure, either as between the two proceedings adopted or as to matters of detail arising under each. We therefore pass all such matters on one side. It also is unnecessary to consider whether the before-mentioned article of our Declaration of Rights is to be limited in its application to the action of magistrates so far as they are left to themselves and the common law, or whether it is to be taken to embody a large general principle equally binding upon all branches of the Government, or at least binding upon magistrates and courts of law even when the Legislature has undertaken to establish a punishment by its act. Finally it is unnecessary to go into any nice argument upon the words of the article, and to decide whether, inasmuch as those words are "cruel or unusual," not "cruel and unusual," a punishment which is unusual but is not cruel is forbidden by them.

Taking all the preliminaries most favorably for the prisoner, we are clearly of opinion that the Constitution is not contravened by the act, and we render our opinion at once that we may avoid delaying the course of the law and raising false hopes in his mind. The answer to the whole argument which has been presented is that there is but a single punishment, death. It is not contended that if this is true the statute is invalid, but it is said that it is not true, and that you cannot separate the means from the end in considering what the punishment is, any more when the means is a current of electricity than when it is a slow fire. We should have thought that the distinction was plain. In the latter case the means is adopted not solely for the purpose of accomplishing the end of death but for the purpose of causing other pain to the person concerned. The so-called means is also an end of the same kind as the death itself, or in other words is intended to be a part of the punishment. But when, as here, the means adopted are chosen with just the contrary intent, and are devised for the purpose of reaching the end proposed as swiftly and painlessly as possible, we are of opinion that they are not forbidden by the Constitution although they should be discoveries of recent science and never should have been heard of before. Not only is the prohibition addressed to what in a proper sense may be called the punishment but, further, the word "unusual" must be construed with the word "cruel" and cannot be taken so broadly as to prohibit every humane improvement not previously known in Massachusetts. *People* v. *Durston,* 119 N. Y. 569; S. C. *In re Kemmler,* 136 U. S. 436.

The suggestion that the punishment of death, in order not to be unusual, must be accomplished by molar rather than by molecular motion seems to us a fancy unwarranted by the Constitution.

No doubt a means might be adopted which, although adopted only as a means, pracically would be part of the punishment and would have to be considered as such. But such a case is not presented by a means chosen precisely because it is instantaneous. There was a hint at an argument based on mental suffering, but the suffering is due not to its being more horrible to be struck by lightning than to be hanged with the chance of slowly strangling, but to the general fear of death. The suffering due to that fear the law does not seek to spare. It means that it shall be felt.

Some criticism was addressed to minor details of the law. The provision that after delivery to the warden of the State prison the prisoner shall be kept in a special cell and only certain persons allowed access to him without an order of the court, does not prevent, and by its true construction is not intended to prevent, the presence of the prisoner in court in any matter which properly still may be brought up in court, and which by the course of law or treaty may require his presence, (see *Commonwealth* v. *Cody,* 165 Mass. 133, 138), as was exemplified in this case.

Leaving it to the warden to select the day of the week appointed by the court for the execution was not intended to aggravate the prisoner's distress, by enhancing his suspense. The purpose is humane, and the possible uncertainty for a brief period as to the exact time is not a part of the punishment. See further *Commonwealth* v. *Costley,* 118 Mass. 1, 35.

Judgment to stand; writ of habeas corpus denied.

EX POST FACTO LAWS
Luigi Storti's Case
180 Mass. 57 (1901)

This is a petition for the writ of *habeas corpus* on the ground that the respondent has no authority to hold the petitioner in custody except such as is derived from St. 1901, c. 520, and that as against the petitioner that statute is unconstitutional and void.

The petitioner had been sentenced to death and had been committed to the warden of the State prison under St. 1898, c. 326. That act required that from the time of delivery to the warden until his execution or discharge a convict under sentence of death should "be kept in a cell provided for the purpose, and no person shall be allowed access to him without an order of the court, except the officers of the prison, his counsel, his physician, a priest or minister of religion, if he shall desire one, and the members of his family." Section 2. This was amended by St. 1901, c. 520, Sec. 1, so as to read: "except the officers and employees of the prison, his counsel, and such physicians, priest or minister of religion as the warden may approve, and the members of his family, who are identified to the satisfaction of the warden," and then was added: "If the execution of the death sentence is respited by the governor, or otherwise delayed by process of law, the convict may, in the discretion of the warden, be confined in one of the cells in the solitary prison established by" St. 1894. Resolves, c. 109.

The prisoner's health was bad, and pending dilatory proceedings by his counsel this statute was passed, obviously for the relief of persons in his situation, and, as there was no other person in his situation, it hardly would be too much to say for his relief. It is admitted that it was a relief to him in its practical working, but he relies upon the undoubted proposition that the constitutionality of a law is to be judged by what it authorizes and by what might happen under it, not alone by what actually is done. It is said that by the later act rights of access conferred by the earlier statute are cut down, and that solitary confinement is or may be substituted for confinement which it is said the earlier statute did not permit to be solitary. On these grounds it is argued that the law is *ex post facto* and void.

We are unable to accede to any part of the argument for the prisoner. If all the rest of it were sound, it would not follow that he was entitled to his release, even apart from Put. Sts. c. 3, Sec. 3, cl. 2, and the decisions under it. * * * But we need not go so far. The mode of confinement is no part of the punishment. That already has been decided. *Storti* v. *Commonwealth,* 178 Mass. 549. If we assume that the provision against *ex post facto* laws nevertheless might apply, the answer to one of the objections is that however his actual confinement under the act of 1898 be described, that act more clearly than the later one permitted the confinement to be made solitary. The mode in which the cell in the execution building may have been constructed does not affect the meaning of the statute, and the warden, after its construction, as before, was at liberty to provide a cell in the State prison building in place of that in the execution building, and to put the prisoner there.

The prison established under the resolve of 1894, although referred to in the act of 1901 as "the solitary prison," was to be a prison "for the separate confinement" of such convicts as the warden should think expedient. It is evident that this refers to a milder form of confinement, adverted to in *Medley, Petitioner,* 134 U. S. 160, 168. It is found that the prison is used for that milder form, and that the petitioner has not been in solitary confinement since he was placed there. But whether or not in fact prisoners within it sometimes are given solitary confinement,—whether or not this prisoner was,—still, so far as the provision of the later statute goes, it was intended and purported to be a mitigation of his lot. There is no doubt that it was so in fact.

Then as to the matter of access. The later statute makes no change, or but an infinitesimal one, from what was implied in the former act. It only makes the implications clear and explicit. The act of 1898 of course did not authorize anyone to walk into the prison on his mere statement that he was a member of the prisoner's family. A person presenting himself as a member would have had to satisfy the warden that he was one. So the provision for "a priest or minister" did not require the admission of any priest or minister who asked to come in. It was enough to admit one whom the warden approved. We think that no different construction should be given to the words "his physician."

But apart from details it is a sufficient answer to the petition that neither of the provisions of the act of 1898 adverted to was intended to confer any rights upon the prisoner. They both were matters of prison discipline, restrictions on the warden and directions for keeping the prisoner until execution,—nothing more. The persons mentioned as possibly having access to him are mentioned only by way of exception to the general exclusion of all others. The excepted persons remain subject to Pub. Sts. c. 221, secs. 33–35, requiring a permit and authorizing the warden to exclude any one, "when it appears that such admission would be injurious to the best interests of the prison."

Petition denied.

APPOINTMENT OF TEMPORARY GUARDIAN OF INSANE PERSON WITHOUT NOTICE

Bumpus v. *French*
179 Mass. 131 (1901)

This is an appeal from the allowance of the account of a temporary guardian appointed by the Probate Court without notice to the ward, the appellant, pending a petition for the appointment of a permanent guardian on the ground of insanity. This petition was dismissed after a hearing, and at the same time the appellant was discharged from the temporary guardianship. The objection to the allowance of the account is taken on the single ground that the statute under which the guardian was appointed, St. 1900, c. 345, is contrary to article 12 of the Massachusetts Declaration of Rights, and to the Fourteenth Amendment of the Constitution of the United States. This question is the only one argued, and is the only one which we shall consider. The appellant did not file a petition to revoke the decree appointing the guardian but only a petition that he might be removed.

We shall not consider whether the constitutional provisions relied on apply to proceedings for the protection of persons alleged to be insane. * * * For assuming that they apply we are of opinion that the statute is constitutional. The great provisions intended to protect liberty and property cannot be read as extending with mathematical logic to every case where there is an unpaid-for diminution of property rights or a temporary restraint of personal freedom without a hearing of both sides in court. It does not need argument to show that sometimes it may be necessary to impose such a temporary restraint without the delay required for a hearing and even before notice to the party restrained. Not to mention other instances familiar to the law, the necessity in cases of alleged insanity to protect the property until the principal question is decided has been recognized and acted upon many times under or possibly even without special authority of statute. * * *

'A distinction is taken on the ground that in this case a guardian is appointed, and that this appointment is a judicial act and changes the status of the appellant. But the change is subject to instant revocation if it should appear to have been made under a mistake. Although the appointment may be made without notice, it cannot take effect without the knowledge of the party concerned, who may apply at once to have the decree revoked and is entitled to a hearing if he wants it. The act does not say so in terms, but we are of opinion that the right is implied, and that this is all that the Constitution requires. *Le Donne, Petitioner,* 173 Mass. 550, 552. * * * No doubt caution should be used and would be used to make sure that the temporary ward should have access to the court, and that means should be furnished to those representing him and opposing the principal petition. Shelford, Lunacy, (1st ed.) 127. No doubt, also, the appointment should be and is limited to the time necessary for the decision of the principal matter. St. 1900, c. 345, Secs. 1, 5. *In re Lawler,* Ir. Rep. 8 Eq. 506, 514–516. But the mere fact that the temporary limitation of the ward's power is effected by the order of a judge and the appointment of a guardian, rather than by arbitrary physical constraint relying on necessity alone for its warrant, certainly does not bring up any new constitutional bar.

If, in the light of *Chase* v. *Hathaway,* 14 Mass. 222, * * * we assume that the appointment of a permanent guardian without notice would be void, and that the foregoing reasoning would not be enough to save it even when the court was satisfied that personal notice would be unsafe, (see *Matter of Blewitt,* 131 N. Y. 541, 547), still we are of opinion that an appointment which in form and essence is provisional and temporary, and is founded on and limited by necessity, may be valid without notice, and that it was valid in this case. See *Porter* v. *Ritch,* 70 Conn. 235.

The practical working of the law was exemplified here. The petitions for the appointment of a permanent and a temporary guardian both were filed on October 13, 1900. Notice under the former was issued on the same day and the temporary guardian was appointed. On October 18 the appellant filed a petition for his removal, and this and the principal matter were heard and decided together. As we have said, there was no petition for a revocation of the decree, and it is apparent that when the appellant came before him the judge did not think it proper to review his action until he was ready to dispose of the whole case. No wrong was done, and there is no danger of wrong under a proper administration of the act.

Decree affirmed.

CHAPTER 5

IMPAIRMENT OF THE
OBLIGATION OF CONTRACT

FOREIGN CREDITOR'S RIGHTS IN MASSACHUSETTS

Murphy v. *Manning*
134 Mass. 488 (1883)

This is a suit on a Massachusetts judgment. The defence is a discharge in insolvency granted in this State on proceedings begun after the judgment was rendered. The plaintiffs were New Jersey creditors of the defendant, (a resident of Massachusetts), and it is not denied that the original debt would not have been discharged. * * * *Kelley* v. *Drury,* 9 Allen, 27. But the distinction is taken, that, as the plaintiffs in this case have elected to merge their debt in a Massachusetts judgment, that judgment at all events must be subject to the state laws, and is disposed of by the discharge. A very forcible argument may be made in favor of such a view, but we think that there are stronger considerations on the other side, which is also supported by the weight of authority.

Kelley v. *Drury* establishes that our insolvent laws do not shut out parties whose claims are not subject to or discharged by them from access to our state courts. We may say more broadly that the Legislature has not shown an intention to adopt a local rule as to the procedure within its control, except so far as it has power to dispose of the substantive rights in aid of which the procedure is set in motion. We are speaking, of course, of the statutes affecting the present decision. It follows that, unless the original debt is merged in the judgment in such a sense that the debt, and not merely this form of it, has become subject to Massachusetts law, we must attribute the same validity to the judgment that remains to the debt. We think that the debt is not affected in this respect by the judgment. A judgment does not obliterate the essential features of the obligation on which it is rendered. *Betts* v. *Bagley,* 12 Pick. 572, 580. For instance, when, by reason of the insolvent laws, execution upon a former judgment could have issued only against the estate, and not against the body, of the defendant, execution upon a second judgment recovered upon the first was limited in the same way. *Choteau* v. *Richardson,* 12 Allen, 365. So, the antecedent equities of a surety continue unchanged by a joint judgment against him and his principal; and conduct on the part of the creditor which would have discharged him before will discharge him afterwards. *Carpenter* v. *King,* 9 Met. 511, 516. Conversely, here, the plaintiffs' claim before judgment, not being subject to discharge by our laws, did not lose that characteristic and become more infirm by the change, upon any ground of the substantive law.

We think that the weight of authority is in favor of our conclusion, notwithstanding the dicta in *Ogden* v. *Saunders,* 12 Wheat. 213, 363, 364. * * * See also *Brown* v. *Bridge,* 106 Mass. 563, where the implication is, that, if the plaintiff had not been domiciled in Massachusetts when he recovered the judgment sued upon, it would not have been discharged by the subsequent discharge in insolvency.

This court having deferred to the authority of *Baldwin* v. *Hale,* 1 Wall. 223, in *Kelley* v. *Drury, ubi supra,* it is proper to add that the reasoning of that case applies to the one before us with almost, if not quite, the same force as to *Kelley* v. *Drury*. The debt is still due to citizens of another State, who remain as independent of its jurisdiction and as inaccessible to notice of its proceedings as ever. They were no more bound to resort to Massachusetts in order to get the fruits of their judgment after it was recovered, than they were to go there in the first instance to collect their debt.

Judgment for the plaintiffs.

DISCHARGE IN INSOLVENCY NO BAR TO NON-RESIDENT CREDITOR

Phoenix National Bank v. *Batcheller*
151 Mass. 589 (1890)

This is an action by a Rhode Island national bank, upon a promissory note payable in Massachusetts, and made here by the defendants, citizens of this State. The defence is a discharge in insolvency in this State. It is admitted that the plaintiff did not prove its claim upon the note, and the only question is whether, under these circumstances, the discharge is a bar. It was argued for the defendants, that the decisions of the Supreme Court of the United States that discharges in such cases are not generally valid against citizens of other States do not go upon any constitutional ground, but upon mistaken views of what is called private international law, and therefore are not binding upon us; and we were asked to reconsider *Kelley* v. *Drury,* 9 Allen, 27, in which this court yielded its earlier expressed opinion, and followed the precedent of *Baldwin* v. *Hale,* 1 Wall. 223.   *   *   *

There is no dispute that the letter of the discharge and of our statute covers the plaintiff's claim; Pub. Sts. c. 157, Secs. 80, 81; and the argument in favor of giving them effect according to their letter is, that unless the statute is void we are bound to follow it; that the law of the place where the contract is made and is to be performed, which is in force at the time of making and for performing it, enters into the contract so far as to settle everywhere what acts done at that place shall discharge it (*May* v. *Breed,* 7 Cush. 15); and that a discharge in accordance with that law cannot be said to impair the obligation of a contract which contemplated it, or to deprive the contractee of property without due process of law when that property was created subject to destruction in that way.

We express no opinion upon the weight of this argument. Although it formerly prevailed with this court, (*Scribner* v. *Fisher,* 2 Gray, 43; *Burrall* v. *Rice,* 5 Gray, 539), it may be that there is a distinction as to a discharge by legal proceedings. It may be that statutes providing for a discharge by an insolvency court do not enter into the contract in such a sense as to bind the contractee to adopt and submit himself to the jurisdiction as an implied condition of the promisor's undertaking. It does not follow, because the discharge, if effective, does not impair the obligation of the contract, that absolute liability to it is a part of the substantive obligation. The substantive promise and the obligation of the contract are different things; and apart from this consideration it may be that by sound principle the plaintiff is to be taken to have subjected itself to Massachusetts proceedings only to the extent that, if the Massachusetts courts could acquire jurisdiction over it in the ordinary modes by which jurisdiction of the person is acquired, it would be bound everywhere by a discharge granted here.

However this may be, we see no sufficient reason for departing from what has been accepted as the law for a quarter of a century. We agree that, consistently with our duty, we cannot yield our opinion upon new questions not subject to the final jurisdiction of the Supreme Court of the United States solely out of a desire for uniformity. But when we are asked to overrule a decision of our own court which has been acquiesced in for so long, we should have to be very sure, before doing so, not only that the decision was wrong, but also that the Supreme Court of the United States, whatever we may think about it, either would not regard our decision as subject to review by them, or would abandon opinions which they have expressed repeatedly, and down to the latest volume of their reports.

We should hesitate to overrule *Kelley* v. *Drury,* even if we were ready to say that we disagreed with the principle of *Baldwin* v. *Hale,* and that we thought our decision not subject to review. For when in a particular case the precedents are settled in favor of uniformity, the fact that they do conform to the decisions of the Supreme Court of the United States is a most powerful secondary reason for not disturbing them, and would be likely to outweigh our private opinions upon the original matter. There is, too, a particular reason for uniformity in the present case, because it is manifest that, practicaly at least, the general validity of the discharge, that is, its effect outside this Commonwealth, depends upon the decision of other courts than this, and that the decision of the United States Court upon that question is of more importance than that of any other.

The often repeated view of the Supreme Court of the United States is, that discharges like the present are void for want of jurisdiction, and that statutes purporting to authorize them are beyond the power of the States to pass. * * * Whether that court would regard a decision to the contrary by a State court as subject to review by them upon constitutional grounds, does not appear very clearly from any language of theirs which has been called to our attention, unless it be the following, repeated in *Baldwin* v. *Hale,* 1 Wall. 223, 231, from *Ogden* v. *Saunders,* 12 Wheat. 213, 369: "But when, in the exercise of that power, the States pass beyond their own limits, and the rights of their own citizens, and act upon the rights of citizens of other States, there arises a conflict of sovereign power, and a collision with the judicial powers granted to the United States, which renders the exercise of such a power incompatible with the rights of other States and with the Constitution of the United States." This is somewhat emphasized as the deliberate view of the court, not only by its original mode of statement, but by their adhesion to it after the dissent of Chief Justice Taney in *Cook* v. *Moffat,* 5 How. 295, 310. * * *

This language certainly gives the impression that our decision would be regarded as subject to review, possibly on the ground of an implied restriction on the power to pass insolvent laws reserved to the States (*Denney* v. *Bennett,* 128 U. S. 489, 498); possibly on the ground that the discharge would impair the obligation of contracts with persons not within the jurisdiction (*Cook* v. *Moffat,* 5 How. 295, 308); possibly by reason of the Fourteenth Amendment (*Pennoyer* v. *Neff,* 95 U. S. 714); possibly on some vaguer ground. We feel the force of the reasoning quoted from *Stoddard* v. *Harrington,* 100 Mass. 87, 89, but that case did not profess to weaken the authority of *Kelley* v. *Drury,* and, moreover, the question which we are now considering is not what would be our own opinion, but what seems to be the opinion of the Supreme Court of the United States.

The decision in *Kelley* v. *Drury* did not go upon any nice inquiry whether it was subject to review, but upon the ground that this court deferred to the decision of the Supreme Court of the United States, that discharges like the present were not binding outside the jurisdiction, and that, this being so, a discrimination should not be made in favor of our citizens in proceedings in the State court in distinction from proceedings in the courts of the United States.

This last proposition was conceded by the senior counsel for the defendant. But as some doubt was thrown upon it in the printed brief, we repeat what was again intimated in *Murphy* v. *Manning*, 134 Mass. 488, that there is nothing in the law affecting the question before us which indicates an intent to refuse foreign creditors access to the courts of Massachusetts as a merely local rule of procedure, or otherwise than as a consequence of the substantive right having been barred by the discharge. The form of the discharge in the Pub. Sts. c. 157, Sec. 80, and the language of sec. 81, address themselves directly to the substantive right, and declare the debtor discharged from the specified debts. It being settled that the plaintiff's debt is not barred, an action can be maintained to recover it in a State court.

Judgment for the plaintiff.

DISCHARGE NO BAR TO ACTION ON DEBT DUE A PARTNERSHIP

Chase v. *Henry*
166 Mass. 577, 581 (1896)

[The plaintiffs, Chase, Chamberlain and Griffin, partners, sued Henry on a contract for slippers. Chase and Chamberlain were citizens of Massachusetts; Griffin of New Hampshire. The defendant, Henry, was given a discharge in insolvency but plaintiffs put in no claim at the proceedings. A majority of the court held that the debt was an entirety and was, therefore, not barred by the discharge. Holmes dissented. Chief Justice Field and Justice C. Allen concurred.]

I am unable to agree with the decision of the majority, and, as two other of the judges are of the same way of thinking, I deem it best to state the fact, and to give my reasons. The Commonwealth of Massachusetts at the time of the insolvency proceedings had jurisdiction, and, subject to the Constitution of United States, had sovereign power, over the defendant and over the plaintiffs Chase and Chamberlain. As between those persons, it had the power and the constitutional right to declare all obligations which were entered into after the insolvent law was passed at an end when a discharge should be granted. Its power was derived from its power over the persons of the parties named, and could not be affected by the nature of the obligation, or by the fact that others also were interested in the obligation who were not within its power. Jurisdiction and sovereignty deal with persons and with all legal relations of persons, not with particular kinds of contracts. It is true that Massachusetts could not discharge the claim of a person outside its territory,—in this case the plaintiff Griffin. But that did not affect its power to discharge Chase and Chamberlain, who were within it. It may be that, if it did discharge them, the plaintiff Griffin cannot recover; but that is not because Massachusetts has dealt with his claim or has attempted to deal with it *ultra vires,* but because he cannot recover without joining others whose claim this State could deal with and has discharged. It seems to me an inversion to say that a jurisdiction otherwise perfect is defeated because of the secondary and indirect effects it may have on persons outside the jurisdiction. The true order of subordination appears to me the other way. In fact, in other cases,—for instance, divorce,—courts having jurisdiction of one party do not scruple to deal with obligations between that party and another out of the State, although logically the effect upon the rights of the other party in that case is direct. * * * It appears to me that the suggestion that the debt is an entirety is merely a *petitio principii* clothed in scholastic language. As a fact, in other cases the debt is not dealt with as an entirety. *Stone* v. *Wainwright,* 147 Mass. 201, 203.

One who accepts a promise jointly with others acquires a property which has the inherent vice that anything which disables his fellow contractees from suing will prevent his maintaining a suit. For instance, if one partner has set off his own debt wrongfully against a debt due the firm, the innocent partners cannot recover. * * * So, "when once the statute [of limitations] runs against one of two parties entitled to a joint

action, it operates as a bar to such joint action." * * *
I presume it would make no difference that one of the parties lived out of the State. If the statute of limitations bars an action in such a case, I see no reason why the insolvent law should have a less effect.

FOREIGN CORPORATION DOING BUSINESS IN MASSACHUSETTS

Bergner & Engel Brewing Co. v. *Dreyfus*
172 Mass. 154 (1898)

[Chief Justice Field dissented in a separate opinion in this case.]

This is a suit by a Pennsylvania corporation to recover a debt for goods sold and delivered here. The only defence is a discharge in insolvency under our statutes, which of course commonly is no defence at all. This was reaffirmed unanimously in 1890, after full consideration of the objections now urged, and it was decided, also, not for the first time, that the general language of the insolvent law was not intended to affect access to Massachusetts courts by a local rule of procedure unless the substantive right was barred by the discharge. *Phoenix National Bank* v. *Batcheller*, 151 Mass. 589. The grounds urged for an exception in the present case are that the plaintiff, although its brewery and main offices are in Pennsylvania, has an office in Boston and maintains here a complete outfit for the distribution of its products, and that it has a license of the fourth class under Pub. Sts. c. 100, sec. 10, and that it has complied with the laws regulating foreign corporations doing business here, including, we assume, that which requires the appointment of the commissioner of corporations its "attorney upon whom all lawful processes in any action or proceeding against it may be served." St. 1884, c. 330, sec. 1. See St. 1895, c. 157.

We are of opinion that these facts are not enough to bring the plaintiff under the operation of the State insolvent law. It is settled that doing business here does not have that effect upon a citizen or corporation of another State. * * * It is not pointed out what the license, whether valid or void, has to do with the matter, and we do not perceive that complying with the laws concerning foreign corporations ought to have any greater effect. We think it plain that the words just quoted from St. 1884, c. 330, sec. 1, do not mean that, by appointing the commissioner of corporations their attorney, foreign corporations agree not only that publication of notice in insolvency proceedings shall have the effect of personal service upon them in an action, but also that, as a result, they shall be subject to the jurisdiction of the State insolvency proceedings so as to be bound by a discharge.

The most that could be deduced from the appointment would be that, if on other grounds a foreign corporation were subject to the operations of the insolvent law, publication of notice should have the same effect upon it as upon other creditors in making it a party to the proceedings. But we do not suppose that it would be suggested that a natural person, a creditor who was a citizen of another State, lost his immunity and became a party to the proceedings merely by his accidental presence in the Commonwealth at the moment when the notice appeared. *Olivieri* v. *Atkinson*, 168 Mass. 28. No greater direct effect than the actual presence of a natural person can be attributed to the presence of an attorney authorized to receive service of process. Furthermore, we doubt whether the act of 1884 purports to give the appointment even so much effect as that. The language discloses no thought about insolvent proceedings, and when at a later date it was decided to make foreign corporations subject to be put into insolvency here, it was thought proper to provide expressly that service upon the commissioner of corporations should be a sufficient notice to the corporation of the presentment of the petition by creditors against it. St. 1890, c. 321, sec. 1. If the act of 1884 attempted to do more than we have construed it to attempt, its validity might be drawn in doubt as requiring the corporation to surrender a priivlege secured to it by the Constitution and laws of the United States. *Southern Pacific Co. v. Denton,* 146 U. S. 202, 207.

The independent ground on which it is urged that the plaintiff is subject to the insolvent law in the present case is that the plaintiff is domesticated in this State, as shown by the facts above recited, of which the appointment of an attorney is only one. The word "domesticated," which was used in the argument for the defendant, presents no definite legal conception which has any bearing upon the case. We presume that it was intended to convey in a conciliatory form the notion that the plaintiff was domiciled here,—"resident," in the language of Pub. Sts. c. 157, Sec. 81,—and therefore barred by the language and legal operation of the act. It could not be contended that the corporation was a citizen of Massachusetts. In such sense as it is a citizen of any State, it is a citizen of the State which creates it and of no other. But there are even greater objections to a double domicil than there are to double citizenship. Under the law as it has been, a man might find himself owing a double allegiance without any choice of his own. But domicil, at least for any given purpose, is single by its essence. Dicey, Confl. of Laws, 95. A corporation does not differ from a natural person in this respect. If any person, natural or artificial, as a result of choice or on technical grounds of birth or creation, has a domicil in one place, it cannot have one elsewhere, because what the law means by domicil is the one technically pre-eminent headquarters, which, as a result either of fact or of fiction, every person is compelled to have in order that by aid of it certain rights and duties which have been attached to it by the law may be determined. It is settled that a corporation has its domicil in the jurisdiction of the State which created it, and as a consequence that it has not a domicil anywhere else. * * * The so-called modifications of this rule by statutes like the act of 1884 do not modify it because jurisdiction of the ordinary personal actions does not depend upon domicil, but only upon such presence within the jurisdiction as to make service possible. See *In re Hohorst,* 150 U. S. 653. But the operation of our insolvent law by its very terms may, and in this case does, depend upon the domicil of the creditor, and as there can be no doubt either in fact or in law that the plaintiff was domiciled in Pennsylvania in such a sense that a statute like Pub. Sts. c. 157, Sec. 81, would hit it there, it cannot have been domiciled here for the same purpose at the same time.

Judgment for the plaintiff affirmed.

FOREIGN JUDGMENT CREDITOR'S ANCILLARY ADMINISTRATOR

Adams v. *Batchelder*
173 Mass. 258 (1899)

This is an action of contract brought upon a New Hampshire judgment obtained by a man domiciled in New Hampshire, upon a debt contracted in New Hampshire, against a resident of Massachusetts. The judgment creditor died, and the present plaintiff, also a resident of New Hampshire, was appointed his administratrix there. On April 18, 1881, the plaintiff was appointed ancillary administratrix in Massachusetts. On January 21, 1891, the defendant received a discharge in insolvency in Massachusetts. At the trial there was evidence that the debt never had been paid, but the judge ruled that the discharge was a bar to the action. The case is here upon an exception to that ruling.

The ruling raises the question whether the debt is to be regarded as due to a person resident in Massachusetts, within the meaning of Pub. Sts. c. 157, Sec. 81. The defendant's position is that, as the debt could not be collected except by taking out ancillary administration here, it must be taken to be due to the plaintiff in her capacity of ancillary administratrix, and not as a natural person; and that, as that office has its birth and life in Massachusetts, the plaintiff in that capacity has her residence here, just as a corporation has its domicil in the State which created it. *Bergner & Engel Brewing Co. v. Dreyfus,* 172 Mass. 154. But this argument is working a fiction too hard. An executor or administrator is not a corporation sole. He gets his title or his succession to the rights of the deceased by his appointment, it is true. Nowadays he holds those rights in a fiduciary capacity, and he must account for what he receives. But there is no absolute separation of his artificial from his natural personality, as is shown by the fact that a suit against an executor may end in a judgment *de bonis propriis,* either at common law or under Pub. Sts. c. 166, Sec. 10, and very frequently may lead to a personal judgment for costs, as also that in general his contracts as such bind him only personally, even when he is entitled to indemnity from the estate. *Durkin* v. *Langley,* 167 Mass. 577. A judgment recovered by an administrator is payable to him personally, and may be sued on by him in another State. *Talmage* v. *Chapel,* 16 Mass. 71. And it has been held that, when a chattel is taken from an administrator wrongfully, he may sue for it in another State into which it has been carried. * * * What is true of an executor is even more plainly true of an ancillary administrator. And as one person can have but one domicil, unless the law for this purpose treats the woman and the ancillary administratrix as two persons, the plaintiff is a resident of New Hampshire, since no one would contend that her residence was changed for all purposes by her merely accepting an appointment here.

In the present case there is also another consideration. The debt was not suspended until the appointment of the ancillary administratrix. It was the property of the principal administratrix so far that a payment to her would have been a bar to the present action; * * * or that the debt could have been sued for and collected there before the ancillary letters were issued, and that, if collected in Massachusetts, it would be transmitted to New Hampshire and accounted for there, unless there happened to be local claims against the estate. We presume that the right to sue the debtor in New Hampshire, if service could be got there, was not affected by the ancillary appointment. As is said in *Wilkins* v. *Ellett,* 108 U. S. 256, 258, the objection to the principal administratrix's bringing an action here "does not rest upon any defect of the administrator's title in the property, but upon his personal incapacity to sue as administrator beyond the jurisdiction which appointed him." * * *

Perhaps this branch of the argument so far is not unanswerable. But there is the further fact that the debt already had been reduced to judgment. Whatever may be the law as to simple contract debts, it was laid down three centuries ago, and still is repeated, that judgments are *bona notabilia* where the judgment was given. As applied to this case, at least, we may accept the statement. * * * Taking all the elements into account, it seems to us that in this case, if ever, "the [administratrix] here is only the deputy or agent of the [administratrix] abroad." * * *

Whichever of the foregoing lines of thought we pursue, we are led to the conclusion that the debt is not barred. If we treat the debt as due to the ancillary administratrix, we cannot so far distinguish between her natural and her artificial person, in the present state of the law, as to say that she resides in Massachusetts as administratrix when as a woman she resides in New Hampshire. If we are to consider the question of title more nicely, the debt belongs to the principal administratrix, although she may not receive it except subject to local debts of the estate.

Exceptions sustained.

RIGHT TO BE SECOND ASSISTANT ENGINEER IN A FIRE DEPARTMENT

Donaghy v. Macy
167 Mass 178 (1896)

[Donaghy, the second assistant engineer in the fire department of New Bedford, had been removed from his office two years before the expiration of his term. The ordinance under which he held office had been repealed and a successor chosen under a later ordinance. Donaghy then filed a petition of mandamus to Macy, his chief, to be restored to the office to which he had been elected, contending that he could be removed only for cause by a concurrent vote of the two branches of the city council, and that his successor, Dahill, was not entitled to the office. Additional facts appear in Holmes' opinion.]

On January 1, 1894, under the ordinances then in force, the petitioner was duly elected to his office for the term of four years, ending in January, 1898. Ordinances of 1882, c. 11, Sec. 4. In 1896 this ordinance was repealed, and a new ordinance was adopted, which, so far as it affects the present case, is like the old one, except that the time of election is April instead of January, and the first election under it is for two years, ending in 1898. After that the elections are for four years. The petitioner suggests a doubt whether the powers of the city council were not exhausted by one exercise, so that the second ordinance is void, and argues that, however that may be, inasmuch as by Sec. 5 of the earlier ordinances he was removable for cause, he could not be removed otherwise, but had a contract with the city which no more could be avoided by a repeal of the ordinance than by a more direct attempt to remove him without cause.

We have no doubt that the city council had power to pass the second ordinance. St. 1852, c. 177. It is not necessary to resort to the words "from time to time," in Sec. 1, to convince us that the powers given by that section were not exhausted by a single exercise. This being so, we think that the respondent Dahill lawfully fills the office created by the later ordinance, and, even if it were true that the petitioner has a contract which binds the city, we should hesitate long before requiring the city to keep the earlier created office open for the purpose of specifically performing it. We should be much more likely to leave the petitioner to his remedy by action.

But we know of no decision in this Commonwealth that the petitioner has a contract which binds, or purports to bind, the city to keep him in his office after the office shall have been abolished lawfully, except for the contract. It is going a long way to say that there was any contract, however qualified, to continue the petitioner in office during his term, or to accept the corollary that the petitioner had not a right to resign whenever he saw fit. But the notion that an appointment for a term under an ordinance providing that the officer shall be removable for cause, without more, is a contract that the office shall be kept up for the term irrespective of the public welfare, seems to us to go beyond any possible view, and to be contrary to such decisions as we have seen which bear upon the point.
* * *

It is not to be presumed that the repeal of the ordinance was a mere device to get rid of the petitioner, and the petition does not allege such a case.

Petition denied.

CHAPTER 6

FULL FAITH AND CREDIT CLAUSE

APPLYING THE LAW OF ANOTHER STATE

Richards v. *Barlow*
140 Mass. 218 (1885)

[Richards an indorser sued Barlow and Wilson on an Illinois judgment recovered on a promissory note, which was payable to the order of Jeffery, "ninety days after date," and which contained a power of attorney authorizing a confession of judgment, "at any time hereafter." Although the note was not negotiable in Massachusetts, full faith and credit was given to the judgment confessed by attorney in Illinois and recovery was allowed.]

In the absence of any evidence to the contrary, we must assume that the question whether the note in suit was negotiable is governed by the common law, as amended or declared by the St. of 3 & 4 Anne, c. 9; see *Commonwealth* v. *Leach,* 1 Mass. 59, 61; * * * and we must assume that that law is as declared by the Massachusetts decisions. It has been decided in Massachusetts that a note payable at a future day certain, or earlier at the option of the holder, is not negotiable. *Mahoney* v. *Fitzpatrick,* 133 Mass. 151. * * * The obligation to be gathered from the four corners of the present instrument is similar. The promise, taken by itself, is absolute, to pay in ninety days from date; but the power of attorney on the face of the note authorizes a confession of judgment "at any time hereafter," and we must construe these words as meaning at any time after the date. See *Adam* v. *Arnold,* 86 Ill. 185. We cannot distinguish such a case from *Mahoney* v. *Fitzpatrick.* For this reason, without considering whether there are any others, we must decide that the note was not negotiable. We do not rely upon the fact that it seems to have been under seal, because there was some difference between counsel as to the meaning of the bill of exceptions.

The ruling that an action could not be maintained against Wilson on the judgment recovered against him in Illinois was erroneous. The form of the ruling shows that it was not made on the technical ground that there was a misjoinder of counts against Wilson alone and against Barlow and Wilson jointly. No such objection seems to have been made at the trial, and no attempt is made to support the ruling on that ground. But it is argued that the jurisdiction of the Illinois court depended on the power of attorney contained in the note; and that, if the note was not negotiable, the scope of the power—"to confess a judgment without process in favor of the holder of this note"— was confined to Jeffery, the payee. But we think it clear that the word "holder" was used in a sense which embraces any indorsee of the note. See *Ransom* v. *Jones,* 1 Scam. 291. The form of the instrument plainly imports that it was drawn on the assumption that it would be negotiable, and, even if this assumption was erroneous, it must be taken into account none the less, if necessary, in interpreting the meaning of the power. It is not argued that the power of attorney was invalid, or that we are not to assume proceedings in accordance with its terms to have been regular. See *Keith* v. *Kellogg,* 97 Ill. 147.

The jurisdiction of the Illinois court being established, we should be bound to respect the judgment, even if there were error of law apparent on the face of the record. But we cannot say that there is any such error, because, apart from other reasons, we cannot say that Illinois may not have statutes authorizing the assignee of a chose in action not negotiable to recover in his own name, although no such statute was put in evidence. See Ill. Rev. Sts. c. 98, Sec. 4; c. 110, Sec. 66.

If there is a statute as supposed, the jurisdiction might perhaps be supported, even if the word "holder" were confined to Jeffery, the original payee. For we are not prepared to say, that if, for any reason, he found it convenient to take a judgment in the name of an agent, that would not still be a judgment in his favor within the meaning of the power, and it does not appear that the plaintiff was not acting on his behalf.

Exceptions sustained.

JUDGMENT IN ANOTHER STATE WITHOUT SERVICE OF PROCESS

Stone v. Wainwright
147 Mass. 201 (1888)

This is an action of contract upon four promissory notes, brought by the payee against the five makers, who were copartners under the name of the Olympian Roller Skating Club. Two only of the defendants, Wainwright and Noble, were within the jurisdiction, or were served. These defendants set up a judgment recovered in New York as a bar. The New York judgment was rendered against all five; but the defendant Wainwright lived in Massachusetts, and was never served with process in New York. The New York summons and complaint were served upon him in Boston, in pursuance of an order of one of the justices of the New York court. In the present action the court found for the defendant Noble, but declined to rule that Wainwright was entitled to judgment, or that his liability was to be determined by the common law, and found against him. The case comes up on Wainwright's exceptions to the refusal to rule as stated.

In the absence of any evidence of the New York statutes, the New York judgment would be no bar to the present suit against Wainwright, because it would be void as against him for want of jurisdiction; and being a joint judgment, it would be void altogether.
* * *

In our opinion the sections of the New York Code put in evidence do not change the result. Sec. 438–445, 1932–1938, 1946. By Sec. 1932, the plaintiff, in an action against defendants jointly indebted upon a contract, may proceed against the defendants served with process, and, if he recovers, may take judgment against all the defendants. By Sec. 1933, when such a judgment is taken against a defendant upon whom the summons was served without the State, pursuant to an order for that purpose, it has the effect specified in Sec. 445, by which the defendant, upon good cause shown, and upon just terms, may be allowed to defend after final judgment, within certain times limited. And Sec. 1933 further provides that, as against such defendant who is allowed to defend after judgment, the judgment is evidence only of the extent of the plaintiff's demand, after the liability of that defendant has been established by other evidence.

We see no reason to doubt, and we assume, that this case was one in which Sec. 438 *et seq.* purported to authorize service without the State by order, that Sec. 1932 purported to authorize the judgment against all the defendants, including Wainwright, and that the judgment had the effect above stated, so far as the statute could give it that effect.

At the same time, it is very plain that the judgment against Wainwright would not be recognized outside of New York if a suit were brought upon it, and it can have no greater effect as a bar than it would have as a cause of action. It would be a singular conclusion, that, because a record established Wainwright's liability in New York, he was not liable anywhere else in any form of action.

If all the defendants in an ordinary action at law live out of the State, and none of them are served with process or voluntarily appear, it is settled that a judgment against them is only valid so far as to warrant the application of property attached to its satisfaction, and will have no general operation *in personam,* even in the State where it is rendered. Statutes cannot confer jurisdiction over persons not subject to the legislative power. * * *

It is only by very subtle reasoning that the fact that the New York court had power to enter judgment against the other defendants could be held to enlarge their power against Wainwright, even so as to give the judgment against him a local validity. Clearly the judgment can have no force against him outside of the State. The result is the same, whether the judgment be pronounced void as against Wainwright, and therefore void as against all, notwithstanding the statute, or whether, since it is in statutory form, it be held valid as against those with whom the statute had power to deal. In either view it cannot bar a suit against Wainwright on the notes.

For if the judgment be held valid against the defendants who were within the jurisdiction, the judgment is in effect (at least outside the State of New York) a judgment against those defendants only, although in form it also embraces Wainwright. By immemorial practice, founded on necessity, and embodied in a declaratory statute in this Commonwealth, if an action of contract is brought against several defendants, some of whom cannot be served, by reason of their absence from the State, the action may proceed against those who are duly served. But when a judgment is taken for this reason against less than the whole number of joint contractors, an action on the same contract may be maintained afterwards against any of those not served. * * *

It follows from the same necessity, and has been settled by repeated decisions, without the aid of statute, that similar judgments in other States can have no greater effect in barring an action here. * * *

Exceptions overruled.

EFFECT OF INVALID MARRIAGE UPON RIGHT OF ISSUE TO INHERIT

Adams v. *Adams*
154 Mass. 290 (1891)

This is a bill in equity by which the plaintiff seeks to establish his right to a share in a fund left by the will of Seth Adams, of Newton, Massachusetts, to the "present wife" of his brother, Charles W. Adams, "for the benefit of herself and all the children of said Charles in equal proportions." The testator died in this State on December 7, 1873, and the will was dated February 15, 1872. The question is whether the plaintiff is one of the children within the meaning of the will. The wife referred to is admitted to be the defendant Anne T. Adams, who was married to Charles W. in Maine, in 1854, he then being a resident of New York. The plaintiff is the child of Charles W. Adams and Hannah Phillips, was born in California on August 28, 1881, and was then illegitimate. At that time Charles W. Adam's domicil was in Texas. In October, 1881, Charles W. Adams changed his domicil to California, and on December 3, 1881, he began an action there for divorce against the above mentioned Anne, and got a decree on April 13, 1882. It is found that he had not been a resident of the State for six months next preceding the commencement of the action, as required by the California Civil Code, sec. 128, and that for this reason the court had no jurisdiction of the action, but that the court was imposed upon by Charles W. Adams. We may also mention, that it is found that the wife of Charles W. Adams was then residing in Massachusetts, and had no actual notice of the action, and that it might be a question, if material, whether her domicil followed that of her husband. * * * On April 20, 1882, Charles W. Adams married Hannah Phillips in California, then having his domicil there, and after the marriage recognized the plaintiff as his son. By the law of California a child born before wedlock becomes legitimate by the subsequent marriage of its parents. Civil Code, sec. 215. The law of Texas is similar, if the child is recognized by the father. Rev. Sts. sec. 1656 (1879).

The word "children" in a Massachusetts will means legitimate children. Kent v. Barker, 2 Gray, 535, 536. Probably the meaning would be the same, even if the parents referred to and the child were domiciled in a State where illegitimate children were recognized as children for some purposes. *Lincoln* v. *Perry,* 149 Mass. 368, 373, 374. But we do not need to consider this at length, as it does not appear that the law of California or of Texas would recognize the plaintiff as the child of Charles W. Adams for the present purpose unless he were legitimated, as Charles W. Adams in any case was only domiciled in California for a short time, long after the testator's death, and after the birth of his child, and died domiciled in Massachusetts. The plaintiff's case is put wholly upon his having been legitimated. We assume for the purposes of our decision, that, if he has been legitimated, he is entitled to a share under the will. * * * We may as well add here, that, if the Texas domicil of Charles W. Adams at the time of the birth of his son was material, * * * no difference based on that fact, and favorable to the plaintiff, has been called to our attention. We shall speak only of the law of California in dealing with this part of the case. We shall not consider whether, if it were necessary to satisfy the requirements of the Texas statute, a marriage in California would do so.

It may be assumed that the California statute to which we have referred (Civil Code, sec. 215) requires a valid marriage to legitimate an earlier born child. * * * For Charles W. Adams's marriage to be valid it was necessary that he should have obtained a valid divorce. But if we should assume that the decree of divorce was valid in California, so that Charles W. Adams had a capacity to marry there, and that his marriage conferred the status of a legitimate child upon his son by the law of that State, we should encounter doubts like those expressed by Lord Colonsay, in *Shaw v. Gould*, L. R. 3 H. L. 55, 97, whether at any distance of time we were to reopen the inquiry into the circumstances of Charles W. Adams's resort to the California court. The California record shows that the court there found that Charles W. Adams had been a resident of the State for the necessary time. There is color in the California decisions put in evidence for the argument that this finding could not be impeached collaterally in California, and thus that the case supposed is the case before us.

Taking the case this way for a moment, we still are unable to decide it in favor of the plaintiff. The rule that the status of the domicil is the status everywhere must yield when the status is constructed on principles which are contrary to those which are generally recognized, or which can be admitted by the law of the forum resorted to. See *Ross* v. *Ross*, 129 Mass. 243.

We should agree with the English decisions so far as this, that the fact that a marriage has taken place on the faith of a previous divorce does not preclude an inquiry by the courts of another State into the capacity of the divorced party, and thus into the validity of the divorce, or a denial of the validity of the marriage if the divorce is one which would be decreed void if it were directly in issue. A purely voluntary contract of marriage cannot be allowed to impart a conclusive character to a decree which before could have been examined. * * *

The present case offers remarkably little ground for hesitation in going into this inquiry. Marriage in California is, or may be, a pure matter of private contract, entered into without intervention of the State except for purposes of registration. * * * The mother's rights are not in question, and if they were, she did not stand at all in the position of a purchaser for value without notice. She is found to have known all the facts, and her belief in Charles W. Adams's capacity to contract marriage was simply an opinion about California law. (We are not now considering the conditions of a putative marriage, as to which different views have been expressed. * * *) The plaintiff is claiming a purely gratuitous benefit as an incidental result of the proceedings in California, at the expense of other children who were not parties to any of those proceedings, or entitled to be heard at any stage of them, but who nevertheless are to be precluded from denying their validity.

If the validity of the divorce were immediately in issue, it could be impeached here for want of jurisdiction, notwithstanding the recitals in the record, and those recitals could be contradicted by parol evidence.

* * * For instance, if Charles W. Adams had married Hannah Phillips in this State and had been indicted for polygamy. * * * Or even in a proceeding between the parties to the divorce, if the one raising the objection had not appeared in that cause, and was not domiciled in the State where it was granted. * * * So *a fortiori* where the question is raised, as here, by third persons whose rights are concerned, and who were not parties to or entitled to be heard in the divorce suit. * * * In *Hood* v. *Hood,* 11 Allen, 196, the fact of domicil was tried between the original parties for the purpose of determining the jurisdiction of an Illinois divorce, and in *Hood* v. *Hood,* 110 Mass. 463, it was the Massachusetts, not the Illinois decree, which was held conclusive on third persons, they offering evidence only to impeach the Illinois decree. * * *

There is no doubt that the requirement of six months' residence goes to the jurisdiction of the court. The finding of the judge on this point is confirmed, not only by the plain effect of the California statute, but by the express statement of the Supreme Court of that State, and by its intimation that a divorce granted without that prerequisite would not be binding in any other State. * * *

But although we have made the assumption for a moment, we by no means are prepared to concede that, if the present case arose in California, under a California will, it would be decided differently there. The universal effect of a judgment *in rem* in establishing or changing a status or title, whether given to it by statute or by the tradition of the courts, rests on the practical necessity of the case, because the effect is of a nature to concern strangers to the proceedings. It would be inconvenient for parties to be divorced as between themselves, and yet married towards the world. The same convenience makes it desirable that the effect should be the same wherever the question arises, whether within the jurisdiction or without it, and therefore, in the case of a decree which would be void outside the jurisdiction, that it should not be held conclusive within it. The decree if binding in California would be binding everywhere. *Cheever* v. *Wilson,* 9 Wall. 108. It is desirable, at least, that the converse rule should be applied, and that a decree void elsewhere should not be held binding there. We are aware that some of the cases which we have cited, and others which we have not cited, contemplate the possibility of a divorce which shall be valid only as to the plaintiff within the jurisdiction. But especially in this country, where changes of residence from State to State are frequent, every court must strive so far as possible to bring the local view of a citizen's status into accord with that which would prevail generally elsewhere.

We have tried to show that the decree before us would be regarded as void outside of the jurisdiction, and void on the ground that the condition precedent attached by a California statute to the right of the court to take jurisdiction had not been complied with. The question is whether the statute has a less effect within the State. No conclusive evidence of the law of California upon this point has been called to our attention. If the plaintiff had been rightly in court, and the objection had been that the defendant had not been duly served, it may be that, if the record showed a proper publication, it could not be contradicted. *In re Newman,* 75 Cal. 213, 220. But perhaps even this is doubtful, in view of some of the decisions earlier cited, and however it may be, a distinction has been suggested between a total want of jurisdiction and a failure to get jurisdiction of the person of the defendant in a case which is rightly in court. * * * We feel at liberty to assume the law of California to be in accordance with that generally received elsewhere, and to consider the question on principle.

The argument for the conclusiveness of the decree in California would seem to be, that the parties to a domestic judgment showing jurisdiction on the face of the record cannot impeach it collaterally. * * * And that if a judgment *in rem* is operative as between the parties while it stands, it must be effectual to determine their status as to third persons, although not parties, for reasons already given. * * *

But if the judgment is thus binding to all intents and purposes in California, it would be binding elsewhere, which, as has been shown, is not the law. In New York this consideration has been adduced as a reason for the rule prevailing there, that a domestic record may be impeached collaterally for want of jurisdiction, even by a party. *Ferguson* v. *Crawford*, 70 N. Y. 253, 261, 262. Whether the rule as to parties be regarded as an anomaly established on the principle *Communis error facit jus,* or as a mere rule of procedure, that those who have it in their power to reverse a judgment must do so if they do not want to be bound by it, as possibly may be inferred from some of the cases, *Hendrick* v. *Whittemore,* 105 Mass. 23, 28, the conclusion cannot be admitted that those who have not that power are also bound, if the judgment is *in rem,* to admit the change of status which it purports to effect. Consider what would be the result. In a great majority of divorces neither party wishes to disturb the decree. If their acquiescence should be allowed to have the effect supposed, third persons may be affected in their property and in their most sacred personal rights by the interested action of others, without ever having had a chance to be heard. The cases are few, and we are aware of no binding authority. But in *Perry* v. *Meddowcroft,* 10 Beav. 122, 137, an infant was allowed to impeach a domestic sentence of nullity collaterally for collusion, although the sentence operated *in rem,* and bastardized him if it stood. * * * We cannot doubt that, if the fraud on the court had concerned its jurisdiction rather than the merits, Lord Langdale would have been at least equally ready to hear the evidence. *Cavanaugh* v. *Smith,* 84 Ind. 380. Yet the parties to the collusive decree were bound by it. * * * We have confined our citations mainly to cases of divorce and judgments *in rem.* But where there has been an execution sale under a judgment *in personam,* there is a difficulty not unlike that which arises with regard to judgments *in rem* in allowing the validity of the judgment to be disputed by third persons, for the purpose of destroying the purchaser's title. Yet it has been held that this may be done. *Safford* v. *Weare,* 142 Mass. 231.

We shall not consider further whether this judgment was not absolutely void on the facts reported, and whether, if so, the record could be contradicted by the parties to it on what has been declared in California to be a "fundamental rule that no court can acquire jurisdiction by the mere assertion of it, or by deciding that it has it." *McMinn* v. *Whelan,* 27 Cal. 300, 314.

We are of opinion, for the reasons which we have given, that the validity of the divorce granted Charles W. Adams is open to contradiction in this suit, that the divorce was void and ineffectual as against his legitimate children, and that therefore his marriage with the plaintiff's mother was void, and did not legitimate the plaintiff in such a sense as to entitle him to set up a claim in competition with the legitimate children under a Massachusetts will.

Another and distinct argument has been drawn from another California statute, which provides that, when a marriage is annulled on the ground that a former husband or wife was living, children begotten before the judgment are legitimate. Cal. Civil Code, sec. 84. The California and Texas statutes also provide that the issue of marriages null in law shall be legitimate. Cal. Civil Code, sec. 1387. Texas Rev. Sts. sec. 1656.

The Texas statute may be laid on one side. For, even if we should hold that the Texas law imparted to the plaintiff his capacity for legitimation, which, under the facts of this case, we do not intimate, still, subject to the qualifications heretofore stated, the effects of his parents' marriage upon him must be determined by the law of California, where it took place, and where they and he then were domiciled. We lay on one side, therefore, without further remark, a dictum in a decision by the Supreme Court of Texas, that children born before the parents entered into a void marriage would be legitimated so as to take as children under a Texas will. *Carroll* v. *Carroll,* 20 Texas, 731, 745, 746.

We see no ground for construing the California acts as applying to any children except those born after the void ceremony has been gone through with. They alone can be described as issue of the marriage, according to the express words of sec. 1387. *Greenhow* v. *James,* 80 Va. 636, 638. They alone fall within the obvious reasons for the statute and the earlier Spanish law, from which it would seem that the statute may have been derived, according to the exposition in another Texas case. *Smith* v. *Smith,* 1 Texas, 621, 629. If we assume that sec. 84 applies where there has been no judgment annulling the marriage, the general words, "children begotten before the judgment" must be confined to children born after the marriage, in view of sec. 1387. Neither sec. 84 nor sec. 1387, nor both together, can be taken to enlarge the meaning of sec. 215, discussed at the beginning of this opinion, so that a void marriage shall legitimate children previously born. The view which we take seems to be that of the Supreme Court of California, so far as they have expressed an opinion. * * * We have found no case favoring a different construction, except the few words in *Carroll* v. *Carroll,* 20 Texas, 731, 746.

Bill dismissed.

VALIDITY OF DIVORCE OBTAINED IN ANOTHER STATE

Andrews v. *Andrews*
176 Mass. 92 (1900)

[This case was affirmed by the United States Supreme Court in 188 U. S. 14.]

This is an appeal from the decree of the Probate Court appointing Annie Andrews administratrix of the estate of Charles S. Andrews. The appellant is the first wife of the deceased. The appellee married him later in good faith, after he had obtained a decree of divorce in South Dakota. The questions are whether the divorce is valid in this State, or whether, if it is invalid, the appellant, on the ground of connivance and acquiescence, is estopped to deny its validity. Charles S. Andrews went to South Dakota for the purpose of getting the divorce, and intended to return to Massachusetts as soon as he had done so. Subject to this intention it is found that he intended to become a resident of South Dakota for the purpose of getting a divorce, and to do all that was needful to make him such a resident. The statute of South Dakota forbids a divorce "unless the plaintiff has, in good faith, been a resident of the Territory ninety days next preceding the commencement of the action." Compiled Laws of Territory of Dakota, sec. 2578, St. South Dakota, 1890, c. 105, sec. 1. Andrews lived in South Dakota ninety days; and the Dakota court found in favor of its own jurisdiction, substantially in the words of the section just quoted, and granted the divorce for a cause which would not authorize a divorce by the laws of this Commonwealth.

The consensus of English speaking courts founds jurisdiction of divorce on domicil. It may be that a State might substitute for domicil, by statute, if it chose, simple bodily presence within its borders for a certain number of days. It may be, at least under the Constitution of the United States, that a divorce granted under such a statute between parties, both of whom were before the court, would be entitled to respect here, notwithstanding Pub. Sts. c. 146, sec. 41. But compare *People* v. *Dawell,* 25 Mich. 247, 264; *Dolphin* v. *Robins,* 7 H. L. Cas. 390, 414. But no such question arises in this case, because the language of the South Dakota statute must be taken to require not mere bodily presence, but domicil. In the light of the decisions upon similar acts, and the generally accepted rule making domicil the foundation, the words "resident of the Territory" mean domiciled in the Territory, whether they also mean personally present or not.
* * *

The finding of the single justice clearly means that the deceased did not get a domicil in South Dakota. He meant to stay there ninety days, and such further time, perhaps, as was necessary to get his divorce, and then he meant to come back to Massachusetts. It is true that he meant to do all that was needful to get a divorce, but he meant it because he was mistaken as to what was needful. In other words, he only meant to do what he supposed to be needful, and that was not enough. Whether if he had known what was needful he would have meant that and would have done it, is a speculation. In fact he did not mean or do it, on the facts so far stated. It is clear that the finding of the South Dakota court in favor of its own jurisdiction upon an *ex parte* hearing would not be conclusive, but that the facts would be open to examination here. * * *

But the appellant appeared in the divorce suit and denied the alleged residence of the deceased, although afterwards, upon receiving a certain sum of money, she directed her counsel to withdraw. There is a plain difference between a case in which a respondent has not submitted herself to the power of the court and one in which she has done so. In the former, a foreign State within whose territory she is domiciled may decline to allow her rights to be affected by the decree, whatever the record may allege. In the latter, there is stronger ground for saying that if the libel alleges residence and any other facts necessary to give jurisdiction, the libellee no more can dispute the validity of the decree on the ground that the court was mistaken as to residence than she could upon the ground that it went wrong on the merits. Notwithstanding the language of some decisions which do not distinguish in terms between judgments where there has been no service and those where there has been an apparance, *Sewall* v. *Sewall,* 122 Mass. 156, 161, the decisions in some States where the question has been raised is in favor of the distinction. *Kinnier* v. *Kinnier,* 45 N. Y. 535, 540, 541 * * * *Waldo* v. *Waldo,* 52 Mich. 94, 99. * * *

Supposing the State decisions just mentioned to be correct as to the effect of the decree between the parties, the general consequence would be that it was effective as to the rest of the world. As a general rule it would be inconvenient to admit that parties who were divorced as between themselves were not divorced as against others. *Kinnier* v. *Kinnier* and *Waldo* v. *Waldo, ubi supra. Adams* v. *Adams,* 154 Mass. 290, 295. But a further distinction is taken. The world at large has no interest in the divorce, and therefore may be bound by it; but it is suggested that the State of the domicil has an interest, and that it cannot be concluded by a mere false recital in the record, because the foreign court did not even pretend to jurisdiction over that State. *People* v. *Dawell,* 25 Mich. 247, 257. In *People* v. *Dawell,* this proposition was applied in favor of the State of the domicil as a prosecutor, and at an earlier date it was applied by this court in favor of the State as a legislator. *Chase* v. *Chase,* 6 Gray, 157, 161.

It will be borne in mind that, on the facts before us, the case is not one in which the Legislature of South Dakota has undertaken to allow the grant of a divorce. It is one in which the court of that State has been deceived, and in which it would have refused to act and would have had no right to act, had it known the facts. In such a case as this, the State of the domicil, if it sees fit, may decline to be bound by recitals in a record to which it is not a party. It may say, as Massachusetts has said by Pub. Sts. c. 146, sec. 41, that it will be governed by the fact, not by a possibly collusive record, and therefore that the fact must be ascertained, tried, and found here. Whether or not the statute goes farther than the law would go without it, we are of opinion, in accordance with the decision in *Chase* v. *Chase,* that as applied to this case it does not go beyond the constitutional powers of the State. In *Hardy* v. *Smith,* 136

Mass. 328, 331, it would seem from the papers in the case that there was an appearance for the respondent in the Utah court. The validity of the statute has been affirmed in a general way, more than once (*Sewall* v. *Sewall,* 122 Mass. 156, 161; *Smith* v. *Smith,* 13 Gray, 209; *Dickinson* v. *Dickinson,* 167 Mass. 474), and confined, as it should be, to persons retaining their Massachusetts domicil, (*Clark* v. *Clark,* 8 Cush. 385, 387), it seems to be mainly declaratory of the law (*Lyon* v. *Lyon,* 2 Gray, 367, 368), unless in cases like the present, where, perhaps, apart from it, the parties both having appeared could not dispute the foreign adjudication of jurisdiction disclosed by the record. A further question might arise, as we have suggested, if the State granting the divorce had established a test of jurisdiction other than domicil; but that has not happened, and is not likely to happen.

The Commonwealth having intervened by legislation, the appellant gets the benefit of it irrespective of any merits of her own. The possibility of a distinction such as was sanctioned by *In re Ellis' Estate,* 55 Minn. 401, upholding the divorce as between the parties and so far as concerns property rights, but treating it as void as against the State and for the purposes of the criminal law, is done away with by the act. It is settled that in a case within the statute the divorce is to be treated here as void for all purposes. *Chase* v. *Chase,* 6 Gray, 157, 160. It is settled that there is no estoppel even as against the party instituting the foreign proceedings. *Smith* v. *Smith,* 13 Gray, 209, 210. If the appellant's conduct amounted to connivance, as found, so that she could not have maintained a libel for adultery on the ground of the second marriage, that does not go far enough to constitute an estoppel. *Loud*

v. *Loud,* 129 Mass. 14, 19. All that she did was to withdraw her active opposition to the divorce, in consideration of a payment of money, and thereafter to remain silent. We are compelled to overrule the exceptions.

Exceptions overruled.

CHAPTER 7

DUE PROCESS UNDER THE
MASSACHUSETTS CONSTITUTION

OBLIGATIONS ARISING OUT OF THE MARRIAGE STATUS

Blackinton v. *Blackinton*
141 Mass. 432 (1886)

[Mr. and Mrs. Blackinton were married in Massachusetts and lived together in Attleborough for nine years thereafter, when Mr. Blackington without cause left his wife and moved to New York where he became a citizen and resided for eight years. Subsequently, Mrs. Blackinton sued her husband (under Pub. Sts. c. 147, sec. 33) for separate maintenance of herself and her eleven year old daughter, Effie. No attachment of property was made. Service was had in New York.]

If the petitioner were proceeding for a divorce, there is no doubt that the court would possess and exercise jurisdiction, notwithstanding the husband's change of domicil. Pub. Sts. c. 146, Secs. 1, 5. *Harteau* v. *Harteau,* 14 Pick. 181, 185. * * * The present proceeding contemplates a continuance of the marriage status, instead of its dissolution. But the ground on which it proceeds is a breach of the duties incident to that status,—in this case desertion, that is, a separation of home and interests,—without the petitioner's fault; and the same considerations which are stated in *Harteau* v. *Harteau, ubi supra,* for declining to treat the domicil of the wife as following that of the husband when she seeks a divorce, equally apply when she seeks protection and separate maintenance under the Pub. Sts. c. 147, sec. 33. The statute is general in its terms, and we know of no principle which would warrant our confining its operation to cases where the deserting husband retains his domicile within the State.

Assuming that the Probate Court has jurisdiction of the subject matter in such a case, we are of opinion that its right to proceed is not confined to cases where personal service can be made upon the respondent within the State. The jurisdiction in divorce is not confined to such cases. *Burlen* v. *Shannon,* 115 Mass. 438. And whatever may be thought of decisions like *People* v. *Baker,* 76 N. Y. 78, and *Daughty* v. *Daughty,* 1 Stew. (N. J.) Eq. 581, we do not understand any one to deny that divorces granted against absent defendants, after such notice as the laws of the State prescribe, are valid within the limits of the State granting them.

In like manner, so far as the petitioner seeks a decree protecting her person, and giving her the custody of her child now living in this Commonwealth, we have no doubt that the statute confers power upon the Probate Court to make it. The question whether it also confers power to order the payment of money for maintenance is more difficult, but, in the opinion of a majority of the court, must be answered in the same way. It has been intimated that authority to decree a divorce against a defendant domiciled elsewhere, and not appearing, does not carry with it authority to decree alimony. *Beard* v. *Beard,* 21 Ind. 321. But the statute under which the petitioner proceeds recognizes no such distinction. It does not contemplate a jurisdiction for one of its purposes and a want of jurisdiction for another, and we see no reason why it should be limited beyond its words.

The whole proceeding is for the regulation of a status. The incidents of that status are various,—some concerning the person, some concerning the support, of the petitioner or her child. The order to pay money is not founded on an isolated obligation, as in a case of contract or tort, but upon a duty which is one of those incidents. The status, considered as a whole, is subject to regulation here, although it involves relations with another not here, because such regulation is necessary rightly to order the daily life, and to secure the comfort and support, of the party rightfully living within the jurisdiction. It is quite true that these considerations may not suffice to give the decree extra-territorial force, and that, in general, courts do not willingly pass decrees, unless they think that other courts at least ought to respect them. But that is not the final test. We think that the statute was intended to authorize such decrees as that appealed from, and tacitly to adopt the rules as to service expressly laid down for divorce. Pub. Sts. c. 146, sec. 9. We do not see any sufficient ground for denying the power of the legislature to pass the act. We are therefore of opinion that the decree was within the power of the court, and can be carried out against the defendant's property within the jurisdiction, and against his person if he be found here.

Decree affirmed.

RIGHT OF LEGISLATURE TO LIMIT HEIGHT OF BOUNDARY FENCES

Rideout v. *Knox*
148 Mass. 368 (1889)

[Rideout sued Knox and his wife who were occupants of an adjoining estate to his own, for maintaining a fence over six feet in height. The statute under which the suit was brought provided that any fence, "unnecessarily exceeding six feet in height, maliciously erected or maintained for the purpose of annoying the owners or occupants of adjoining property, shall be deemed a private nuisance." Knox claimed that the statute was unconstitutional.]

This is an action of tort, under the St. of 1887, c. 348. The plaintiff has had a verdict for nominal damages, and the first question raised by the bill of exceptions is the constitutionality of the statute. Another question more or less connected with the former is whether the structure, in order to bring it within the act, must be erected or maintained for the purpose of annoyance as the dominant motive, or whether it is enough if that purpose existed, although subordinate to a *bona fide* use for legitimate purposes.

At common law, a man has a right to build a fence on his own land as high as he pleases, however much it may obstruct his neighbor's light and air. And the limit up to which a man may impair his neighbor's enjoyment of his estate by the mode of using his own is fixed by external standards only. * * *

But it is plain that the right to use one's property for the sole purpose of injuring others is not one of the immediate rights of ownership; it is not a right for the sake of which property is recognized by the law, but is only a more or less necessary incident of rights which are established for very different ends. It has been thought by respectable authorities, that even at common law the extent of a man's rights in cases like the present might depend upon the motive with which he acted. * * *

We do not so understand the common law, and we concede further, that to a large extent the power to use one's property malevolently, in any way which would be lawful for other ends, is an incident of property which cannot be taken away even by legislation. It may be assumed, that, under our Constitution, the Legislature would not have power to prohibit putting up or maintaining stores or houses with malicious intent, and thus to make a large part of the property of the Commonwealth dependent upon what a jury might find to have been the past or to be the present motives of the owner.

But it does not follow that the rule is the same for a boundary fence unnecessarily built more than six feet high. It may be said that the difference is only one of degree: most differences are, when nicely analyzed. At any rate, difference of degree is one of the distinctions by which the right of the Legislature to exercise the police power is determined. Some small limitations of previously existing rights incident to property may be imposed for the sake of preventing a manifest evil; larger ones could not be, except by the exercise of the right of eminent domain. *Sawyer* v. *Davis*, 136 Mass. 239, 243.

The statute is confined to fences and structures in the nature of fences, and to such fences only as unnecessarily exceed six feet in height. It is hard to imagine a more insignificant curtailment of the rights of property. Even the right to build a fence above six feet is not denied, when any convenience of the owner would be served by building higher. It is at least doubtful whether the act applies to fences not substantially adjoining the injured party's land. The fences must be "maliciously erected or maintained for the purpose of annoying" adjoining owners or occupiers. This language clearly expresses that there must be an actual malevolent motive, as distinguished from merely technical malice. The meaning is plainer than in the case of statutes concerning malicious mischief.

* * *

Finally, we are of opinion that it is not enough to satisfy the words of the act that malevolence was one of the motives, but that malevolence must be the dominant motive,—a motive without which the fence would not have been built or maintained. A man cannot be punished for malevolently maintaining a fence for the purpose of annoying his neighbor merely because he feels pleasure at the thought he is giving annoyance, if that pleasure alone would not induce him to maintain it, or if he would maintain if for other reasons even if that pleasure should be denied him. If the height above six feet is really necessary for any reason, there is no liability, whatever the motives of the owner in erecting it. If he thinks it necessary, and acts on his opinion, he is not liable because he also acts malevolently.

We are of opinion that the statute thus construed is within the limits of the police power, and is constitu-

tional, so far as it regulates the subsequent erection of fences. To that extent, it simply restrains a noxious use of the owner's premises, and although the use is not directly injurious to the public at large, there is a public interest to restrain this kind of aggressive annoyance of one neighbor by another, and to mark a definite limit beyond which it is not lawful to go.
* * *

Whether the statute is constitutional with reference to fences already in existence when the act was passed, is a more difficult question. We are compelled to construe the act as applying to all fences maintained after it goes into operation. If a fence which was built before the act, and is simply allowed to stand, may be found to be a nuisance, and abated at the expense of the owner, there is a taking of property without compensation which is more marked and significant than in the case of a simple prohibition to build. *Commonwealth* v. *Alger,* 7 Cush. 53, 103. But the case is not so hard as it seems. If the owner of the fence gave leave to the party complaining to take it down, it would show conclusively that the fence was no longer maintained by him for malevolent motives, and therefore would defeat an action for subsequent annoyance. On the whole, having regard to the smallness of the injury, the nature of the evil to be avoided, the quasi accidental character of the defendant's right to put up a fence for malevolent purposes, and also to the fact that police regulations may limit the use of property in ways which greatly diminish its value, we are of opinion that the act is constitutional to the full extent of its provisions. See *Mugler* v. *Kansas,* 123 U. S. 623; *Kidd* v. *Pearson,* 128 U. S. 1.

We are of opinion, however, that the exceptions must be sustained on the ground that the construction of the statute embraced in the second request for a ruling was substantially correct, as we have stated, whereas it appears that the request was refused, and the jury were instructed otherwise.

This fence was built before the act of 1887 was passed. The statute could not make the conduct of David Knox, in 1886, unlawful retrospectively. Help given by him in lawfully building the fence on his wife's land did not of itself make him liable, whatever his motives, and did not tend to prove that he maintained the fence. There was no evidence that he did so, unless it is to be found in the ambiguous statement that he used it, which does not seem to have been the ground on which the case was allowed to go to the jury. The reply of Mrs. Knox in his absence was not evidence against him. As the exceptions must be sustained upon another ground, it is unnecessary to say more on this branch of the case.

Exceptions sustained.

MORE ABOUT BOUNDARY FENCES

Smith v. Morse
148 Mass. 407 (1889)

[Abby S. Smith, an adjoining landowner of Morse, sued the latter (under St. of 1887, c. 348) for maintaining a fence unnecessarily exceeding six feet in height. Mrs. Smith's property was occupied by tenants. There was no evidence of any injury to Mrs. Smith or her tenants except what might have been gathered upon a view by the jury of the premises.]

These are both actions under St. of 1887, c. 348. We have decided that the statute is constitutional in *Rideout v. Knox,* ante, 368. The plaintiff had never occupied the premises, and there was no evidence of any injury to her or to her tenants, except what the jury may have gathered from a view. The judge ruled that as it appeared that the plaintiff's estate was occupied solely by tenants, she was not entitled to recover, and directed verdicts for the defendant.

Notwithstanding the use of the word "nuisance," sec. 1 of the statute in no sense creates an easement in favor of the plaintiff's land, but only makes it unlawful to do malevolently what the defendant still has a right to do from other motives. This right of action is given by sec. 2 to an "owner or occupant, injured either in his comfort or the enjoyment of his estate by such nuisance." This means, we think, that the owners may have an action under some circumstances, although not in occupation.

This action is for causing personal annoyance for the sake of annoying, and to attempt to answer the question whether the annoyance suffered is within the act, by deciding whether there is an injury to the reversion by the principles of the common law, is likely to mislead. We agree that the comfort or enjoyment which must be enjoyed must be comfort or enjoyment in the use of the premises, and that it is not enough that an owner not in occupation is disturbed in his mind when he thinks about the fence. But we are of opinion that such an owner might suffer an actionable injury. If the fence was likely to diminish his rents, or to make it more difficult to get tenants, the injury to his comfort or the enjoyment of his estate on account of that reasonable anticipation would be within the act. The jury might be able to say upon a view that the fence would have that effect. What they see is evidence in the case. * * *

If the motives for allowing the fence to stand are malicious, as explained in *Rideout* v. *Knox,* the defendant may be liable, although he has done no act upon it since the passage of the statute.

New trials granted.

A RAILROAD SUES A PASSENGER FOR HIS FARE

Boston and Maine Railroad v. Trafton
151 Mass. 229 (1890)

This is an action to recover fares for three journeys by the defendant upon the plaintiff's road in this State. The defendant in each instance tendered a stop-over check, which was refused. These checks were stated on their face to be good only for ten days, and the ten days had expired; but the defendant claimed the right to be carried without further payment, on the ground that he received the checks under protest in exchange for tickets from points in Maine to Boston, which he had purchased of the plaintiff in Maine, and that the Maine statutes made tickets good for six years, and allowed passengers to stop over at will. The court below refused to rule that the statute of Maine was binding upon the plaintiff within this Commonwealth, and the case comes before us on exceptions to this refusal.

It is a sufficient answer to the defendant's argument, that the statute upon which he relies is construed by the Supreme Judicial Court of Maine as applying only to transportation within the limits of that State. *Carpenter* v. *Grand Trunk Railway,* 72 Maine, 388. Obviously, a broader construction would lead to great confusion and trouble, apart from the constitutional questions mentioned by the court. Admitting, then, that the statute entered into the defendant's contract as an implied term, the contract so far as it embodied the statute was only that the defendant might stop over in Maine. As this disposes of the case, we do not consider other difficulties of the defence.

Exceptions overruled.

RIGHT OF STATE TO KILL DISEASED HORSES

Miller v. Horton
152 Mass. 540 (1891)

[Miller sued Horton and another in damages for killing his horse which was condemned by Stockbridge and Winchester—State Commissioners on contagious diseases among domestic animals. At the trial two veterinary surgeons testified that the horse did not have the glanders or any other disease. The statute did not provide compensation for the owner. It was contended that the act under which the Commissioners acted was unconstitutional. Holmes delivered the opinion for the majority in this now famous case. Devens delivered a dissenting opinion with Allen and Knowlton concurring.]

This is an action of tort for killing the plaintiff's horse. The defendants admit the killing, but justify as members of the board of health of the town of Rehobeth, under an order addressed to the board and signed by two of the three commissioners on contagious diseases among domestic animals, appointed under the St. of 1885, c. 378, and acting under the alleged authority of the St. 1887, c. 252, Sec. 13. This order declared that it was adjudged that the horse had the glanders, and that it was condemned, and directed the defendants to cause it to be killed. The judge before whom the case was tried found that the horse had not the glanders, but declined to rule that the defendants had failed to make out their justification, and found for the defendants. The plaintiff excepted.

The language of the material part of Sec. 13 of the act of 1887 is: "In all cases of farcy or glanders, the commissioners, having condemned the animal infected therewith, shall cause such animal to be killed without an appraisal, but may pay the owner or any other person an equitable sum for the killing and burial thereof." Taken literally, these words only give the commissioners jurisdiction and power to condemn a horse that really has the glanders. The question is whether they go further by implication, so that, if a horse which has not the disease is condemned by the commissioners, their order will protect the man who kills it in a subsequent suit by the owner for compensation.

The main ground for reading into the statute an intent to make the commissioners' order an absolute protection is, that there is no provision for compensation to the owner in this class of cases, and therefore, unless the order is a protection, those who carry it out will do so at their peril. Such a construction when once known would be apt to destroy the efficiency of the clause, as few people could be found to carry out orders on these terms.

On the other hand, this same absence of any provision for compensation to the owner, even if not plainly founded on the assumption that only a worthless thing and a nuisance is in question, still would be an equally strong argument for keeping to the literal and narrower interpretation. If the Legislature had had in mind the possible destruction of healthy horses, there was no reason in the world why it should not have provided for paying the owners. Section 12 does provide for paying them in all cases where they are not in fault, unless this is an exception. When, as here, the horse not only is not to be paid for, but may be condemned without appeal and killed without giving the owner a hearing or even notice, the grounds are very strong for believing that the statute means no more than it says, and is intended to authorize the killing of actually infected horses only. If the commissioners had felt any doubt, they could have had the horse appraised under Sec. 12. Whether an action would have lain in that case we need not consider.

The reasons for this construction seem decisive to a majority of the court, when they consider the grave questions which would arise as to the constitutionality of the clause if it were construed the other way.

Section 13 of the act of 1887, by implication, declares horses with the glanders to be nuisances, and we assume in favor of the defendant that it may do so constitutionally, and may authorize them to be killed without compensation to the owners. But the statute does not declare all horses to be nuisances, and the question is, whether, if the owner of the horse denies that his horse falls within the class declared to be so, the Legislature can make the *ex parte* decision of a board like this conclusive upon him. That question is answered by the decision in *Fisher* v. *McGirr,* 1 Gray, 1. It is decided there that the owner has a right to be heard, and, further, that only a trial by jury satisfies the provision of Article XII of the Declaration of Rights, that no subject shall be deprived of his property by the judgment of his peers, or the law of the land.

In *Belcher* v. *Farrar,* 8 Allen, 325, 328, it was said, "It would violate one of the fundamental principles of justice to deprive a party absolutely of the free use and enjoyment of his estate under an allegation that the purpose to which it was appropriated, or the mode of its occupation, was injurious to the health and comfort of others, and created a nuisance, without giving the owner an opportunity to appear and disprove the allegation, and protect his property from the restraint to which it was proposed to subject it." * * * Of course there cannot be a trial by jury before killing an animal supposed to have a contagious disease, and we assume that the Legislature may authorize its destruction in such emergencies without a hearing beforehand. But it does not follow that it can throw the loss on the owner without a hearing. If he cannot be heard beforehand, he may be heard afterward. The statute may provide for paying him in case it should appear that his property was not what the Legislature has declared to be a nuisance, and may give him his hearing in that way. If it does not do so, the statute may leave those who act under it to proceed at their peril, and the owner gets his hearing in an action against them.

An illustration, although not strictly an instance, of the former mode may be found in the statute authorizing fire-wards or engineers of fire departments to order houses to be pulled down in order to prevent the spreading of a fire, and making the town answerable to the house owner, except in certain cases in which the house is practically worthless because it would have been burned if it had not been destroyed. Pub. Sts. c. 35, Secs. 3–5. No doubt the order would be conclusive in its legislative capacity, or "so far as the *res* is concerned," as is said in *Salem* v. *Eastern Railroad*, 98 Mass. 431, 449, that is to say, that the house should be pulled down. But the owner is preserved his right to a hearing in a subsequent proceeding for compensation. On the other hand, a case where a party proceeds at his peril is when he pulls down a house for the same object without the authority of statute. It is said that if the destruction is necessary he is not liable. But by the common law as understood in this Commonwealth, "if there be no necessity, then the individuals who do the act shall be responsible." *Shaw,* C. J., in *Taylor* v. *Plymouth,* 8 Met. 462, 465. * * * This means that the determination of the individual is subject to revision by a jury in an action, and is not conclusive on the owner of the house.

So in *Blair* v. *Forehand,* 100 Mass. 136, where it was held that a statute might constitutionally authorize the killing of unlicensed dogs as nuisances, it was assumed, at page 143, that the question whether the particular dog killed was unlicensed was open in an action against the officer who killed it, and that if he killed a licensed dog he would be liable in tort; in other words, that he proceeded in that respect at his own risk, citing *Shaw,* C. J., in *Tower* v. *Tower,* 18 Pick. 262. It could have made no difference in that case if a board of three had been required to decide *ex parte* beforehand whether the dog was licensed.

In *Salem* v. *Eastern Railroad,* 98 Mass. 431, it was decided, in agreement with the views which we have expressed, that the decision of a board of health that a nuisance existed on certain premises, and the order of the board that it be removed at the expense of the owner, were not conclusive upon the owner in a subsequent action against him to recover the expense, he having had no notice or opportunity to be heard. The general rule is, that a judgment *in rem,* even when rendered by a regularly constituted court after the fullest and most formal trial, is not conclusive of the facts on which it proceeds against persons not entitled to be heard and not heard in fact, although, if the court has jurisdiction, the judgment does change or establish the status it deals with as against all the world, from the necessities of the case, and frequently by express legislation. *Brigham* v. *Fayerweather,* 140 Mass. 411, 413.

It is true that it is said in *Salem* v. *Eastern Railroad* that the board's determination of questions of discretion and judgment in the discharge of their duties would protect all those employed to carry such determinations into effect. The remark is *obiter,* and it is doubtful perhaps, on reading the whole case, whether it means that the determination would protect them in an action for damages, when the statute provides no compensation for property taken which is not a nuisance. To give it such an effect as a judgment merely, would be inconsistent with the point decided, and with *Brigham* v. *Fayerweather.* We are not prepared to admit that a condemnation by the present board under Sec. 13 could be made conclusive in the present action of the fact that the plaintiff's horse had the glanders.
* * *

But we are led by the dictum in *Salem* v. *Eastern Railroad* to consider another possible suggestion. It may be said, suppose that the decision of the board is not conclusive that the plaintiff's horse had the glanders, still the Legislature may consider that self-protection requires the immediate killing of all horses which a competent board deem infected, whether they are so or not, and, if so, the innocent horses that are killed are a sacrifice to necessary self-protection, and need not be paid for.

In *Train* v. *Boston Disinfecting Co.* 144 Mass. 523, it was held that all imported rags might be required to be put through a disinfecting process at the expense of the owner. Of course, the order did not mean that the Legislature or board of health declared all imported rags to be infected, but simply that the danger was too great to risk an attempt at discrimination. If the Legislature could throw the burden on owners of innocent rags in that case, why could it not throw the burden on the owners of innocent horses in this? If it could order all rags to be disinfected, why might it not have ordered such rags to be disinfected as a board of three should determine, summarily, and without notice or appeal? The latter provision would have been more favorable to owners, as they would have had a chance at least of escaping the burden, and it would stand on the same ground as the severer law.

The answer, or a part of it, is this. Whether the motives of the Legislature are the same or not in the two cases supposed, it declares different things to be dangerous and nuisances unless disinfected. In the one it declares all imported rags to be so; in the other, only all infected rags. Within limits it may thus enlarge or diminish the number of things to be deemed nuisances by the law, and courts cannot inquire why it includes certain property, and whether the motive was to avoid an investigation. But wherever it draws the line, an owner has a right to a hearing on the question whether his property falls within it, and this right is not destroyed by the fact that the line might have been drawn so differently as unquestionably to include that property. Thus, in the first case, the owner has a right to try the question whether his rags were imported; in the second, whether they were infected. His right is no more met in the second case by the fact that the Legislature might have made the inquiry immaterial by requiring all imported rags to be disinfected, than it would be in the first by the suggestion that possibly the Legislature might require all rags to be put through the same process, whether imported or not. But if the property is admitted to fall within the line, there is nothing to try, provided the line drawn is a valid one under the police power. All that *Train* v. *Boston Disinfecting Co.* decided was that the line there considered was a valid one.

Still it may be asked, if self-protection required the act, why should not the owner bear the loss? It may be answered, that self-protection does not require all that is believed to be necessary to that end, nor even all that reasonably is believed to be necessary to that end. It only requires what is actually necessary. It would seem doubtful, at least, whether actual necessity ought not to be the limit when the question arises under the Constitution between the public and an individual. Such seems to be the law as between private parties in this Commonwealth in the case of fires, as we have seen. It could not be assumed as a general principle, without discussion, that even necessity would exonerate a party from civil liability for a loss inflicted knowingly upon an innocent person, who neither by his person nor by his property threatens any harm to the defendant. It has been thought by great lawyers that a man cannot shift his misfortunes upon his neighbor's shoulders in that way when it is a question of damages, although his act may be one for which he would not be punished. * * * Upon this we express no opinion. It is enough to say, that in this case actual necessity required the destruction only of infected horses, and that was all that the Legislature purported to authorize.

Again, there is a pretty important difference of degree, at least (*Rideout* v. *Knox*, 148 Mass. 368, 372), between regulating the precautions to be taken in keeping property, especially property sought to be brought into the State, and ordering its destruction. We cannot admit that the Legislature has an unlimited right to destroy property without compensation, on the ground that destruction is not an appropriation to public use within Article X of the Declaration of Rights. When a healthy horse is killed by a public officer, acting under a general statute, for fear that it should spread disease, the horse certainly would seem to be taken for public use, as truly as if it were seized to drag an artillery wagon. The public equally appropriate it, whatever they do with it afterwards. Certainly the Legislature could not declare all cattle to be nuisances, and order them to be killed without compensation. * * * It does not attempt to do so. As we have said, it only declares certain diseased animals to be nuisances. And even if we assume that it could authorize some trifling amount of innocent property to be destroyed as a necessary means to the abatement of a nuisance, still, if in this Sec. 13 it had added in terms that such healthy animals as should be killed by mistake for diseased ones should not be paid for, we should deem it a serious question whether such a provision could be upheld. * * *

For these reasons, the literal, and as we think the true construction of Sec. 13, seems to us the only safe one to adopt, and accordingly we are of opinion that the authority and jurisdiction of the commissioners to condemn the plaintiff's horse under Sec. 13 was conditional upon its actually having the glanders. If this be so, their order would not protect the defendants in a case where the commissioners acted outside their jurisdiction. *Fisher* v. *McGirr,* 1 Gray, 1, 45. The fact as to the horse having the disease was open to investigation in the present action, and on the finding that the horse did not have it, the plaintiff was entitled to a ruling that the defendants had failed to make out their justification.

In view of our conclusion upon the main question, we have not considered whether an order signed by two members of the board, upon an examination by one, satisfies the statute, or whether cases like *Ruggles* v. *Nantucket,* 11 Cush. 433, and *Parsons* v. *Pettingell,* 11 Allen, 507, apply.

Exceptions sustained.

POWERS OF BOARD OF ALDERMEN

Commonwealth v. *Parks*
155 Mass. 531 (1892)

[Parks and Riley were prosecuted and fined under a city ordinance of Somerville (Pub. Sts. c. 27, Sec. 17) for blasting rock with gunpowder without the written consent of the board of aldermen. It appeared that several houses were located near the quarry where the blasting was done; that a public street ran by it; and that the ordinance was passed because of complaints from people who resided near by and apprehended the danger. It was contended that the ordinance was unconstitutional.]

It is settled that, within constitutional limits not exactly determined, the Legislature may change the common law as to nuisances, and may move the line either way, so as to make things nuisances, although by so doing it affects the use or value of property. * * * It is still plainer that it may prohibit a use of land which the common law would regard as a nuisance if it endangered adjoining houses or the highway, and the Legislature may authorize cities and towns by ordinances and by-laws to make similar prohibitions. * * * Furthermore, what the municipal body may forbid altogether, it may forbid conditionally, unless its written permission is obtained beforehand. We see nothing in *Newton* v. *Belger,* 143 Mass. 598, or in *Yick Wo* v. *Hopkins,* 118 U. S. 356, and *Baltimore* v. *Radecke,* 49 Md. 217, to make us doubt the correctness of the decision in *Quincy* v. *Kennard,* 151 Mass. 563. Nor do we think it matters that the permission required is that of the aldermen, and not that of the whole city council.

In view of the foregoing principles and decisions, we are of opinion that the power, when deemed necessary for public safety, to prohibit blasting rocks with gunpowder without written consent, is among the powers given by the Pub. Sts. c. 27, Sec. 15.* Equal powers are conferred upon the city council of Somerville by its charter. St. 1871, c. 182, Sec. 23. It would be a mere perversion to construe the Pub. Sts. c. 102, Secs. 60, 61, authorizing cities and towns to make ordinances and by-laws in regard to the use of explosive compounds, defined in Sec. 68, so as not to include gunpowder, as cutting down the power which is given in the earlier chapter, and which we have no doubt extended to this case before the passage of the St. of 1877, c. 216, from which the sections first cited are taken. It would be a still greater perversion to construe the sections giving authority over offensive trades to town boards of health as having such an effect. Pub. Sts. c. 80, Sec. 84 *et seq.*

The prohibition which the Pub. Sts. c. 27, Sec. 15, as construed by us, purport to authorize, is not such a taking of property as always to be beyond the police power. Under *Miller* v. *Horton,* 152 Mass. 540, 547, blasting might be a private or a public nuisance. * * * Forbidding it does not trench upon the rights of ownership to such an extent as necessarily to require compensation.

---

* The part of Sec. 15 of the Pub. Sts. c. 27, referred to in the opinion, is as follows: "Towns may make for the following named purposes, in addition to other purposes authorized by law, such necessary orders and by-laws, not repugnant to law, as they may judge most conducive to their welfare, and may fix penalties, not exceeding twenty dollars for one offence, for breaches thereof; For directing and managing the prudential affairs, preserving the peace and good order, and maintaining the internal police thereof . . ."

It may be that a by-law absolutely prohibiting blasting would be invalid in some towns in this Commonwealth. It may be that, in order to determine the question, we should have to take into account facts touching the mode in which the particular town was occupied and the nature of its industries, whether we listened to evidence of such facts or noticed them judicially. * * * But however this may be, we find nothing in the facts before us to lead us to doubt the reasonableness of the ordinance of Somerville.

The ordinance being valid, the defendants have had their hearing in this case on the only question upon which they were entitled to one, namely, whether they had done the prohibited act. *Miller* v. *Horton,* 152 Mass. 540, 546.

Exceptions overruled.

VALIDITY OF ORDINANCE FORBIDDING SELLING IN STREETS

Commonwealth v. Ellis
158 Mass. 555 (1893)

[Ellis was prosecuted for selling flowers in a public street in Boston without a permit as required by city ordinance. The ordinance provided that, "No person shall, except in accordance with a permit from the superintendent, in any street or from any building, sell any goods or articles to any person on the street. . . ." Ellis contended that the ordinance was unjust, unreasonable, in restraint of trade, and unconstitutional.]

We must assume that the defendant was guilty of a breach of the Boston city ordinance against selling in the streets. Rev. Ord. 1892, c. 43, sec. 35. The only question brought before us by the exceptions is whether the ordinance is valid. It must be construed in a rational way. See *Commonwealth* v. *Plaisted,* 148 Mass. 375, 382. Of course it does not mean that two persons walking together on a highway cannot make a bargain in their private conversation, and execute it on the spot. The sales referred to are sales in pursuance of an offer to the public,—sales in the course of a business generally conducted at a standstill, or at least with frequent stops, and tending to collect a crowd. Formerly the prohibition was confined to standing in the street for the sale of any article. Rev. Ord. 1885, c. 28, sec. 44. Probably the change was made to avoid nice questions as to what was standing, such as were raised in *Commonwealth* v. *Elliott,* 121 Mass. 367, but the object is the same, as appears also from the context. *Commonwealth* v. *McCafferty,* 145 Mass. 384, 385.

Anyone who has observed the obstruction to travel and the general inconvenience which are caused by a stationary object in our crowded and narrow streets, would be slow to declare unreasonable a prohibition intended to prevent that inconvenience. We are of opinion, both on principle and on authority, that for this purpose the city council lawfully may forbid public selling in the streets. * * * This being so, the ordinance is none the worse for the exception in case of a permit from the superintendent of streets. * * * The fact that the defendant had a license as a peddler from the Commonwealth is not material on these exceptions. But the license did not authorize him to violate the ordinances of the city. * * * In the opinion of a majority of the court, the exceptions must be overruled.

Exceptions overruled.

BEING PRESENT WHERE GAMING INSTRUMENTS ARE FOUND

Commonwealth v. Smith
166 Mass. 370 (1896)

[Denton, a police officer, by virtue of a search warrant granted under the provisions of a statute (St. 1895, c. 419, Sec. 9) searched certain premises described in the complaint and found a blackboard "on which were written, in six different columns, the names of race horses entered in six different races, and one hundred and twenty blank tickets for the making of memoranda of bets found in a compartment designed for the sale of such memoranda. The defendant, Smith, was present when the above described implements, which were in plain view of any person in the room, were found, and when searched at the stationhouse a ticket containing a memorandum of a bet on a horse race was found on his person." The defendant claimed that "the mere presence of the instruments of gaming in the alleged room . . . was not prima facie evidence of any unlawful game" and that section 2, 3 and 4 of the statute of 1895 were unconstitutional.]

The offence of being present where gaming implements are found, created by St. 1895, c. 419, sec. 9, is created by the words "every person found . . . so present shall be punished." "So" refers back to the words "all persons present, . . . if any . . . materials of any form of gaming are found in said place." "Said place" by reference means a place which has been complained of under oath as a common gaming house. But the words last quoted are used in that part of the sections which authorizes an arrest on the complaint. When we come to the words constituting the offence, and first above quoted, it is plain that we must not take the word "so" literally, with the result of making it criminal to be in the same place with gaming implements if the place merely has been complained of as a common gaming house. The place must be used unlawfully as a common gaming house in fact. The word "so" is an abbreviation, and not so accurate an abbreviation as might be wished in a criminal statute, since it seems to have misled the pleader; but we are of opinion that the meaning is clear. Therefore it is material to allege that the place was "unlawfully used as and for a common gaming house."

The allegation in the complaint before us is, "And so the said Denton . . . doth say that the said room, in manner and form aforesaid, was unlawfully used as and for a common gaming-house," etc. It is argued for the defendant that the words "and so" import that the allegation following is a legal consequence of facts previously alleged; and that although there may be no objection to the form of expression as argumentative if the earlier allegations justify it (*Commonwealth* v. *Desmarteau*, 16 Gray, 1, 16), if they do not justify it the complaint must be quashed. *Commonwealth* v. *Whitney*, 5 Gray, 85, 86. The previous allegations here, after those which superfluously state the preliminary complaint and the warrant, are, in substance, that the present complainant, Denton, entered the room complained of and there found the defendant present at the time gaming implements were found by Denton in the room; and that Denton seized the implements and arrested the defendant. All this might be true if the room was a chapel, if the defendant had been attending divine service, and if a thief had hidden the implements under a cushion in a remote corner of the place. It is not enough to warrant a conviction; it does not even amount to *prima facie* evidence under Secs. 3, 4. The sole argument, it will be seen, turns on the effect of the words "And so." But the court are of opinion that the words as here used do not have the effect of limiting the following allegation to the legal conclusion from what precedes. They think that it sufficiently appears that the complainant intends to allege as a distinct substantive fact that the room was used as and for a common gaming house.

The objection that the defendant and those indicted with him cannot be joined in one complaint, although plausible, seems to us unsound in view of the precedents. As was said of a different offence, the act is more analogous to the maintaining of a public nuisance than to those which necessarily are the separate acts of single persons. * * *

It is unnecessary under the statute to allege the defendant's knowledge of the presence of the implements or the character of the place. The statute means that people enter such places at their peril. It goes no further than other statutes which have been enforced by this court. When according to common experience a certain fact generally is accompanied by knowledge of the further elements necessary to complete what it is the final object of the law to prevent, or even short of that, when it is very desirable that people should find out whether the further elements are there, actual knowledge being a matter difficult to prove, the law may stop at the preliminary fact, and in the pursuit of its policy may make the preliminary fact enough to constitute a crime. It may say that, as people generally do know when they are selling intoxicating liquors, they must discover at their peril whether what they sell will intoxicate. * * * It may say that, if a man will have connection with a woman to whom he is not married, he must take the chance of her turning out to be married to someone else. * * * In like manner it may say that people are not likely to resort to a common gaming house without knowing it, and that they must take the risk of knowing the character of the place to which they resort, if the implements of gaming are actually present.

The evidence warranted a conviction. St. 1895, c. 419, Secs. 2, 3, 4. These sections are constitutional. * * * Apart from them the evidence was competent, and leaves no reasonable doubt as to the character of the place. * * * The mode in which the ticket was obtained did not make it inadmissible, even if the right of objecting to it had been reserved in the agreed facts, which is not the case. * * * We believe we have dealt with all the questions before us. Some others were argued, which are not open.

Exceptions overruled.

FLIMSY EXCEPTIONS

Commonwealth v. *Brown*
167 Mass. 144 (1896)

[Indictment, for obtaining property by false pretenses. The jury returned a verdict of guilty and the defendant alleged exceptions.]

The case went to the jury only on certain allegations in two counts, the second and fifth. The allegations in the second count are of false representations to one Martin that the daily receipts of a certain business then carried on by the defendant at a certain shop "then averaged, and for some time theretofore had averaged, from twenty to twenty-five dollars," and that the defendant "had occupied said store in carrying on said business for the period of five years theretofore." It is alleged that Martin was induced by these pretences to pay the defendant three hundred and fifty dollars for one-half interest in the business.

The allegations in the fifth count are of false representations to one Day, that the amount of business done by the defendant in a certain shop in Boston "had been more than four hundred dollars per week," and that the defendant "had no other store than said store except one" on Dudley Street in Boston. It is alleged that Day was induced by these pretences to give the defendant a check of the amount and of the value of three hundred and eighty-five dollars for a half interest in the business.

A great number of points are raised by the exceptions, many of them of a very flimsy character, and we shall confine our discussion to those for which the defendant has offered some reason in argument, or which seem to us important, and shall follow in the main the order adopted by his counsel.

The defendant was sentenced, notwithstanding his exceptions, as required by St. 1895, c. 469. It is suggested that this statute is unconstitutional. No reason is offered for the suggestion. A statute looking in the same direction has long been in force and unquestioned. * * *

The judge was right in refusing to stay the sentence or execution of the sentence, and was not called on to state his reasons for doing so.

It is suggested, again without argument, that St. 1895, c. 504, under which the defendant was sentenced, is unconstitutional. This statute requires the sentence in certain cases to be for a term of not less than two and one half years, and not more than a maximum fixed by the court, and not longer than the longest term fixed by law for the punishment of the offence. Such a sentence is in effect a sentence for the maximum fixed by the court, unless a permit to be at liberty is issued as provided by Sec. 2. But the form of the sentence is made to recognize and carry out a policy familiar to our legislation and acted on heretofore without question. * * * Such a form of sentence does not make the punishment more severe than it otherwise would have been, and we see no reason why the law should not be construed to apply to all sentences, in the cases referred to, passed after the act goes into operation. * * *

With regard to the substance of the offence it is argued that what the defendant received became partnership funds at once, and therefore continued to belong in part to the defrauded party. *Regina* v. *Watson*, 7 Cox C. C. 364. But this was left to the jury, with directions to acquit if they found that to be the fact, as, no doubt, much of the testimony tended to show that it was. It was possible, however, on the evidence, for the jury to find that the money was paid to the defendant as his own for an interest in the firm, and that he merely gave a personal undertaking to put a certain sum out of his own money into the business afterwards, as occasion should require. On that state of facts a conviction was warranted. This consideration disposes of the general objections to testimony on the ground that the defendant was forming a partnership, as well as of the request for a ruling that, if the prosecutors afterwards treated the partnership as existing, the defendant could not be convicted. The request, no doubt, was based on the suggestion as to the possible effect of rescinding the contract of partnership when the money was a contribution to capital, made in *Regina* v. *Watson*, 7 Cox C. C. 364, 371, but has no application to the facts which the jury must have found under the very clear instructions of the court. On these facts, it does not matter if the payment was made after the partnership was begun. The payment did not become an item in the partnership accounts for that reason, if it was not made as an advance of capital.

We may as well say, in this connection, that the representations are sufficient to constitute false pretenses. * * * It is not necessary for us to consider nicely whether the latitude allowed to sellers of chattels would apply to representations made as the inducements to enter into confidential relations with the person making them.

Next it is said that there was a variance under the fifth count, because it is alleged that Day was induced by false representations to part with a check for three hundred and eighty-five dollars, whereas it appeared by the evidence that ten dollars of the amount was for that sum in cash handed back by the defendant. But the check was delivered as alleged, and, under the instructions of the court, the representations must have been found to have given a motive without which the transaction of which the payment was part would not have been entered into. That is enough for conviction. * * * The time of the representations alleged in the second count did not have to be proved as laid. It would be overrefining to no useful purpose to say that, inasmuch as the representations referred as a starting point to the time when they were made, therefore the time when they were made entered into the description of the offence. The representations referred to the time of speaking, whatever it might be, but went no further, and they were not changed or enlarged by an allegation as to what the time was.

No exception was taken to the instruction that the defendant was not to be prejudiced because he had not testified, and the instruction was proper. * * *

The judge was not requested to instruct the jury not to consider the evidence on the counts which were thrown out. If he had been asked to, doubtless he would have done it. No exception was taken on the matter.

The releases of all demands, etc. to the defendant from Martin, one of the defrauded parties, did not purge the crime. *Commonwealth* v. *Coe,* 115 Mass. 481, 502, 503.

A previous indictment had been found against the defendant in respect of the fraud on Day, on which a trial had been had and a verdict of guilty rendered, but the verdict had been set aside on the defendant's motion, and the indictment had been placed on file. These facts were pleaded. The pendency of this indictment is no defence. * * * The effect of the verdict is no greater than if it had been rendered on the fifth count now before us, and the prevailing view in such a case is, that, when a verdict is set aside on the prisoner's own motion and for his benefit, he may be tried anew. * * *

Exceptions overruled.

STATUTE GIVING LABOR AN ADDITIONAL REMEDY

Callahan v. *Boston*
175 Mass. 201 (1900)

[Callahan sued the city of Boston under a statute which provided that in certain cases a laborer was permitted to sue the city if he worked for a third person who was authorized to contract for the city.]

It is not denied that the defendant is liable to the plaintiff under St. 1892, c. 270, if that statute is constitutional. The effect of that act is that if a city or town sees fit voluntarily to order the construction of public works owned by it, then *nolens volens,* it must assume a part of the responsibility of an employer to the workmen employed by the contractor with whom it deals. It is intended to be a milder application of the principle of the mechanic's lien laws. We see no constitutional objection to the law. It is a familiar type of statute, and has been upheld heretofore. *Hart* v. *Boston, Revere Beach, & Lynn Railroad,* 121 Mass. 510. A compulsory relation of master and servant is not unknown even to the common law. *Benjamin* v. *Dockham,* 134 Mass. 418.

Judgment for the plaintiff.

RIGHT OF CITY COUNCIL TO FIX SEWAGE CHARGES

Carson v. Sewerage Commission of Brockton
175 Mass. 242 (1900)

[Carson, a resident of Brockton, claimed his sewage assessment was too high and petitioned to have it quashed contending that both the State statute and the city ordinance under which the Commissioners acted were unconstitutional. This case was later appealed to the United States Supreme Court and Chief Justice Holmes' opinion was affirmed, see 182 U. S. 398.]

This is a petition for a writ of certiorari for the purpose of quashing the assessment of an annual charge for the use of a common sewer. The assessment was authorized by St. 1892, c. 245, Sec. 1, and by an ordinance in pursuance of that section. It is objected that both statute and ordinance are unconstitutional.

By the statute the City council of any city except Boston, or a town, with sewers laid out under Pub. Sts. c. 50, Secs. 1–3, or with a system of sewerage under Sec. 7, may establish just and equitable annual charges or rents for the use of such sewers, to be paid by every one who enters his sewer into the common sewer. The ordinance charges for "unmetered" water service eight dollars, and for "metered" water service thirty cents per thousand gallons of sewage delivered to the sewer, but no charge to be less than eight dollars subject to certain possible discounts. It is argued that the statute is subject to the objections which prevailed in *Sears v. Street Commissioners,* 173 Mass. 350, that the charge is a tax which properly should be borne by the public generally, and that there are no provisions for a hearing.

We are of opinion that the petitioner received a special benefit for which he might be charged, and that this case is free from the elements which in *Sears v. Street Commissioners* led to the conclusion that the petitioner was assessed without regard to the benefits received by him. No one denies that it was a special benefit to the petitioner to have a sewer built in front of his land. That benefit was the probability that the sewer would be available for use in the future. But the city, by building it and receiving a part of the cost from the petitioner, did not impliedly bind itself or the general taxes that the sewer should be maintained forever and that the petitioner should be at liberty to use it free of further expense. If building the sewer was a special benefit, keeping the sewer in condition for use by such further expenditure as was necessary was a further special benefit to such as used it.

The charge allowed by the act is a charge for using the sewer, a benefit distinct from that originally conferred by building it. By the statute the charge must be a "just and equitable" charge. These words have been held insufficient to save the constitutionality of a statute in *State* v. *Commissioners of Streets & Sewers,* 9 Vroom, 190, and in *Barnes* v. *Dyer,* 56 Vt. 469. But the facts of those cases were too different to make them conclusive. Here the words are applied solely to those who actually use the sewer. Therefore the benefit to the parties assessed is established. The assessment in order to be equitable must be proportional to the benefit and not in excess of it. The words in this connection sufficiently express an intent to confine the charge within constitutional limits. They are so construed by the ordinance. For by the ordinance the charge is in proportion to the extent of the use, which is a reasonable way of estimating the extent of the benefit received. See *Parker* v. *Boston,* 1 Allen, 361, 367. There is no charge unless the sewer is used. The charge to the plaintiff was $42.53, and therefore under the terms of the ordinance which we have stated must have been determined by meter.

It is said that there is no provision for a hearing. But under the ordinance the only questions are whether the petitioner's sewer enters the common sewer, and what amount of sewage is shown by the meter readings to have been delivered to the sewer. If the petitioner wished to be heard on either of these facts, no doubt he could resort to the courts. On the rate per thousand gallons fixed by the ordinance he was not entitled to be heard. So far as appears, if he is dissatisfied with the rate he is not obliged to use the sewer. But if he were compelled by law to use it and to pay as now for the use (St. 1890, c. 132), and recognizing as we must the possibility that, in spite of the meaning which we attribute to the statute, the rate fixed by the ordinance might be in excess of the benefit received, still in our opinion the act and ordinance would be valid, notwithstanding that mere possibility in the absence of any allegation that the rate fixed did exceed, in fact, the benefit received. In cases of this sort the petitioner has no right of appeal to a jury. *Howe* v. *Cambridge,* 114 Mass. 388. The final decision must be somewhere, and may as well be left to the city council as to anyone. *New London Northern Railroad* v. *Boston & Albany*

Railroad, 102 Mass. 386, 387, 388. If it is left to them they are not obliged to hear the several parties who may be affected before fixing a general rate. Clearly the rate might have been fixed by the Legislature without a hearing. *Parsons* v. *District of Columbia,* 170 U. S. 45. And whatever differences there may be between the Legislature of the State and inferior although legislative bodies in cases where particular property is to be valued, still when a uniform and self-adjusting rate is adopted under which no question as to proportion can arise, or any other question except the general one whether the rate is high, we are of opinion that the Legislature has power to authorize a city council to determine that question as it has done here. *United States* v. *New Orleans,* 98 U. S. 381. * * *

If under the pretence of fixing an equitable rate the ordinance should do what amounted to the taking or destruction of property, very possibly that might afford a ground for judicial interference as in other cases where the Legislature fixes rates. * * *

Petition denied.

ASSESSING ABUTTERS FOR BETTERMENTS

Lincoln v. Street Commissioners
176 Mass. 210 (1900)

This is a petition for a writ of certiorari to quash an assessment for betterments made under St. 1893, c. 339, and St. 1894, c. 439. Under these acts the street commissioners of Boston constructed a portion of Boylston Street, with sewers, and established building lines outside of and parallel with the lines of the highway. They assessed upon the abutters, and no others, so much of the cost of the whole work (subject to the exceptions mentioned in Sec. 2 of the act of 1893) as was equal to what they adjudged to be the total special benefits received, and in estimating the special benefits they took the whole improvement as one, instead of separating the items and setting the cost of the sewer against the benefit of the sewer, the cost of the building lines against the benefit of the building lines, and the cost of the street against the benefit of the street, alone. This is one ground upon which the assessment is attacked.

Another ground is that the commissioners confined the assessment to abutters, although the statute of 1893 did not, and that other estates not abutting on the way were benefited specially. In support of this allegation proof was offered at the hearing that the value of estates near the end of Boylston Street was increased by having a shorter and more pleasant avenue to important points, and was increased much more than that of more remote estates. The evidence was rejected, the judge ruling that the alleged benefits were not special and peculiar within the meaning of the statute, and also that the omission of estates which ought to have been assessed could not be shown upon certiorari, unless, which did not appear, the omission occurred through a mistake of law and not through a mistake of fact.

It is objected further that to make the assessment proportional a valuation should have been set upon the public benefit, or at least upon the benefit to all Boston real estate as well as upon the special benefits to individuals, and both should have been assessed equally. The statute itself is attacked as imposing a disproportionate tax.

The first objection goes to the course adopted by the commissioners in considering the benefits from the whole improvement as one. The assessment cannot exceed the special benefit, (*Norwood* v. *Baker,* 172 U. S. 269; *Sears* v. *Boston,* 173 Mass. 71, 78), and therefore in determining what the petitioners can be called on to pay it may make a great difference if an item which cost but little, but added much to the value of their estate, can be lumped with another of which the cost was large but the benefit small. Still "the question was as to the benefit to the petitioner's land by the whole construction of the street." *Alden* v. *Springfield,* 121 Mass. 27, 28. The statute seems to contemplate the course which was adopted, so that strictly the question would be, perhaps, whether the statute could not authorize it. But if we assume the statute to be neutral, the question is whether it can be said as a matter of law that the commissioners were not warranted in finding street, sewer, and building lines all to be portions of one improvement. We are of opinion that they were warranted in their finding. The different elements are combined in the unity of a single though complex design. A sewer is one of the recognized incidents of a way, although it serves a different purpose from that of the pavement; just as a chimney is part of a house, although it serves a different end from that of the roof or walls. The right to lay sewers is paid for when a way is laid out although not specially mentioned in the taking. *Lincoln* v. *Commonwealth,* 164 Mass. 1, 10.

Next as to the refusal to receive evidence that other estates beside those of abutters were benefited by having a shorter and more pleasant way to central points. The statute did not limit the assessment to abutters. It allowed lands specially benefited to be assessed "whether situated on said street or otherwise." St. 1893, c. 339, Sec. 2. This being so, the petitioners say that they are entitled to be heard at some time on the question whether others should not have been called on to contribute and so to tighten the petitioners' burden. We must take this contention with the petitioners' offer of evidence. If any amendment were necessary to give the respondent the advantage of the actual state of facts as shown by that offer, it would be allowed as of course. But the benefits which the petitioners offered to prove were those common to all lands in the vicinity, and these, it is settled, are not to be regarded as special. * * *

All these last cited cases start from *Meacham* v. *Fitchburg Railroad,* 4 Cush. 291, 297, 298, and it is said that this distinction between special and general benefits had its beginning in a mere rule of damages for determining the sum to be deducted from the amount to be paid when land was taken for a public improvement. It is argued that constitutional difficulties have no place in a case of that sort, but arise only when the special benefits are made the subject of an assessment. A suggestion that the deduction of benefits may be referred to the right of eminent domain will be found in *Harvard College* v. *Boston,* 104 Mass. 470, 490, 491. See *Sears* v. *Boston,* 173 Mass. 71, 76. The distinctions of constitutional law must be pretty technical if taking a man's money is unlawful in the latter case and is not equally so in the former. It may be that the line between special and general benefits is fixed by a somewhat rough estimate of differences. But all legal lines are more or less arbitrary as to the precise place of their incidence, although the distinctions of which they are the inevitable outcome are plain and undeniable. This one we regard as sanctioned by legislation and judicial determination.

In what we have said last we have approached the grounds on which the statute is argued to be unconstitutional. The petitioners say that if there is a benefit to other estates in the neighborhood, or to all the land in Boston, or to the public generally, no matter how you distinguish it from that received by the petitioners' land, they are entitled to have those benefits share proportionately with their own in the expense. They deny that their special benefits can be assessed before calling on the others. Notwithstanding the effort of their counsel in his able and ingenious argument to distinguish the case, we must regard the whole contention as disposed of by *Dorgan* v. *Boston,* 12 Allen, 223. It is suggested that we are to take the decision as assuming merely such a minimum public benefit as would justify the exercise of the right of eminent domain; but this seems to us excluded when it is said, although in a different connection, that the Legislature deemed the work to be "so essential to common convenience as to warrant them in authorizing its execution in a certain contingency at the common expense." 12 Allen, 242.

This disposes of the claim to contribution in respect of the public benefit, and we think that the court had the general benefit to real estate in the neighborhood no less clearly in mind, when, after having earlier referred to "the well established rule as recognized in *Meacham* v. *Fitchburg Railroad*," it laid down its conclusion that "taxes levied for public purposes of a local character are not unconstitutional, as being unreasonable and unproportional, solely because they are imposed only . . . on persons residing or owning property in a particular locality, and that an assessment made on persons in respect of their ownership of certain property which receives a peculiar benefit from the expenditure of the money raised by a tax, or by reason of their residence in the vicinity of a proposed public improvement, and the special advantage or convenience which will accrue to them and their property therefrom, will not be held invalid, although it does not operate on all persons and property in the community in the same manner as taxes levied for general purposes." The argument for the petitioners cuts at the root of all betterment assessments upon abutters, because in almost every case there must be a public benefit and some general benefit to other land in the neighborhood which are neglected in the assessment. We should be slow to believe that anything in *Nor-*

wood v. *Baker,* 172 U. S. 269, or in any other authoritative decision threw doubt on the validity of such assessments on the ground supposed, provided they did not exceed the special benefits to the estates concerned. See further *Springfield* v. *Gay,* 12 Allen, 612, 615, 616; * * *

A subordinate objection taken to the act of 1893 needs a word. The board in determining the cost of the work is to exclude "the expenses for gas pipes, water pipes, their connections and the laying thereof," but is to assess a proportional share of the cost upon the real estate "which said board shall adjudge receives any benefit and advantage from such laying out, construction, and laying of sewers and pipes as aforesaid, beyond the general advantages to all real estate in such city, to the extent of the total amount of such adjudged benefit and advantage," c. 339, Sec. 2. It is urged that the benefit of the gas pipes cannot be treated as part of the benefit conferred by the laying out of the street, that it is a benefit paid for and furnished by a private company. Our answer is that the statute here is merely indicating in general terms the benefits to be assessed for, not precisely describing the elements and laying down a legal rule for assessments; that there was not intended or expected by the insertion of the word "pipes" any improper enhancement of the estimated benefits; that the word "pipes," if of any importance, is satisfied by water pipes which are laid by the city; and that the board seems from its return to have considered only the benefits of the laying out and construction of the streets, the laying out of sewers and the establishment of building lines, and that that is all that the statute meant it to do.

Although it is not necessary, we recur to the ruling of the justice at the hearing. A second ground on which the evidence offered was rejected was that it was not admissible on certiorari. That is in accordance with the well understood rule. *Prince* v. *Boston,* 111 Mass. 226, 232; *Farmington River Water Power Co.* v. *County Commissioners,* 112 Mass. 206. It is argued from *Butler* v. *Worcester,* 112 Mass. 541, 556, * * * that if not admissible on certiorari it would not be admissible at all. We do not so understand those cases. The first two only decide that you cannot show an assessment to be void for the omission of proper parties in an action to recover a sum paid under protest. They say that an error of omission may be remedied on certiorari. *LeRoy* v. *York,* 20 Johns. 430, the only one of the cases cited by Chief Justice Gray in the earlier decision needing notice, shows that he had in mind a case where the record disclosed an omission of estates standing like the petitioners', and omitted because of the adoption of a mistaken principle. The error was broader and more fundamental than a mistaken finding that this or that piece of land was not specially benefited. A mistaken finding upon that point would not invalidate the assessment. * * * *Prince* v. *Boston and County Commissioners, Petitioners,* show that, so far as necessary to fix the amount due from the petitioners, the matter can be gone into before the jury, if a jury is asked for to revise the assessment. See also *Whiting* v. *Boston,* 106 Mass. 89, 97. But we repeat that the offer would have to go further than the one made to give the petitioners a right to put in the evidence anywhere.

Petition dismissed.

RIGHTS OF A NON-RESIDENT ALIEN
Mulhall v. *Fallon*
176 Mass. 266 (1900)

This is an action under St. 1887, c. 270, Sec. 2, for causing the death of the plaintiff's son. The plaintiff is an Irishwoman who, so far as appears, never has left Ireland. In the Superior Court she had a verdict, and the case is here on exceptions to a refusal to direct a verdict for the defendants, either on the ground that the statute conferred no rights upon the plaintiff, or on the ground that she did not appear to have been dependent upon the wages of her son for support. Exceptions were taken also upon some matters of evidence.

On the question of the plaintiff's dependence upon her son we are of opinion that there was evidence for the jury. It appeared from declarations of the deceased, properly admitted under St. 1898, c. 535, that his mother was very poor, and that he sent over money repeatedly, and regretted not being able to do more. The money, it is true, was received by his father while alive; but the father was a paralytic, and died nearly a year before his son. The plaintiff in her deposition confirmed the statements of her son. She testified that she bought food with his money, among other things, and that she wished she had more to eat.

In answer to the question to what extent, if at all, she was dependent upon her son for support, she answered that she was almost entirely dependent upon him for the last two years. This question was objected to, but was admissible. The extent to which particulars may be summed up in a general expression is a matter involving more or less discretion, and cannot be disposed of by the suggestion that the general expression involves the conclusion which the jury is to draw, or that it is law rather than fact. * * * The question to what extent she was dependent upon her son called for details of fact in a perfectly proper way. Whether the answer showed a sufficient dependence to satisfy the statute remained for the jury to answer under the instructions of the court. Even more plainly admissible were interrogatories whether the son contributed to her support, and if so how much. The plaintiff also testified that she "had to turn around and go three miles to earn [her] support," that she had a boy that was hard set to earn from 8d. to 1s. a day, and another boy an invalid. How far these statements should outweigh the others was for the jury. * * * Partial dependence for the necessaries of life would be enough, as it is made in terms by the English statute. 60 & 61 Vict. c. 37, sec. 7, cl. 2. * * * In *Hodnett* v. *Boston & Albany Railroad,* 156 Mass. 86, there was nothing to show that the plaintiff did not support herself by her own earnings.

We come then to the more difficult question, whether the plaintiff can claim the benefit of the act. However this may be decided, it is not to be decided upon any theoretic impossibility of Massachusetts law conferring a right outside her boundary lines. In *Mannville Co.* v. *Worcester,* 138 Mass. 89, where a Rhode Island corporation sought to recover for a diversion of waters from its mill in Rhode Island by an act done higher up the stream in Massachusetts, it was held, following earlier decisions, that there was no such impossibility, although the point was strongly urged. It is true that legislative power is territorial, and that no duties can be imposed by statute upon persons who are within the limits of another State. But rights can be offered to such persons, and if, as is usually the case, the power that governs them makes no objection, there is nothing to hinder their accepting what is offered. The same principle is recognized without discussion in *Lumb* v. *Jenkins,* 100 Mass. 527, where a non-resident alien was held entitled to take land by descent. So, after discussion, as to a non-resident's right to sue. *Peabody* v. *Hamilton,* 106 Mass. 217. So the Supreme Court of the United States holds that a right to recover for wrongfully causing death under a State law similar to Lord Campbell's act may be asserted by an administrator appointed in another State. *Dennick* v. *Central Railroad,* 103 U. S. 11. See 8 Am. & Eng. Encyc. of Law (2d ed.) 879, "Death by wrongful act." It is true that the arguments which prevailed in this case did not prevail in *Richardson* v. *New York Central Railroad,* 98 Mass. 85, and perhaps would not have prevailed in England. *Adam* v. *British & Foreign Steamship Co.* 79 L. T. (N.S.) 31. But so far as the principle for which we cite the case is concerned, it is in accord with our own decisions, assuming that, like Lord Campbell's act, the statute was regarded as conferring a new right of action on the foreign executor or administrator, and not as giving a right of action to the deceased which went to the executor by survival only. * * * The cause of action survived in *Higgins* v. *Central New England & Western Railroad,* 155 Mass. 176. This distinction seems to be lost sight of by many of the cases given in the Encyclopædia as following *Dennick* v. *Central Railroad,* so that their reasoning is not very satisfactory. But see *Bruce* v. *Cincinnati Railroad,* 83 Ky. 174, 182 *et seq.*

The question then becomes one of construction, and of construction upon a point upon which it is probable that the Legislature never thought when they passed the act. In view of the decisions to which we have referred, we lay on one side as too absolute some expressions which are to be found in the English cases, and some of which are cited in *Adam* v. *British & Foreign Steamship Co.* 79 L. T. (N.S.) 31. Our different relation to our neighbors politically and territorially is a sufficient ground for a more liberal rule, at least as to inhabitants of the United States.

One or two cases may be found where a general grant of a right of action for wrongfully causing death has been held to confer no rights upon non-resident aliens. * * * On the other hand, in several States the right of the non-resident to sue is treated as too clear to need extended argument. * * *

Under the statute the action for death without conscious suffering takes the place of an action that would have been brought by the employee himself if the harm had been less, and by his representative if it had been equally great, but the death had been attended with pain. St. 1887, c. 270, Sec. 1, cl. 3. In the latter case, there would be no exception to the right of recovery if the next of kin were non-resident aliens. It would be strange to read an exception into general words when the wrong is so nearly identical, and when the different provisions are part of one scheme. In all cases the statute has the interest of the employees in mind. It is on their account that an action is given to the widow or next of kin. Whether the action is to be brought by them or by the administrator, the sum to be recovered is to be assessed with reference to the degree of culpability of the employer or negligent person. In other words, it is primarily a penalty for the protection of the life of a workman in this state. We cannot think that workmen were intended to be less protected if their mothers happen to live abroad, or less protected against sudden than against lingering death. In view of the very large amount of foreign labor employed in this State, we cannot believe that so large an exception was silently left to be read in. Whether if the statute were of a different kind we could make a distinction between a mother living just across the boundary line between Massachusetts and Rhode Island and one living in Ireland, need not be considered now.

We are of opinion that the Superior Court was right in letting the case go to the jury. A similar decision has been rendered upon this statute by the United States Circuit Court for this district. *Vetaloro* v. *Perkins,* 101 Fed. Rep. 393.

Exceptions overruled.

PAYMENT FOR PUBLIC WORKS
Hall v. Street Commissioners of Boston
177 Mass. 434 (1901)

[Hall, a Boston taxpayer and landowner filed a petition of certiorari to quash the proceedings of the board of street commissioners, contending among other things, that the statute under which the sewer assessments were made against him did not apply to a sewer already built and if it did it was unconstitutional. Holmes said that the statute did apply and upheld it.]

This is a petition for a writ of certiorari to quash a sewer assessment laid under St. 1899, c. 450, Sec. 3, which took the place of St. 1897, c. 426, Sec. 7, declared unconstitutional in *Sears v. Street Commissioners,* 173 Mass. 350.

The act of 1899, in the first part of Sec. 3, enacts that the board of street commissioners "at any time within two years after any new sewer or drain . . . is completed, shall assess upon the several estates especially benefited by such sewer or drain, a proportional part of the cost thereof, not exceeding in amount the sum of four dollars per linear foot," and goes on to provide for a reassessment of any such assessment which shall have been found to be invalid and is unpaid, or which shall have been recovered back. This act took effect June 1, 1899. The sewer in question was built under an order of August 5, 1897, the work being finished on April 5, 1898. There was an old sewer in the street, but it was on the other side, no part of it was used in the new construction, and it fairly is to be taken from the respondents' answer that they found it broken down and useless.

It is objected to the assessment that the sewer was not a new sewer, that the act does not apply to a sewer already built, and that if it does it is unconstitutional for that and other reasons. It is objected further, that the answer does not show that the petitioner has not paid for the sewer within a proviso further on in the section, but this and some other objections go on the footing that the action of the board in this case is to be referred to a later power to "assess upon any estate heretofore or hereafter connected with a public sewer a reasonable part of the cost of construction thereof" subject to the proviso just referred to. As we are of opinion that the board acted under the words first quoted from the beginning of the section and not under this later power, we shall say no more about these other objections beyond adding that so far as they go on a failure of the answer to state matters obviously true with technical fulness, we should not grant a certiorari on that ground.

We are of opinion that the sewer was a new sewer within the meaning of the act, and that it is sufficiently shown to have been so by the facts which we have stated. The suggestion that it is not a new sewer seems to have been an afterthought and contrary to the purport of the petition. In view of our opinion on this point and of the fact that the words of the act which we shall discuss require a new sewer, it is unnecessary to consider whether the Legislature would not have had power to authorize an assessment for reconstructing an old sewer or a new part of an old system.

* * *

We are of opinion in the next place that this sewer is within the words first above quoted from the act. It is true that the words "within two years after any new sewer . . . is completed" taken by themselves would seem to refer to a completion in the future. But we have to consider the whole section and the circumstances. Later on, as we have said, there is a general power to assess upon any estate heretofore or hereafter connected with a sewer, about which we say nothing except that it shows that the Legislature had past work in its mind. But what is more important is that the section is enacted to replace the one which was held unconstitutional by this court, and its whole frame shows that it was intended among other things to enable the city to collect the special assessment which it had failed to get under the earlier act. Indeed this is the petitioner's argument, although aimed at a different conclusion. Taking this into account, and also that the section which we are construing was passed as an amendment to the act of 1897, we are of opinion that the words embrace at least sewers completed after the act of 1897 went into effect. We are not laying down a general rule of construction for amendments, but simply are construing this particular act as we think that the Legislature meant it to be construed. No doubt if the amendment in a new clause not repeated from the amended section, had read "is hereafter completed," the general rule would take "hereafter" as referring to the date of the amendment, not to the date of the act. * * *

Finally we are of opinion that the act of 1899 is constitutional, so far as it applies to this case. The greater part of the petitioner's argument is made inapplicable by our decision that this was a new sewer and is within the opening words of the section. We see no objection to the statute in the fact that the statute does not apply to any sewer built before a certain date, it does not matter precisely what. Such a limit of liability by time is no more unreasonable or contrary to any principle of constitutional right than is a statute of limitations. Again, it is not unconstitutional to levy special assessments for sewers already built. One must not let one's mind be led astray by the false analogy of executed consideration in contracts. Public works must be paid for although they have been constructed before any tax has been levied on their account. If the tax otherwise is levied properly as a special assessment for betterments, then, in view of the fact that the benefit and payment both are compulsory, not matter of contract, a betterment already executed when the law authorizing the tax was passed will sustain the tax as well as a work built with express notice that it is under the law. * * *

It is suggested that this statute is an attempt to exercise judicial functions and to revise the decision in *Sears* v. *Street Commissioners*. We perceive no such attempt except that the Legislature is trying now to give a valid authority where formerly it gave a void one. * * *

It is urged that the method of assessment is bad as not being limited to the benefit received. It is unfortunate that the petitioner's argument is directed against the later clause authorizing the board to assess a reasonable part of the cost upon any estate heretofore or hereafter connected with a public sewer. But we assume that he would wish to urge the same objection to the clause at the beginning of the section which we have decided to be applicable. That clause confines the assessment in terms to the estates especially benefited and limits it to a proportional part of the cost, not exceeding four dollars per linear foot, but does not limit it in clear terms to the special benefit received. We are of opinion, however, that the word "proportional" as here used must be taken to mean proportional to the special benefit received. See *Carson* v. *Brockton,* 175 Mass. 242. We believe that we have dealt with all the objections to the assessment insisted on in the petitioner's argument so far as they are applicable to our view of the facts and our construction of the statute.

Petition dismissed.

A STATUTE IS HELD UNCONSTITUTIONAL

Lorden v. *Coffey*
178 Mass. 489 (1901)

[This is the only case during Holmes' State court career that he wrote an opinion holding a Massachusetts statute unconstitutional.]

This is an action on the covenant against encumbrances in a deed conveying land on Burbank Street in Boston. A few days before the date of the deed the street commissioners had ordered that the so-called street should be laid out as a highway under St. 1891, c. 323, as amended by St. 1892, c. 418. After the date of the deed the street commissioners determined the assessable cost which subsequently the plaintiff paid. It is not denied that the lien for this cost was an encumbrance (*Blackie* v. *Hudson,* 117 Mass. 181), if the statute under which it was assessed is constitutional, and the case comes here on exceptions to a refusal to rule that the act is void. No other question is argued.

By St. 1892, c. 418, Sec. 8, the assessable cost of the work is made a lien upon the land without personal liability, and the amount for which each parcel shall be liable shall be determined by the street commissioners "in accordance with the proportions in which said board shall determine that the said parcels of land are increased in value by the aforesaid order and the carrying out thereof." It is argued that, although the cost is to be divided among the estates liable in proportion to the benefit, the cost may be greater than the benefit, and that therefore an attempt to charge it all unconditionally to the benefited estates is void under recent decisions. *Dexter* v. *Boston,* 176 Mass. 247, 251.

We are of opinion that the argument is sound, and that the statute cannot be sustained. At first we had the impression that the required proportion to the increase in value could be construed to save it, as the word "proportional" was deemed sufficient to save St. 1899, c. 450, Sec. 3. *Hall* v. *Street Commissioners,* 177 Mass. 434. But the statute of 1899 simply fixed a maximum of not more than four dollars per linear foot as the sum which was to be charged in proportion to the benefit received. Under the statute before us the whole assessable cost is to be paid by the adjoining estates. "The said assessable cost of the work done under said order shall be assessed upon the several parcels of land," St. 1892, c. 418, Sec. 8, or as it read before amendment, "The said assessable cost . . . shall be repaid with interest to the city, by the owners of the several parcels of land." St. 1891, c. 323, Sec. 15. There is no escape from the construction that the whole assessable cost is to be paid. What this cost is is defined in St. 1892, c. 418, Sec. 7. It includes the expenses of taking land and all the main items to be expected. Plainly it may be greater than the benefit to the adjoining estates. The proportion in which the board shall determine that the parcel of land is increased in value determines the amount for which each parcel is to be liable, it is true, but as the total cost is to be divided among the several parcels, there is no chance to read the reference to this proportion as implying that the charges shall not be more than the benefit. The only effect which it can have is to determine the distribution of the tax among the different parcels which collectively must pay the whole. We are unable to construe the statute in such a way as to make it consistent with the Constitution.

Exceptions sustained.

WHAT IS GAMBLING?
Commonwealth v. Sisson
178 Mass. 578 (1901)

[Sisson was prosecuted in the Police Court of Brockton under a Massachusetts statute (St. 1884, c. 277, as amended by St. 1898, c. 576) for selling a hair brush and giving trading-stamps or coupons to the purchaser. The purchaser was entitled to turn in the stamps to another firm for selected articles of value. Sisson was found guilty but excepted, contending that the statute was unconstitutional.]

This court has construed St. 1884, c. 277, and its decision had been public for two years when St. 1898, c. 576, was passed. *Commonwealth* v. *Emerson*, 165 Mass. 146. It must be presumed that the Legislature knew the construction of the earlier act and adopted it when it passed the later one. The former act punished selling property upon the inducement that something other than what is specifically stated to be the subject of the sale is to be delivered. This was construed in *Commonwealth* v. *Emerson* to refer only to the offer of bargains that appeal to the gambling instinct and induce people to buy what they do not want by the gift or promise of a prize, the nature of which is not known at the moment of making the purchase. When then it is enacted by the later statute that the provisions of the one last mentioned shall apply to the giving of a stamp or coupon entitling the purchaser to other property from other persons, the same limitation to the generality of the words used must be understood.

The act of 1898 cannot be taken to prohibit a rebate on the nominal price of goods, or the giving of this rebate in the form of another symbol of purchasing power instead of money, as for instance a draft upon another merchant, payable in goods. It prohibits the giving of coupons only to the same extent that the act of 1884 prohibits the giving of goods. Those who framed the act very probably had in mind the accomplishment of more than we take the act to effect, and of results which have been held unconstitutional elsewhere. * * * But on the other hand it is no less probable that some at least of those who concurred in passing the statute saw that its effect necessarily would be cut down by the construction already given to the act upon which it was engrafted. The fact that it is thus limited makes it unnecessary to consider the above decisions or to compare them with *Lansburgh v. District of Columbia,* 11 App. D. C. 512.

So far as appears there was no gambling element in the defendant's transaction, and his acts were not prohibited by law.

Exceptions sustained.

MORTGAGEE'S RIGHT OF
REDEMPTION—CLASS LEGISLATION

Barry v. Lancy
179 Mass. 112 (1901)

This is a bill to redeem from a tax sale. The premises were mortgaged to the plaintiff on November 12, 1895. On September 4, 1896, they were sold on a foreclosure sale, and on December 4, 1896, the purchasers conveyed their title to the plaintiff, on the ground, it is suggested, that they thought that the foreclosure sale was bad for want of a previous entry. One day before this conveyance, that is, on December 3, the premises were sold to the defendant for taxes. The plaintiff had a decree, and the case is here by the defendant's appeal on the evidence. We shall mention briefly the chief points argued.

Assuming the foreclosure of the mortgage to have been valid, the right of a purchaser at a foreclosure sale and of his assignee to redeem is settled. *McGauley v. Sullivan*, 174 Mass. 303; *Lancy v. Abington Savings Bank*, 177 Mass. 431, 433. * * * In the second case, as in this, the mortgage was given after the lien for taxes had attached. In this there is the further fact that the foreclosure was before the tax sale. But in our opinion the intention of the statute to protect *bona fide* mortgagees, who but for it might lose their security before they ever heard that the taxes were unpaid, extends as well to such intervening securities and to those who claim title under them as to mortgages outstanding at the time of the sale. See *Clark* v. *Lancy,* 178 Mass. 460.

It is rather late to attack the constitutionality of the statute. The objection urged is that the right given to mortgagees to redeem is confined to mortgages of record. St. 1888, c. 390, Sec. 57. In view of the general policy of our law to require registration of titles, and the special reasons for requiring this evidence of good faith as a condition for extending the ordinary time of redemption, we think no further argument necessary to sustain the act.

It is objected that the bill does not appear to have been brought within two years after the plaintiff had actual notice of the sale. We shall not consider which side has the burden of proof, or whether the plaintiff has to go forward with evidence, or whether there was not sufficient evidence in the absence of anything calling special attention to the matter. If all those questions should be decided against the plaintiff, as we are far from intimating that they should be, the bill would be maintainable under St. 1888, c. 390, Sec. 76. It was brought within five years, and the defendant evidently endeavored to evade the plaintiff and to prevent a redemption. *Clark* v. *Lancy,* 178 Mass. 460.

The right given to the plaintiff by Secs. 58, 59, to pay the city treasurer, was a cumulative remedy and did not cut down her right to equitable relief. *Clark* v. *Lancy,* 178 Mass. 460.

Decree affirmed.

MORE BETTERMENT ASSESSMENTS
Sears v. Street Commissioners
180 Mass. 274 (1902)

[The burdens of betterment assessments in this case moved the petitioners to file twelve petitions to have the assessments quashed. It was ingeniously contended that the statute under which they were levied was unconstitutional. Two writs were later filed for an appeal to the United States Supreme Court but were dismissed. See, 189 U. S. 515, and 189 U. S. 516.]

These are petitions for writs of certiorari to quash assessments made by the defendants under St. 1896, c. 516, Sec. 14. The act created a corporation with power to build the southern union passenger station in Boston. The stock was to belong to the five railroads that were to use the station, and the corporation was to purchase or take the specified land and to build the station. By Sec. 11, in order to render the station and passenger facilities accessible and convenient for public use, the defendants were ordered to make certain changes in the streets of Boston, the chief of which were the widening and extension of Cove Street and the extension of Summer Street, and then by Sec. 14 they were directed to assess upon any real estate in Boston which in their opinion "receives any benefit and advantage from the location and construction of said union station, Summer Street and Cove Street, beyond the general advantage to all real estate in said city, a proportionate part of one half of the expense incurred by said city therefor, but in no case exceeding such benefit and advantage." The defendants have made their assessment, reciting that "the Union Station, Summer Street, and Cove Street provided for by" the act "have been located, constructed and completed," adjudicating that each of the estates in a schedule "received benefit and advantage from such location and construction beyond the general advantage to all real estate in said city, and that said estates are all the estates receiving such benefit and advantage," determining the amount of "one half of the expense incurred by the city for such location and construction," and thereupon assessing upon each estate a certain sum "as the part of said one half of said expense, proportionate to, and not exceeding, said benefit and advantage so received by the estate."

Against the assessment it is argued that by a true construction of the words quoted from the statute the cost and benefit ought to have been severed, so that half the cost of the extension of Summer Street, for instance, should have been assessed to those benefited by that extension, and to no others, instead of lumping the cost of both streets and the benefit of the whole improvement, as was done. It is argued further that, at least when construed as the defendants have construed it, the statute is unconstitutional, because it makes the petitioners pay for changes which did not benefit them, and further because it does not limit the sum with which they may be charged by the benefit accruing from the outlay of the city, but only by the benefit of the whole establishment of the union station. It is said that even if it had been a public building an assessment of cost to the extent of the benefit from the station to the petitioners' land would not have been warranted, both because the benefit was merely the general public benefit and also was too remote and uncertain, and because, whatever its kind, it was an accidental result of a change made not for the purpose of improving the petitioners' land but with a different intent. But the station was not a public building, and a further objection still is based upon the fact that it was built with the money of a private corporation and belonged to that corporation when built. Some minor matters were mentioned, but these are the main points.

We shall spend no time upon the construction of the statute, because we hardly could make it plainer than it is made by the literal meaning of the words of the act that the improvement was treated by the Legislature as a unit, the station being impossible without a change in the streets, the extension of the streets being unnecessary apart from the building of the station, two means of continuous public travel being thus brought together according to a single plan. The unity of the plan is emphasized by taking the completion of the station as the time from which the two years allowed for making the assessment shall begin to run.

The most serious question, and that to which the greater part of the argument was directed, is whether the statute is constitutional. The first subdivision of this question concerns the power of the Legislature to lump the cost of the streets, treating it all as the contribution of the city to a single object. As to this we have no doubt. It is easy to put cases of absurd attempts to unite by legislative fiat things which have nothing to do with each other. But such illustrations do not carry the argument far. There is no doubt that the Legislature within the limits of reason can group as one the distinguishable elements of a public improvement. *Lincoln* v. *Street Commissioners,* 176 Mass. 210, 212. To a greater or less extent it is necessary and habitual to group them in this way. *Alden* v. *Springfield,* 121 Mass. 27, 28. The only thing to be considered is whether the attempt to do so is unjustifiable in the particular case. We are of opinion that in this case the action of the Legislature was fully justified. We are of opinion that if, for instance, the whole enterprise had been carried out by the city, supposing other objections out of the way, and considering the power of the Legislature only with reference to treating the cost as one whole for the purpose of assessment, it would have been warranted in so doing by the organic relation of part to part, upon plain principles of common sense. It was argued that if the Legislature treated the scheme as one, then it should have provided for the assessment of estates benefited by the station in connection with other changes beside those made in Summer Street and Cove Street. But it will be remembered that the assessment is for a part of the cost of Summer Street and Cove Street alone, and that the benefit from the location and construction of the station and streets is only a limit. Reasons of detail for the decision of the Legislature were offered by the city solicitor. We deem it a sufficient answer that we cannot say that the Legislature was wrong. If we are right in our general view, of course it was proper to take the time of finishing the station as the moment for estimating the benefit, although the work of the city should be finished at an earlier moment.

But supposing that the Legislature could lump the cost to the city, it is said, it was bound to limit the assessment to the benefit to the petitioners' land from the city's expenditure and could not include that from any other source. With regard to this it is to be remembered, that, in the language of Chief Justice Gray, "The estates are assessed, not for the benefit conferred, but for the cost of the public improvement." *Chase v. Aldermen of Springfield,* 119 Mass. 556, 563. The petitioners are called on to repay a part of what the city of Boston has spent, they are not specially taxed for the gain to their lands. The benefit is referred to only as a justification and a limit. If an outlay by the city has made it possible for the petitioners to enjoy special benefits otherwise justifying an assessment, we are at a loss to see why it should be any more necessary that the city should have created the benefit *in toto* than that it should have created the matter out of which the station was built. The foundation on which the statute puts the petitioners' liability plainly is that although the city did not pay for the whole thing, no part of it would have been called into being without the city's payment, and the city's payment was in fact so far the cause of the advantage to the petitioners that it was entitled to assess on the footing that its expenditures brought the improvement about. Certainly we cannot say that the Legislature was wrong.

Assuming all that we have decided thus far in favor of the defendants, still, it is said, this particular scheme considered as a whole was not a public improvement, and on that account payments toward it as a whole and special benefits from it as a whole would not warrant an assessment. So far as this objection is based on the general nature of the dominant purpose of the union station, it is settled that that purpose is sufficiently public to authorize the exercise of the power of eminent domain, *Eastern Railroad* v. *Boston & Maine*

Railroad, 111 Mass. 125, or of general taxation, *Kittredge* v. *North Brookfield,* 138 Mass. 286, even for purposes of a pure gift, *Railroad Co.* v. *Otoe County,* 16 Wall. 667, 673, 675. * * * And we see no reason why it is not sufficiently public for special assessment also. It is implied that it might be in *Brown* v. *Providence, Warren & Bristol Railroad,* 5 Gray, 35, 39. We are not now dealing with the objection that the purpose is public in such a sense that a local tax or assessment cannot be levied for it, that it is too public, so to speak, *Dyar* v. *Farmington Village Corp.* 70 Maine, 515; that comes later. We are considering the opposite objection, urged however in the same breath, that it is not public at all. The cases cited are sufficient perhaps to answer the argument based on the fact that the ownership of the station was private, that the city did not get back a title for what it gave (see also *Gleason* v. *Waukesha County,* 103 Wis. 225, 234), and that the present use might be transitory. But further, as was observed by the city solicitor, in the care of streets it very well may happen that neither the city nor the persons assessed get any title and that the service is far more transitory than here, and yet that an assessment will be valid. * * *

We come now to the question whether there is anything in the nature of the benefit that enables us to say that the Legislature could not do what it attempted to do. It would be a matter for regret if the law as worked out by the courts with regard to the constitutional powers of the Legislature should be found to have taken so scholastic a form that an actual effect upon a well defined and limited part of a city which might be so distinct as to change the character of its use and to double its market value could not be recognized as a benefit when it came to the imposition of a tax. The truth is that the supposed objections are of so shadowy a form and consist so largely of rhetorical expressions that it is hard to grapple with them, and yet that they derive a kind of life from the atmosphere of the cases.

Upon a question of set-off against the payment for property taken for public uses, the line might be drawn strictly in order to give full effect to the constitutional requirement that what is taken shall be paid for. * * * But it has been recognized that benefits which could not be set off might justify an assessment. *Upham* v. *Worcester,* 113 Mass. 97, 98. And even by way of set-off in a proceeding for damages caused by the taking of land for a railroad it has been held that any peculiar increase of value in the market could be allowed. *Meacham* v. *Fitchburg Railroad,* 4 Cush. 291, 294, 298.

It is plain that the fact that the rise in value is common to all or many of the estates upon a street would not prevent the benefits being sufficiently peculiar for a betterment tax. * * * No doubt it might be hard to draw the line between some cases where the benefit might be held special and a general advance of real estate in the vicinity which often has been said not to be sufficient for set-off, *Meacham* v. *Fitchburg Railroad,* 4 Cush. 291; * * * although it is to be noticed that Mr. Chief Justice Gray, in speaking of benefits that cannot be assessed for, describes them as those which extend to all estates in the same town or city, *Upham* v. *Worcester,* 113 Mass. 97, 99, * * * and that the same limit is adopted by Sec. 14. But this difficulty does not arise where the source of the benefit is the direction given to public travel along a special channel. There the benefit is accurately localized.

Again the fact that the improvement is for a public purpose of course is no objection to the tax. *Harvard College* v. *Aldermen of Boston,* 104 Mass. 470, 486. * * * To invalidate the betterment assessment, the general public benefit must be the only result of the improvement. Such a change may have a double aspect of general public benefit and also of peculiar local advantage. *Gleason* v. *Waukesha County,* 103 Wis. 225, 237. It is suggested, to be sure, that the special benefits cannot be made the basis of a tax when they are only incidental and not the object to which the improvement was directed. See *Morgan Park* v. *Wiswall,* 155 Ill. 262, 274. But we see nothing in the Constitution to prevent it, or to make the power of the Legislature depend upon which of two resultant advantages is especially before its mind when it makes a change in the streets. In this case, plainly it contemplated improving the petitioners' land as it provided for making them pay their share of the cost of the improvement.

As to the remoteness or speculative character of the advantage, we do not see what trouble there is on the former ground if the Legislature says that the advantage is near enough. It certainly does not affect the power of the Legislature that a loss of value caused by diversion of travel is not allowed for under some general provisions for the payment of damages, or, by decisions not without their difficulties, in case of the discontinuance of a way. *Stanwood* v. *Malden,* 157 Mass. 17. We are aware that the phrases "remote" and "speculative" have been used in that connection. But, as often has been pointed out, anticipations of the future are the main element in all values. *Johnston* v. *Faxon,* 172 Mass. 466, 467. With regard to speculativeness, the possible changes in the future use of the station and all the elements of doubt are discounted by the public and allowed for in market value.

A minor objection taken to the assessment is that although it is provided by Sec. 14 that the city of Boston shall assume all assessments upon land of the terminal company, such an assessment should have been made in the first place, as thereby the share of the petitioners would be diminished. If it is not absurd, as the city solicitor contends, to assess for a public improvement land taken by eminent domain for that very improvement, it is enough to say that the defendants in their order adjudicated that the estates assessed were all the estates receiving benefit beyond the general advantage to all real estate in the city. We cannot go behind the adjudication on certiorari.

Finally it is objected that the terminal company had not conveyed certain lands to the city as required in a proviso of Sec. 14, and that the conveyance was a condition precedent to the right to assess. The land had been laid out as a public street although the form of taking a deed was not gone through with until later. We are of opinion that the proviso was intended merely to attach some subsidiary requirements favorable in part to the city and in part to the terminal company, in the mode in which provisos often do, but not to attach a condition precedent to the right to assess. See *Considine* v. *Metropolitan Ins. Co.* 165 Mass. 462, 465.

We have considered all the numerous briefs submitted to us, in all their detail, and have dealt with such points of the combined argument as seemed to us most important. We are of opinion that none of the objections to the statute are valid, and that the assessment must stand.

Petitions dismissed.

VALIDITY OF A SEWER ASSESSMENT

Smith v. Mayor and Aldermen of Worcester
182 Mass. 232 (1902)

This is a petition for a writ of certiorari to quash a sewer assessment levied under St. 1867, c. 106. The question whether the petition could be sustained was reserved by a single justice of this court.

We are asked to declare the statute unconstitutional on the ground that the assessment which it purports to authorize may exceed the benefit to the estate assessed, and therefore is bad under the recent decisions of this court. * * * It is admitted that the statute has been before the court repeatedly, and has been upheld after argument as to its validity. * * * But it is said that the rule of the recent cases cited was not understood at the time of these decisions, and that the latter no longer are authority so far as the present question is concerned.

It would be a misfortune if we were driven to the conclusion contended for by the plaintiff, after the act has stood so long under the shelter of an express decision, and after, as we may presume, very great and costly improvements have been made and probably titles passed in reliance upon the authority which the statute purports to confer. It is only justice to require an argument from which there is no possible escape before we accept such a result. But we do not suppose the recent decisions of this court to have made such slaughter among the older cases as the petitioner's counsel is inclined to believe, and we find it unnecessary to consider what effect, if any, is to be given to the modification by *French* v. *Barber Asphalt Paving Co.* 181 U. S. 324, * * * and the other cases in the same volume, of the law as laid down in *Norwood* v. *Baker,* 172 U. S. 269, a decision to which while it stood unqualified we were bound to defer.

We are of opinion that the act may be sustained. Under the recent decisions it may be true that when the Legislature is passing a law of general future application, and when therefore it cannot be supposed to have compared the local benefit with the cost, the only mode in which it can be made certain, apart from the police power, that constitutional rights are preserved, is by limiting each assessment upon an estate to the benefit received by that estate. But when the Legislature has contemplated a certain region and may be supposed to have acted in view of a specific scheme, there is no doubt that within reasonable limits it may determine that the cost of an improvement shall fall upon a designated district and may fix the principles upon which the cost shall be apportioned. * * * It may deal with the whole improvement as a unit and charge those assessed with a share of the total expense. * * * How far it may authorize an inferior body to constitute a special taxing district need not be considered here.

In *Sears* v. *Street Commissioners,* 173 Mass. 350, and *Lorden* v. *Coffey,* 178 Mass. 489, the statutes under consideration were general provisions for such sewers and streets as should be constructed or laid out in Boston thereafter, and the Legislature could not be taken to have passed upon a scheme. In the former case, the act authorized the street commissioners to take into consideration other matters beside the benefit received by the estate, and showed on its face that the Legislature had not undertaken to decide anything with regard to that. Of course there may arise cases in which it is difficult to say how far the Legislature has a particular region and a particular plan in mind. Perhaps we should have hesitated over the Worcester statute if it had come before us now for the first time. But as it stands now, the act before us fairly may be supposed to have contemplated a system and a more or less specific scheme even if the scheme was not then complete in its details. This was indicated in *Butler* v. *Worcester,* 112 Mass. 541, 552, and in view of that and later decisions must be assumed. On that footing the Legislature determined that the real estate on the line of the sewers, together with possibly some other land, would be benefited as a whole to the extent of the charge put upon it. *Butler* v. *Worcester,* 112 Mass. 541, 555. The language is "Every person owning real estate upon any street," etc., "or whose real estate may be benefited thereby." The antithesis expressed is between estates on the line of the sewer, and thus obviously benefited, and those others which are benefited although not upon the line. * * * The statute, we may remark in passing, does not purport to embrace all the real estate in the city as the region to be taxed, but the real estate along the line of the sewers and some other specially benefited land. The argument that the city is treated as a unit and that therefore the cost should have gone into the general taxes proceeds on a false premise.

When the Legislature has determined that the cost or a proportion of it shall be thrown upon a designated region, the determination must be assumed to have been reached on constitutional principles, unless the court can see that it was unreasonable. On that assumption the right of individual owners within the designated region is narrowed. When they go before a jury they may contest the apportionment, but they cannot show that they have received no benefit at all. That the Legislature has decided. See *French* v. *Barber Asphalt Paving Co.* 181 U. S. 324, 341. For if any one, then every one might contest in detail the question which the Legislature has answered once for all. Of course in the case of an estate not identified by the statute as falling within the region but made to depend for its doing so upon the question whether it was benefited or not, the owner would have the right to deny the benefit by the terms of the statute itself. After the benefit is established, probably he could not go on to inquire into the amount of the benefit. To that extent at least it seems likely that the old decisions would stand. * * * It will be noticed further that it was held or implied in *Clark* v. *Worcester,* 125 Mass. 226, that the assessment was not for the special benefit to the particular estate but an assessment of a proportional share of a tax laid on a legislatively constituted taxing district in respect, it may be presumed if necessary, of the benefit common to all that region and peculiar to it, but not of the special benefits peculiar to the several estates.

It is suggested that the language of the act extends to expenditure for maintaining the sewer and is bad on that ground. We do not understand it to have that meaning. Therefore it is unnecessary to discuss *Carson* v. *Brockton,* 175 Mass. 242, and *Sears* v. *Street Commissioners,* 173 Mass. 350, which seem to have appeared to the Supreme Court of the United States to be less reconcilable than we had supposed. *Carson* v. *Brockton Sewerage Commission,* 182 U. S. 398, 404.

If it were necessary in order to sustain the constitutionality of the statute, we should read the words, "shall pay such sum as the mayor and aldermen shall assess upon him as his proportionate share of the expenditure," etc., as meaning a share not in excess of the special and peculiar benefit which his estate is adjudged to receive, thus bringing the case under *Hall* v. *Street Commissioners,* 177 Mass. 343, rather than under *Lorden* v. *Coffey,* 178 Mass. 489. But this interpretation would be contrary to the tenor of the decisions and would give the act an entirely different meaning and scope from that which it has been adjudged to have and which we have assumed it to have, for the purpose of deciding this case.

Petition dismissed.

CHAPTER 8

DUE PROCESS UNDER THE
FEDERAL CONSTITUTION

RIGHT OF LEGISLATATURE TO ESTABLISH LAND COURT

Tyler v. *Court of Registration*
175 Mass. 71 (1900)

[Tyler petitioned the Supreme Judicial Court to prohibit the Court of Registration from proceeding further in registering the title and determining the boundaries of his land. Tyler contended that the statute establishing the court was unconstitutional in that the "original registration deprives all persons except the registered owner of any interest in the land without due process of law (14th Amendment Const. U. S.; Declaration of Rights, Art. 12)," and that the statute gives judicial powers to the recorder and assistant recorders after the original registration, although not judicial officers under the Constitution (Const. Mass. c. 2, sec. 1, Art. 9; c. 3, Art. 1. Declaration of Rights, Art. 30)." Chief Justice Holmes upheld the statute; Justice Loring dissented with Lathrop concurring. Later a writ of error was taken to the United States Supreme Court but was dismissed, see 179 U. S. 405.]

This is a petition for a writ of prohibition against the judges of the Court of Registration established by St. 1898, c. 562, and is brought to prevent their proceeding upon an application concerning land in which the petitioner claims an interest. The ground of the petition is that the act establishing the court is unconstitutional. Two reasons are urged against the act, both of which are thought to go to the root of the statute and to make action under it impossible. The first and most important is that the original registration deprives all persons except the registered owner of an interest in the land without due process of law. There is no dispute that the object of the system, expressed in sec. 38, is that the decree of registration "shall bind the land and quiet the title thereto," and "shall be conclusive upon and against all persons, "whether named in the proceedings or not, subject to few and immaterial exceptions. And this being admitted, it is objected that there is no sufficient process against, or notice to, persons having diverse claims, in a proceeding intended to bar their possible rights.

The application for registration is to be in writing and signed and sworn to. It is to contain an accurate description of the land, to set forth clearly other outstanding estates or interests known to the petitioner, to identify the deed by which he obtained title, to state the name and address of the occupant if there is one, and also to give the names and addresses so far as known of the occupants of all lands adjoining. Sec. 21. As soon as it is filed, a memorandum containing a copy of the description of the land concerned is to be filed in the registry of deeds. Sec. 20. The case is immediately referred to an examiner (appointed by the judge, Sec. 12), who makes as full an investigation as he can and reports to the court. Sec. 29. If in the opinion of the examiner the applicant has a good title as alleged, or if the applicant after an adverse opinion elects to proceed further, the recorder is to publish a notice by order of the court in some newspaper published in the district where any portion of the land lies. This notice is to be addressed by name to all persons known to have an adverse interest, and to the adjoining owners and occupants so far as known, and to all whom it may concern. It is to contain a description of the land, the name of the applicant, and the time and place of the hearing. Sec. 31. A copy is to be mailed to every person named in the notice whose address is known, and a duly attested copy is to be posted in a conspicuous place on each parcel of land included in the application, by a sheriff or deputy sheriff, fourteen days at least before the return day. Further notice may be ordered by the court. Sec. 32.

It will be seen that the notice is required to name all persons known to have an adverse interest, and this of course includes any adverse claim, whether admitted or denied, that may have been discovered by the examiner, or in any way found to exist. Taking this into account, we should construe the requirement in Sec. 21 concerning the application, as calling upon the applicant to mention not merely outstanding interests which he admits, but equally all claims of interest set up although denied by him. We mention this here to dispose of an objection of detail urged by the petitioner, and we pass to the general objection that, however construed, the mode of notice does not satisfy the Constitution, either as to persons residing within the State upon whom it is not served, or as to persons residing out of the State and not named.

If it does not satisfy the Constitution, judicial proceeding to clear titles against all the world hardly is possible, for the very meaning of such a proceeding is to get rid of unknown as well as known claims,—indeed certainty against the unknown may be said to be its chief end,—and unknown claims cannot be dealt with by personal service upon the claimant. It seems to have been the impression of the Supreme Court of Ohio, in the case most relied upon by the petitioner, that such a judicial proceeding is impossible in this country. *State* v. *Guilbert,* 56 Ohio St. 575, 629. But we cannot bring ourselves to doubt that the Constitutions of the United States and of Massachusetts at least permit it as fully as did the common law. Prescription or a statute of limitations may give a title good against the world and destroy all manner of outstanding claims without any notice or judicial proceeding at all. Time and the chance which it gives the owner to find out that he is in danger of losing rights are due process of law in that case. *Wheeler* v. *Jackson,* 137 U. S. 245, 258. The same result used to follow upon proceedings which, looked at apart from history, may be regarded as standing half way between statutes of limitations and true judgments *in rem,* and which took much less trouble about giving notice than the statute before us. We refer to the effect of a judgment on a writ of right after the *mise* joined and the lapse of a year and a day; Booth, Real Actions, 101, *in margine;* Fitz. Abr. Continual Claim, pl. 7, *Faux Recovere,* pl. 1; Y. B. 5 Ed. III. 51, pl. 60; and of a fine with proclamations after the same time or by a later statute after five years. 2 Bl. Com. 354. 2 Inst. 510, 518. St. 18 Ed. I., *modus levandi fines.* 34 Ed. III. c. 16, 4 & 5 Hen. VII. c. 24. 32 Hen. VIII. c. 36. It would have astonished John Adams to be told that the framers of our Constitution had put an end to the possibility of these ancient institutions. A somewhat similar statutory contrivance of modern days has been held good. *Turner* v. *New York,* 168 U. S. 90. Finally, as was pointed out by the counsel for the petitioner, a proceeding *in rem* in the proper sense of the word might give a clear title without other notice than a seizure of the *res* and an exhibition of the warrant to those in charge. 2 Browne, Civ. & Adm. Law, 398.

The general requirement of advertisement in admiralty cases is said to be due to rules of court. U. S. Adm. Rule 9. Betts, Adm. Practice (1838), 33, 34, App. 14.

The prohibition in the Fourteenth Amendment of the Constitution of the United States against a State depriving any person of his property without due process of law, and that in the twelfth article of the Massachusetts Bill of Rights, refer to somewhat vaguely determined criteria of justification, which may be found in ancient practice; *Murray* v. *Hoboken Land & Improvement Co.* 18 How. 272, 277; or which may be found in convenience and substantial justice, although the form is new. * * * The prohibitions must be taken largely, with a regard to substance rather than to form, or they are likely to do more harm than good. It is not enough to show a procedure to be unconstitutional to say that we never have heard of it before. *Hurtado* v. *People,* 110 U. S. 516, 537.

Looked at either from the point of view of history or of the necessary requirements of justice, a proceeding *in rem* dealing with a tangible *res* may be instituted and carried to judgment without personal service upon claimants within the State or notice by name to those outside of it, and not encounter any provision of either Constitution. Jurisdiction is secured by the power of the court over the *res*. As we have said, such a proceeding would be impossible, were this not so, for it hardly would do to make a distinction between the constitutional rights of claimants who were known and those who were not known to the plaintiff, when the proceeding is to bar all. *Pennoyer* v. *Neff,* 95 U. S. 714, 727. * * * In *Hamilton* v. *Brown,* 161 U. S. 256, a judgment of escheat was held conclusive upon persons notified only by advertisement to all persons interested. It is true that the statute under consideration required the petition to name all known claimants, and personal service to be made on those so named. But that did the plaintiffs no good, as they were not named. So a decree allowing or disallowing a will binds everybody, although the only notice of the proceedings given be a general notice to all persons interested. And in this case, as in that of escheat just cited, the conclusive effect of the decree is not put upon the ground that the State has an absolute power to determine the persons to whom a man's property shall go at his death, but upon the characteristics of a proceeding *in rem*. * * * Admiralty proceedings need only to be mentioned in this connection, and further citation of cases seems unnecessary.

Speaking for myself, I see no reason why what we have said as to proceedings *in rem* in general should not apply to such proceedings concerning land. In *Arndt* v. *Griggs,* 134 U. S. 316, 327, it is said to be established that "a State has power by statute to provide for the adjudication of titles to real estate within its limits as against non-residents who are brought into court only by publication." In *Hamilton* v. *Brown,* 161 U. S. 256, 274, it was declared to be within the power of a State "to provide for determining and quieting the title to real estate within the limits of the State and within the jurisdiction of the court, after actual notice to all known claimants, and notice by publication to all other persons." I doubt whether the court will not take the further step when necessary, and declare the power of the States to do the same thing after notice by publication alone. * * * But in the present case provision is made for all known claimants by the recorder, who is to mail a copy of the published notice to every person named therein whose address is known. Sec. 32. We shall state in a moment our reasons for thinking this form of notice constitutional. See further *Cook* v. *Allen,* 2 Mass. 462, 469, 470. * * *

But it is said that this is not a proceeding *in rem.* It is certain that no phrase has been more misused. In the past it has had little more significance than that the right alleged to have been violated was a right *in rem.* Austin thinks it necessary to quote Leibnitz for the sufficiently obvious remark that every right to restitution is a right *in personam.* So as to actions. If the technical object of the suit is to establish a claim against some particular person, with a judgment which generally, in theory at least, binds his body, or to bar some individual claim or objection, so that only certain persons are entitled to be heard in defence, the action is *in personam,* although it may concern the right to or possession of a tangible thing. *Mankin* v. *Chandler,* 2 Brock. 125, 127. If, on the other hand, the object is to bar indifferently all who might be minded to make an objection of any sort against the right sought to be established, and if anyone in the world has a right to be heard on the strength of alleging facts which, if true, show an inconsistent interest, the proceeding is *in rem.* Freem. Judgments (4th ed.) sec. 606 *ad fin.* All proceedings, like all rights, are really against persons. Whether they are proceedings or rights *in rem* depends on the number of persons affected. Hence the *res* need not be personified and made a party defendant, as happens with the ship in the admiralty; it need not even be a tangible thing at all, as sufficiently appears by the case of the probate of wills. Personification and naming the *res* as defendant are mere symbols, not the essential matter. They are fictions, conveniently expressing the nature of the process and the result, nothing more.

It is true as an historical fact that these symbols are used in admiralty proceedings, and also, again merely as an historical fact, that the proceedings *in rem* have been confined to cases where certain classes of claims, although of very divers sorts,—for indemnification for injury, for wages, for salvage, etc.,—are to be asserted. But a ship is not a person. It cannot do a wrong or make a contract. To say that a ship has committed a tort is merely a shorthand way of saying that you have decided to deal with it as if it had committed one, because some man has committed one in fact. There is no *a priori* reason why any other claim should not be enforced in the same way. If a claim for a wrong committed by a master may be enforced against all interests in the vessel, there is no juridical objection to a claim of title being enforced in the same way. The fact that it is not so enforced under existing practice affords no test of the powers of the Legislature. The contrary view would indicate that you really believed the fiction that a vessel had an independent personality as a fact behind the law. Furthermore, naming the *res* as defendant, although a convenient way of indicating that the proceeding is against property alone, that is to say, that it is not to establish an infinite personal liability, is not of the essence. If, in fact, the proceeding is of the sort, and is to bar all the world, it is a proceeding *in rem*.

Then as to seizure of the *res*. It is convenient in the case of a vessel, in order to secure its being on hand to abide judgment, although in the case of a suit against a man jurisdiction is regarded as established by service without the need of keeping him in prison to await judgment. It is enough that the personal service shows that he could have been seized and imprisoned. Seizure, to be sure, is said to be notice to the owner. *Scott v. Shearman,* 2 W. Bl. 977, 979; *Mankin v. Chandler,* 2 Brock. 125, 127. But fastening the process or a copy to the mast would seem not necessarily to depend for its effect upon the continued custody of the vessel by the marshal. However this may be, when we come to deal with immovables there would be no sense whatever in declaring seizure to be a constitutional condition of the power of the Legislature to make a proceeding against land a proceeding *in rem. Hamilton v. Brown,* 161 U. S. 256, 274. The land cannot escape from the jurisdiction, and, except as security against escape, seizure is a mere form, of no especial sanctity, and of much possible inconvenience.

I do not wish to ignore the fact that seizure, when it means real dispossession, is another security for actual notice. But when it is considered how purely formal such an act may be, and that even adverse possession is possible without ever coming to the knowledge of a reasonably alert owner, I cannot think that the presence or absence of the form makes a constitutional difference; or rather, to express my view still more cautiously, I cannot but think that the immediate recording of the claim is entitled to equal effect from a constitutional point of view. I am free to confess, however, that, with the rest of my brethren, I think the act ought to be amended in the direction of still further precautions to secure actual notice before a decree is entered, and that, if it is not amended, the judges of the court ought to do all that is in their power to satisfy themselves that there has been no failure in this regard before they admit a title to registration.

The quotations which we have made show the intent of the statute to bind the land, and to make the proceedings adverse to all the world, even if it were not stated in sec. 35, or if the amendment of 1899 did not expressly provide that they should be proceedings *in rem*. St. 1899, c. 131, sec. 1. Notice is to be posted on the land just as admiralty process is fixed to the mast. Any person claiming an interest may appear and be heard. Sec. 34.

But perhaps the classification of the proceeding is not so important as the course of the discussion thus far might seem to imply. I have pursued that course as one which is satisfactory to my own mind, but for the purposes of decision a majority of the court prefer to assume that in cases in which, under the constitutional requirements of due process of law, it heretofore has been necessary to give to parties interested actual notice of the pending proceeding by personal service or its equivalent in order to render a valid judgment against them, it is not in the power of the Legislature, by changing the form of the proceeding from an action *in personam* to a suit *in rem*, to avoid the necessity of giving such a notice, and to assume that under this statute personal rights in property are so involved and may be so affected that effectual notice and an opportunity to be heard should be given to all claimants who are known or who by reasonable effort can be ascertained.

It hardly would be denied that the statute takes great precautions to discover outstanding claims, as we already have shown in detail, or that notice by publication is sufficient with regard to claimants outside the State. With regard to claimants living within the State and remaining undiscovered, notice by publication must suffice of necessity. As to claimants living within the State and known, the question seems to come down to whether we can say that there is a constitutional difference between sending notice of a suit by a messenger and sending it by the post office beside publishing in a newspaper, recording in the registry, and posting on the land. It must be remembered that there is no constitutional requirement that the summons, even in a personal action, shall be served by an officer, or that the copy served shall be officially attested. Apart from local practice, it may be served by any indifferent person. It may be served on residents by leaving a copy at the last and usual place of abode. When we are considering a proceeding of this kind, it seems to us within the power of the Legislature to say that the mail, as it is managed in Massachusetts, is a sufficient messenger to convey the notice, when other means of notifying the party, like publishing and posting, also are required. We agree that such an act as this is not to be upheld without anxiety. But the difference in degree between the case at bar and one in which the constitutionality of the act would be unquestionable seems to us too small to warrant a distinction. If the statute is within the power of the Legislature, it is not for us to criticise the wisdom or expediency of what the Legislature has done.

We do not think it necessary to refer to the elaborate collection of statutes presented by the Attorney General for the purpose of showing that the principle of the present act is old.* Although no question is made on that point, we may mention that an appeal is given

---

* See, citations in note 175 Mass. 79–80.

to the Superior Court with the right to claim a jury. In our opinion, the main objection to the act fails. * * *

The other objection to the constitutionality of the statute is with regard to the powers and duties of the recorder and assistant recorder. It is said that they are given judicial powers after the original registration, although not judicial officers under the Constitution. The act of registration is the operative act to convey title, sec. 50; and by the act of 1898 the assistant recorder does it unless in doubt. Sections 53, 55, 57, 58, 61, 62, 63. It is said that as his decision affects title it must be judicial. But here again it is necessary to use a certain largeness in interpreting broad constitutional provisions. The ordinary business of registration is very nearly ministerial. There is no question to be raised or which can be raised. If there is a question, either raised by any party in interest or occurring to the assistant recorder, it is to be referred to the judge for decision. Sec. 53. But whatever may be thought of the original act, by amendment even the ordinary business is to be done only "in accordance with the rules and instructions of the court." St. 1899, c. 131, sec. 8. Under this amendment registration is the act of the court. The fact that it may be done by the assistant recorder under general orders when there is no question is not different from the power of the clerk to enter judgment in cases ripe for judgment under a general order or rule of the Superior Court. It should be observed that by sec. 55 the production of the owner's duplicate certificate whenever any voluntary instrument is presented for registration is conclusive authority from the registered owner for the entry of a new certificate or the making of a memorandum of registration, and that a registration procured by presenting a forged certificate, etc., is void.

Finally, it is said that there is no provision for notice before registration of transfers or dealings subsequent to the original registration. It must be remembered that at all later stages no one can have a claim which does not appear on the face of the registry. The only rights are registered rights, and when land is brought into the registry system there seems to be nothing to hinder the Legislature from fixing the conditions upon which it shall be held under that system. *People* v. *Simon*, 176 Ill. 165, 176. By sec. 45, the obtaining of a decree of registration, which is a voluntary act, is an agreement running with the land that the land shall be and remain registered land and subject to the provisions of the act. Furthermore, in deciding whether substantial justice is done it is to be borne in mind that ordinary cases will present no question at all. It is contemplated, as we have said, that if there is a question to be discerned it shall be referred to the court, and of course that the court will order notice to any party interested. The act shows throughout the intent that no one shall be concluded without having a chance to be heard and, although some of its methods are new to this Commonwealth, we cannot say that the precautions as to notice are insufficient in substance or form.

Petition denied.

LIABILITY OF FOREIGN CORPORATION IN CROSS-ACTION

Aldrich v. *Blatchford*
175 Mass. 369 (1900)

This is an appeal from an order of the Superior Court denying the defendant's motion to dismiss the action on the ground that the defendant is a foreign corporation and that there has been no service upon it or attachment of its property. The service was made upon Mr. Charles A. Jewell as the defendant's attorney. If we may trust the defendant, for the slipshod papers do not give us the dates, this motion to dismiss followed, and the plaintiffs then amended their writ by inserting an allegation that the defendant was a foreign corporation and was plaintiff in a former action in the same court against the present plaintiffs, and that said Charles A. Jewell was the attorney of the plaintiff in the former suit. Afterwards this motion was brought up and was overruled.

It is provided by Pub. Sts. c. 164, Sec. 2, that if a person who is not an inhabitant of this commonwealth and who cannot be found here to be served with process, brings an action, he shall be held to answer to any action brought against him by the defendant, if the demands in the two cases are of such a nature that the judgments or executions can be set off against each other. It is further provided, by Sec. 4, that the writ in the cross action may be served on the person who appears as the attorney of the plaintiff in the original suit. The plaintiff relies upon these provisions. The defendant denies that the act applies to foreign corporations, suggests that it is unconstitutional under the Fourteenth Amendment of the Constitution of the United States, that the judgments are not of a nature to be set off against each other, and sets up some other subordinate matters which we shall mention so far as necessary.

We see no reason to doubt that the act applies to foreign corporations. The grounds of convenience which led to the enactment are as strong in the case of corporations as when natural persons come here to sue, and the word "person" is sufficient to include them. Pub. Sts. c. 3, Sec. 3, cl. 16.

We should have seen equally little reason to doubt the constitutionality of the act, were it not for a slight ambiguity in some of the expressions in *Dewey* v. *Des Moines*, 173 U. S. 193. In that case the plaintiff, a resident of Illinois, filed a petition to set aside certain assessments of land in Iowa belonging to him. A counterclaim was set up for a sale of the land under the lien for the assessment, and also for a personal judgment. The Supreme Court of the United States held, very naturally, that the Iowa law, so far as it undertook to impose a liability upon a non-resident in excess of the benefit to his land, p. 201, or indeed a personal liability at all, pp. 202, 204, was invalid. That, as we understand the case, is all that is decided or intimated. It is said that "by resorting to the State court to obtain relief from the assessment and from any personal liability provided for by the statute, the plaintiff did not thereby in any manner consent, or render himself liable, to a judgment against him providing for any personal liability." Of course he did not, because there was no such liability; but we do not understand the court to mean that where the liability exists, a plaintiff by resorting to the courts of a State may not consent to counter process which may result in a judgment. We do not understand the court to have had any such question in mind.

We need not refer to the often repeated assertion of the right of the States to determine the conditions upon which foreign corporations shall be permitted to do business within their jurisdiction. * * * We come nearer to the case when foreign insurance companies are required by statute to appoint an attorney for the service of process. There is no doubt of the validity of such statutes. *Lafayette Ins. Co.* v. *French,* 18 How. 404. * * * In the first of these cases it was held that jurisdiction was acquired by service on the resident agent of a foreign company, by force of a State law that such an agent making contracts within the State should also be deemed agent to receive service of process in suits founded upon such contracts. The Supreme Court, speaking through Mr. Justice Curtis, said that when the company sent its agent into the State with authority to make contracts of insurance, then it must be taken to assent to the condition upon which alone such business could be done there. So here. The foreign company by employing an attorney to begin an action against the defendant in Massachusetts, thereby assents to the attorney's receiving service in a counter suit, and gives him such powers as make the service sufficient. See further *Nations* v. *Johnson,* 24 How. 195.

We agree that the analogy which we have suggested is not perfect, but, if it is not sufficient, still we cannot bring ourselves to doubt the validity of the statute in question. If a State law provided that in all cases all cross demands should be open, an entirely possible piece of legislation, no one would doubt the constitutionality of the law. No service would be necessary in order to entitle the defendant to judgment if on a general taking of accounts he came out ahead. We do not suppose that the legislation would be any worse if it made service of a writ on the plaintiff's attorney a condition of the cross judgment. We do not perceive why the law would not be equally good if confined to foreigners suing in this State, the ground of the discrimination being obvious and reasonable.

The other objections may be dealt with very shortly. If the plaintiffs recover a judgment, that judgment will be for a definite sum, and is none the less proper for set-off that the cause of action was for unliquidated damages. Nothing appears on the record before us with regard to several matters touched in the plaintiffs' brief. If it be true as alleged that the Superior Court refused to order a continuance of the original action under Sec. 5, that is not an adjudication that the judgment will not be proper to be set off when reached. Moreover, the decision may have gone on grounds having nothing to do with the question. If it be true as alleged that the claim in the original action has been satisfied since the service of the cross writ, the fact cannot affect the jurisdiction after it has attached. The writ did not need to be served over again after the amendment showing that the mode of service adopted was justified by the facts. * * * The justification lay in the facts, not in the allegation of the facts, and the allegation was necessary, if at all, only to show on the face of the record that the case was within the statute. *Motion denied.*

HOLDING ACT OF A NEIGHBORING STATE UNCONSTITUTIONAL

Woodward v. Central Vermont Railway
180 Mass. 599 (1902)

This is an action upon a judgment obtained by the plaintiff against the Central Vermont Railroad Company a different corporation from the defendant, and upon a Vermont statute, St. 1900, No. 142, requiring the defendant to pay certain judgments of which the plaintiff's was one. The defendant was incorporated for the purpose of taking over the property of the judgment debtor, the Central Vermont Railroad Company, by means of a foreclosure sale. In payment it was authorized to give its own stock and bonds, and the charter provided, expressly and by reference to a preliminary agreement in pursuance of which the charter was obtained, who were to receive the stock and bonds, and in what amounts. The plaintiff was not mentioned or included in the arrangement. Vt. St. 1898, No. 159. The charter however provided that it should be "subject to alterations, amendment or repeal, as the public good may require," and the later statute justifies itself by its title as such an amendment, although in its enacting part it simply adds the requirement of these new payments to those which are in the original act. The defence is that the so-called amendment is contrary to the Constitution of Vermont and of the United States.

We regret very much that the former question at least should not be answered by the Supreme Court of Vermont rather than by ourselves. But as it arises in a suit properly before us we must deal with it to the best of our ability, as our predecessors and the courts of other States have done in similar cases. * * *

The statute requires the defendant to pay a sum of money to a stranger, to whom, so far as appears, the defendant was under no previous legal, equitable, or moral obligation. A purchaser at a mortgage sale is not bound to pay creditors of the mortgagor who are less well secured than himself. It does not appear and is not contended, that, when the charter was granted, there was even an intention on the part of anyone that the defendant should pay judgments like the present. It rather may be said to appear that there was no such intention, so far as any expression can be found in the documents. Such an intention cannot be presumed, because one purpose of a foreclosure is to withdraw property from the reach of creditors of the mortgagor who have inferior liens or none. In short, we cannot deal with the act as correcting a mistake and carrying out the understanding on which the defendant was called into being, and therefore uphold it upon the somewhat swampy ground of *Danforth* v. *Groton Water Co.* 178 Mass. 472.

The statute is an attempt to require private property to be applied to a private use, and therefore encounters those provisions of the Vermont constitution which declare the right to possess property, and, by making express provisions for compensation, etc., "whenever any person's property is taken for the use of the public," implicitly prohibit the taking of it for uses not public. Vt. Const. c. 1, arts. 1, 2 and 9. * * * We presume that these provisions would not be limited by construction to cases where the statute identified the specific property taken, but would apply equally where the act required some property to be appropriated to the specified use. Indeed, as in this case the appropriation is to be in the form of money, the further question is raised whether even if the use were public the taking of property in that form is within the power of the State. *Cary Library* v. *Bliss,* 151 Mass. 364, 378, 379.

It follows that the statute is void unless it is saved by the reservation of the power to amend the charter in the original act. We are of opinion that it is not saved. No doubt under a general reservation of such power amendments have been held valid which directly affected the property of a corporation by cutting down the tolls which the charter allowed it to charge, or by increasing the share of profits which the charter required it to pay over to another institution. * * * But cases like these are in the strictest and most literal sense amendments of the charter, and do not lead to the conclusion that the power to take away property rights is unlimited. The contrary proposition of Chief Justice Shaw now is accepted by most courts as elementary law. An unqualified power to amend authorizes a modification of the franchise conferred, but does not authorize a departure from the general restrictions on legislation with regard to property acquired and owned by the company, by the devise of inserting a confiscation clause in the charter by way of amendment. * * *

The so-called amendment would not have fallen within the power of the Legislature had the power to amend the charter been general. But the power reserved is qualified by the words "as the public good may require," and this qualification presents a further objection to the act. We agree that every reasonable presumption is to be made in favor of the validity of the act, and that there are cases where the payment of public money to an individual not legally entitled to it may serve a public end. But we cannot invent fictions to save acts of the Legislature. We are unable to see how the public good can be said to require that the defendant should be compelled to pay another person's debt.

Judgment for defendant.

CHAPTER 9

MISCELLANEOUS CONSTITUTIONAL CASES

WHAT IS A TAKING OF PROPERTY UNDER THE CONSTITUTION?

Bent v. Emery
173 Mass. 495 (1899)

[In this case the plaintiffs who were owners of certain lands and flats on the South Bay in Boston sued the board of harbor and land commissioners to restrain them from dredging the same.]

It is admitted that the defendants, the board of harbor and land commissioners, intend to dredge flats belonging to the plaintiffs, and to remove from them a substantial quantity of earth, and the question is whether they have power to do it under St. 1897, c. 486, sec. 5, or more especially, St. 1898, c. 278, sec. 3. More specifically, the questions are whether the dredging amounts to a taking of property, and if so, whether adequate provision is made for compensation, or whether the dredging can be justified under the police power or otherwise without compensation.

We think that it must be understood that at least the earth which is to be removed from the plaintiffs' flats is to be taken. That is the natural meaning of the statement that it is to be removed, and besides, whether the earth is taken out to sea or used, as the contract for dredging contemplates, to fill other flats, we cannot assume that the plaintiffs will or can furnish a place for it. Apart from the appropriation of the earth, the change in the surface of the flats in such a way as to bring it permanently under water is a very appreciable diminution of the owner's rights. It is true, that at present they have no right to fill or build upon the flats. But it is agreed to be probable that in a few years the growth of the city will require a change, and this probability may be taken into account in deciding whether the theoretic damage is one of those minima which the law does not take into account.

It would be open to argument at least that an owner might be stripped of his rights so far as to amount to a taking without any physical interference with his land. On the other hand, we assume that even the carrying away or bodily destruction of property might be of such small importance that it would be justified under the police power without compensation. We assume that one of the uses of the convenient phrase, police power, is to justify those small diminutions of property rights, which, although within the letter of constitutional protection, are necessarily incident to the free play of the machinery of government. It may be that the extent to which such diminutions are lawful without compensation is larger when the harm is inflicted only as incident to some general requirement of public welfare. But whether the last mentioned element enters into the problem or not, the question is one of degree, and sooner or later we reach a point at which the Constitution applies, and forbids physical appropriation and legal restrictions alike unless they are paid for.

In the case at bar, the act of 1898, authorizing the changes, was passed on the petition of the Roxbury Central Wharf Company, the owner of adjoining wharves, which will be benefited by them. The dredging is to be done to improve navigation and sanitary conditions, but in view of the probable future of the

region, already referred to, and of the fact that the place of the dredging is above seven bridges, we do not feel called upon to strain the police power in aid of public needs. We are of opinion that, under the circumstances of this case, the combined effect of removing the plaintiff's earth and sinking the surface of their flats under water is such a taking of their property as to require compensation in order to satisfy the law.
* * *

It is argued for the respondents, that, irrespective of the police power, the Commonwealth, as trustee of the *jus publicum* by force of the ordinance of 1647, may do what the Legislature has purported to authorize, under its property rights, so that in strictness no interference with the rights of the plaintiff is threatened, as thus far we have assumed. To this it is enough to say that, if what is proposed to be done cannot be justified under the police power over the subject matter, taking the position of the Commonwealth into account, it stands less well as an act of ownership alone. The right to submerge the plaintiffs' flats and to carry off their soil is less readily justified by any right reserved by the Commonwealth as grantor than by its power as sovereign to exact relatively small sacrifices from individuals for the common good. * * * Cases like *Sage* v. *New York,* 154 N. Y. 61, throw no light upon this question, because there the plaintiff had no title to the flats, but only such riparian rights as were recognized in *Rumsey* v. *New York and New England Railroad,* 133 N. Y. 79. * * *

If the plaintiffs' property must be paid for, the question remains whether sufficient provision is made for payment. There has been no taking of flats or rights in the manner provided for in St. 1897, c. 486. By sec. 4 of the act of 1898, "Any person suffering injury by the doings hereinbefore authorized may have the same determined in the Superior Court . . . in the manner provided for the recovery of damages sustained by reason of the laying out of ways." But it is not said by whom the damages are to be paid. We do not feel warranted in construing these words as by implication pledging the faith of the Commonwealth to the payment. We really are left uncertain who was intended to be charged by the Legislature, or whether it had any one in particular in mind. The act is not at all like the Metropolitan Park Act, St. 1893, c. 407. There the Commonwealth was to take and own the parks, sec. 4, and, to meet the expenses incurred under the act, was to issue bonds, sec. 9, so that there was no doubt who was to pay the damages estimated as provided in sec. 7. If the provision in sec. 3, that the board may expend for dredging and filling any moneys received as compensation for displacement of tidewater in South Bay, refers to payment for anything except the labor engaged in the work, the charge upon a special and limited fund is not enough to satisfy the Constitution. *Connecticut River Railroad* v. *County Commissioners,* 127 Mass. 50.

Decree for the plaintiffs.

LIMITING HEIGHT OF BUILDINGS NEAR THE STATE HOUSE

Parker v. *Commonwealth*
178 Mass. 199 (1901)

[In 1899 the Legislature of Massachusetts passed a statute prohibiting the building of any structure more than seventy feet in height within a restricted area near the State House. At the time the statute was enacted there were no buildings in this area exceeding seventy feet. The petitioners subsequently sued under the statute for an assessment of damages which they had sustained. Holmes said that the statute did not contain an adjudication of public necessity by the Legislature, and therefore, deprived the landowners of their right without compensation of building beyond seventy feet.]

These are petitions by owners of land affected by St. 1899, c. 457, to have the amount of damages assessed which have been sustained by them in their property by reason of the act. The statute in question limits the height of buildings on a small tract west of the State House to seventy feet, and allows these petitions if and in so far as the act, or proceedings to enforce it, may deprive the petitioners of rights existing under the Constitution. The cases are reported upon demurrer and agreed facts.

In some of the arguments addressed to us it was assumed that the only view which it was possible to take of this statute was that it was intended to benefit the State House considered as a dominant estate, and to annex to it an easement or quasi easement, whether for prospect or security it does not matter. Manifestly this is not true. It may be argued that the statute was passed at least as much in the interest of the public at large as travellers on the highway as it was in the interest of the Commonwealth as an owner of property —that one object at any rate was to save the dignity and beauty of the city at its culminating point, for the pride of every Bostonian and for the pleasure of every member of the State. It is on this footing that it is argued for the Commonwealth that the act is a valid exercise of the police power; that a building law would be valid within reasonable limits; * * * that a limitation to seventy feet is reasonable, and that such a law is no less valid when passed to satisfy the love of beauty than when passed to appease the fear of fire. 174 Mass. 479, 480.

It will be observed that this argument avoids the objection that a police law could not be limited to this narrow tract. For all that appears, and probably in fact, the symmetry of Beacon Hill and the domination of the State House as seen from the western approaches, the Mill Dam or the Cambridge Bridge for instance, are or may be secured without restricting a larger tract, and if so the statute is coextensive with the public need.

The language of the act is, we repeat, that in so far as it "may deprive any person of rights existing under the constitution" those in the petitioners' situation may have a remedy. Of course it is possible to read this as the Attorney General would have us read it, as importing an exercise of the police power so far as the Legislature constitutionally could go, and as saving a remedy for all damages beyond the limit. If interpreted in that way it lets in the argument just stated. The objection to the interpretation is that it supposes the Legislature without clear words to have used the police power in one of its extreme manifestations for a purpose which, although conceded to be public, is a purpose which may be described as of luxury rather than necessity, and which, in part after all, is for the benefit of the State House land and its proprietor merely as such. So that to sustain the restriction to its whole extent under the police power would be a startling advance upon anything heretofore done. If it should be suggested that the restriction might be sustained under the police power beyond a certain number of feet from the ground and compensation allowed for the restriction between that height and seventy feet, apart from the difficulty of fixing a constitutional limit by feet and inches, which might not be insuperable, see *Quinn v. New York, New Haven & Hartford Railroad*, 175 Mass. 150, 151, the answer is that the constitutional difficulty would not grow appreciably less until we reached a point at which the restriction became nugatory because it was beyond the height to which anyone would wish to build. Apart from the difficulties which we have stated, and simply reading the words without consideration of consequences, while we can gather that the Legislature was willing to take anything without paying for it that this court should say that it could, we do not find anything that even suggests a legislative adjudication that the public welfare requires that the petitioners' property should be restricted without compensation to them.

For the foregoing reasons we are of opinion that the construction adopted by the Attorney General must be rejected, and therefore we do not find it necessary to express an opinion whether a law, in which the Legislature, either with a declaration of purposes such as we have imagined for this act or without it, should give clear expression to its intent to restrict these buildings in the exercise of its police power without payment, would infringe the Constitution. Such a law certainly would present grave difficulties even when approached with all the presumptions that exist in favor of a legislative decision, and with the duty to uphold it unless it was impossible to do so. * * *

On the construction of the act which we adopt it treats the limits of the police power as if they were a matter which might be left to this court to fix in the first place without any preliminary exercise of legislative judgment. If it stopped here it would raise new difficulties, but it does not. It goes on and gives a remedy if the act deprives the parties of rights existing under the Constitution. In the absence of an adjudication by the Legislature that the public needs require the petitioners' property to be restricted without compensation, the statute does deprive the parties of such rights, and on the construction of the statute which we adopt there has been no such adjudication. The exercise of the police power always deprives a party of what would be his rights under the Constitution but for such an adjudication. The right to build the seventy-first foot from the ground is just as much a right under the Constitution as the right to build the sixty-ninth or the first. It may be of less importance, but it is the same in kind. The justification of a building law is not that it does not qualify or affect a right under the Constitution; if that were the justification the petitioners would be entitled to nothing because no right of theirs would have been infringed. The justification is that although the law affects or even takes away such rights it may do so within reasonable and somewhat narrow limits upon considerations which the Constitution cannot be supposed to have been intended to exclude.

If it be deemed more logical, instead of saying that a constitutional right is cut down or taken away under an implied constitutional power, to say that the right is limited to the extent of the lawful exercise of the police power, it does not leave the petitioners' case less strong. For under that form of statement also the right exists until the Legislature adjudicates that the public welfare requires its termination without being paid for. That, as we have said, the Legislature has not adjudicated but has left to this court.

Demurrers overruled.

IS THE PRACTICE OF MEDICINE A BUSINESS?

Earle v. *Commonwealth*
180 Mass. 579 (1902)

[Earle, a physician, filed a petition under statute for damages sustained to his practice caused by the taking by eminent domain of practically all the business part of the town of West Boylston. It appeared that Earle resided and had an office in this town and his business had been affected to a considerable extent. The Commonwealth contended, among other things, that if the statute applied to a case like this, it was unconstitutional. Other facts appear in the opinion.]

This is a petition brought by a practicing physician to recover for damage to his business by the carrying out of the metropolitan water supply act. St. 1895, c. 488, sec. 14. The case was referred to a commission. It reports that the plaintiff lived and had his office in West Boylston and had a practice which extended through that and some neighboring towns. The taking of land at West Boylston necessarily affected his business to a considerable extent, and the damages are assessed at alternative sums according to the rules suggested by the plaintiff and defendant respectively. The questions of law arising on the report were reserved by one of the justices for the consideration of the full court.

The Commonwealth in the first place contends that the material portion of the statute, if it applies to cases like this, is unconstitutional. The ground seems to be that taxes cannot be levied for purposes of this sort, except to pay for property taken or destroyed, and that the business of a doctor is not property within the principle. The test of what may be required to be paid for if destroyed or damaged under the power of eminent domain, is not whether the same thing could have been sold, nor is it whether the destruction or harm could have been authorized without a provision for payment. Very likely the plaintiff's rights were of a kind that might have been damaged if not destroyed without the constitutional necessity of compensation. But some latitude is allowed to the Legislature. It is not forbidden to be just in some cases where it is not required to be by the letter of paramount law. We think it so plain that, as was assumed by everybody in *Sawyer* v. *Metropolitan Water Board,* 178 Mass. 267, the provision is constitutional, that we prefer to say so without stopping to consider whether the question is open. * * *

Next it is contended that the petitioner was not an "individual . . . owning . . . an established business on land in the town of West Boylston" within the meaning of sec. 14. A majority of the court does not see why not. The defendant cites *Ex parte Breull,* 16 Ch. D. 484, for the proposition that the word "business" has no definite technical meaning. We agree, and think it quite wide enough to include the practice of a doctor. It is suggested that the practice was not established on land in West Boylston. It is true that a doctor can give advice elsewhere than in his office, and that in fact he does so to a greater axtent than a shopkeeper sells his goods outside his shop. But no less than a shopkeeper a doctor usually has, as the petitioner had, a locally established centre to which patients resort, and from which he goes his rounds. There is even a certain amount of salable good will, as is made familiar to us by English law and literature as well as by an occasional case in our own reports. *Smith* v. *Bergengren,* 153 Mass. 236.

The respondent demanded a finding or ruling that the petitioner's business was not decreased in value by the carrying out of the act, because of the figures given for his income in 1894 and 1895, and later. But the commission may have found and, for all that we can see, rightly, that the diminution of income before April 1, 1895, was due to precautions taken by the petitioner in anticipation of the change, and we are unable to say that the respondent's request should have been granted.

The respondent next contends that the measure of damages is the difference in the market value of the business between April 1, 1895, and after the act was carried out. This recurs to the notion that the only interests which the law will recognize are salable, and that the petitioner can recover only for such good will as might have been transferred for cash. The word "owning" in the statute is invoked. We shall not speculate whether ownership of an equitable life estate would be denied to a legatee deprived of the right of alienation. It is enough to say that, if the petitioner's business is within the protection of the act and "is decreased in value," damages are to be paid for "such injury," that is to say, for the actual decrease in value of that business, not for the decrease in the value of such elements in it, only, as admitted of being sold. There is no practical difficulty in the way of carrying out the statute according to its meaning. The money value of the petitioner's business could be estimated, even though absolutely personal to himself.

But the rule suggested by the petitioner also seems to us unsafe on the facts before us. The damage theoretically would be the difference in value between the business as it had been and as it was left. Perhaps it might be reached by taking the difference in value between the business carried on as it was in West Boylston and a similar business carried on by the petitioner in the nearest available place, bearing in mind the effect of requiring all West Boylston patients to move. It may be that the commission will find as a practical matter that the method suggested by the petitioner is as near as can be got to the thing to be determined, but as the case stands we do not feel warranted in adopting it. The commission has not said that it could not make an estimate on more obviously correct principles. It has confined itself to finding the damages according to the rules suggested on the two sides.

A request for a ruling that what the petitioner had earned as a specialist since his abandonment of his general practice could not be considered, went too far. Undoubtedly the evidence was not very important, and probably it was not regarded as being so.

Report recommitted.

IS INJURY TO A BUSINESS AN APPROPRIATION OF PROPERTY?

Sawyer v. *Commonwealth*
182 Mass. 245 (1902)

This is a petition for the determination of damages caused by a decrease in value of the petitioners' business, in consequence of the carrying out of the metropolitan water supply act. St. 1895, c. 488, sec. 14. After the decision in *Sawyer* v. *Metropolitan Water Board*, 178 Mass. 267, the case was referred to a commission upon the present petition, and the petitioners, being dissatisfied with the determination, again claim a trial by jury—this time under sec. 15 of the act. The material words are as follows: "Said water board, or any persons whose property is taken under the right of eminent domain, or entered upon or injured by the taking of said water, if dissatisfied with any determination of damages made by any commission, may . . . claim a trial by jury," etc. The question is whether the petitioners come within these words, and have the right which they claim.

A majority of the court is of opinion that the petitioners are not entitled to a jury. If indeed the loss which they have suffered were within the protection of the Constitution, there would be the strongest reason for construing the statute as giving them whatever rights the Constitution secures, * * * but it hardly would be contended that the Constitution is concerned. It generally has been assumed, we think, that injury to a business is not an appropriation of property which must be paid for. There are many serious pecuniary injuries which may be inflicted without compensation. It would be impracticable to forbid all laws which might result in such damage, unless they provided a *quid pro quo*. No doubt a business may be property in a broad sense of the word, and property of great value. It may be assumed for the purposes of this case that there might be such a taking of it as required compensation. But a business is less tangible in nature and more uncertain in its vicissitudes than the rights which the Constitution undertakes absolutely to protect. It seems to us, in like manner, that the diminution of its value is a vaguer injury than the taking or appropriation with which the Constitution deals. A business might be destroyed by the construction of a more popular street into which travel was diverted, as well as by competition, but there would be as little claim in the one case as in the other. * * * It seems to us that the case stands no differently when the business is destroyed by taking the land on which it was carried on, except so far as it may have enhanced the value of the land. See *New York, New Haven, & Hartford Railroad* v. *Blacker,* 178 Mass. 386, 390.

We believe that what we have said is in accord with the general understanding of the profession, although the cases sometimes cited for the proposition may not have gone far enough to decide it. * * *

Assuming that the petitioners have no right under the Constitution, we have only to construe the statute in a natural way. The words which we have cited seem to us inapt to give the right which the petitioners claim. Their business is not "taken under the right of eminent domain," or alleged to be. It could not be "entered upon." It is not "injured by the taking of said water." Its value is decreased by the carrying out of the act,—that is, we presume, by the occupation of the land where it was carried on and the adjoining land where customers dwelt,—matters quite different from those mentioned. Their business is not "property" within the meaning of the act, unless it be held that the statute gives it the character of property by providing compensation and thereupon in sec. 15 uses the word in a looser and broader sense than that in which it had used it before. In secs. 12, 13, "property" seems to be used with what may be called its constitutional meaning, as was intimated in *Sawyer* v. *Metropolitan Water Board,* 178 Mass. 267, 270. Moreover we may notice for what it is worth that the remedy given to the petitioners by sec. 14 is to have their damages determined in the manner "hereinbefore" provided. That which they claim is provided thereinafter in sec. 15. It seems to us that the provision relied upon plainly corresponds to the first part of sec. 14 and has nothing to do with the petitioners, who come in by an after clap at the end of the section. The statute has provided for ordinary constitutional rights in secs. 12, 13, including a jury trial. Then in sec. 14 it gives a commission to certain owners of real estate taken or injured by the taking of the waters of the Nashua River, or directly or indirectly decreased in value. It will be seen how closely related the words of sec. 15 are to the rights thus given. The rights dealt with are constitutional rights or very near to such, and the jury is preserved. But when the statute did an act of supererogation, however just, it did not enhance its gratuity by leaving it to be determined by a tribunal not peculiarly adapted to deal with the problems involved. It certainly did not do so with any clearness, and the petitioners' rights must be confined to what the statute distinctly says.

Motion denied.

PART II

EXCERPTS AND EPIGRAMS

HAMMOND, J.　　LATHROP, J.　　KNOWLTON, J.　　HOLMES, C. J.　　MORTON, J.　　BARKER, J.　　LORING, J.

SUPREME JUDICIAL COURT
1899–1902

1

. . . It is contrary to the analogies of the law to allow an appeal for the sole purpose of enhancing the punishment. *Smith* v. *Dickinson,* 140 Mass. 171, 173 (1885).

2

A specialty deriving its validity from an estoppel *in pais* is perhaps somewhat like Nebuchadnezzar's image with a head of gold supported by feet of clay. *White* v. *Duggan,* 140 Mass. 18, 20 (1885).

3

It is more important to respect decisions upon a question of property than to preserve a simple test. *Carpenter* v. *Walker,* 140 Mass. 416, 420 (1886).

4

An expert in real estate is no more competent than anyone else to determine just what effect measured in money the dislike of litigation may have had on a given person's mind. *Sawyer* v. *Boston,* 144 Mass. 470, 471 (1887).

5

We cannot disturb a rule of property which has been acted on so long, on the strength of general reasoning. *Sewall & Co.* v. *Boston Water Power Co.* 147 Mass. 61, 64 (1888).

6

There is no law that we know of to prevent a man's friends combining to help him by honest means to an acquittal from a false charge. *Commonwealth* v. *McParland,* 148 Mass. 127, 129 (1888).

7

The general rule is, that a licensee goes upon land at his own risk, and must take the premises as he finds them. An open hole, which is not concealed otherwise than by the darkness of night, is a danger which a licensee must avoid at his peril. *Reardon* v. *Thompson,* 149 Mass. 267, 268 (1889).

8

In view of the general considerations, we are to construe the statute liberally in favor of employees, and we ought to be slow to conclude that indirectly, and without express words to that effect, it has limited the workman's common law rights most materially in respect to the conditions and time of bringing an action, and the amount which he can recover. . . . General maxims are oftener an excuse for the want of accurate analysis than a help in determining the extent of a duty or the construction of a statute. *Ryalls* v. *Mechanics' Mills,* 150 Misc. 190, 193, 194 (1889).

9

We do not construe declarations quite so adversely nowadays as indictments were construed a hundred years ago. *Coughlin* v. *Boston Tow-Boat Co.* 151 Mass. 92, 94 (1890).

10

When we can gather from the whole declaration that it is intended to present a certain case, we do not pronounce it bad for a want of technical accuracy of allegation, unless the specific defect is unmistakably pointed out. *Windram* v. *French,* 151 Mass. 547, 552 (1890).

11

Legislation is often tentative, beginning with the most obvious case, and not going beyond it, or to the full length of the principle upon which its act must be justified. . . . We think it safer to take the words as we find them in their ordinary and literal sense. *Beard* v. *Boston,* 151 Mass. 96, 97, 98 (1890).

12

A married woman must be supposed to be capable of receiving advice to separate from her husband without losing her reason or responsibility. . . . Good intentions are no excuse for spreading slanders. *Tasker* v. *Stanley,* 153 Mass. 148, 150 (1891).

13

. . . You cannot prove a mere private convention between the two parties to give language a different meaning from its common one. . . . It would open too great risks if evidence were admissible to show that when they said five hundred feet they agreed it should mean one hundred inches, or that Bunker Hill Monument should signify the Old South Church. As an artificial construction cannot be given to plain words by express agreement, the same rule is applied when there is a mutual mistake not apparent on the face of the instrument. *Goode* v. *Riley,* 153 Mass. 585, 586 (1891).

14

. . . A man does not take the risk of every danger which may arise from certain causes merely because, in a general way, he is aware of the existence of those causes. *Powers* v. *Boston,* 154 Mass. 60, 63 (1891).

15

. . . A tribunal cannot establish its own jurisdiction by adjudicating it to exist. *Taft* v. *Commonwealth,* 158 Mass. 526, 551 (1893).

16

. . . If it is a bad rule, that is no reason for making a bad exception to it. *Ayer* v. *Philadelphia & Boston Face Brick Co.* 159 Mass. 84, 88 (1893).

17

The law constantly is tending towards consistency of theory. *Hanson* v. *Globe Newspaper Co.* 159 Mass. 293, 302 (1893).

18

A man cannot be said to live on an estate which he does not occupy and which he has no right to enter. *Greenfield* v. *Buckland,* 159 Mass. 491, 492 (1893).

19

All values are anticipations of the future. *Lincoln* v. *Commonwealth,* 164 Mass. 368, 378 (1895).

20

A boy who is dull at fifteen probably was dull at fourteen. *Laplante* v. *Warren Cotton Mills,* 165 Mass. 487, 489 (1896).

21

Nowadays we do not require pleadings to be guarded against all the possible distortions of perverse ingenuity. *Braithwaite* v. *Hall,* 168 Mass. 38, 39 (1897).

22

The possibility of an occasional jolt is a thing which everyone who gets upon a street car must be taken to contemplate. *McCauley* v. *Springfield Street Railway Co.* 169 Mass. 301, 302 (1897).

23

A libel does not need the categorical certainty of an indictment at common law. An insinuation may be as actionable as a direct statement, and nothing is better settled than that a defendant cannot escape liability merely by putting the insinuation or statement into the mouth of somebody else. *Haynes* v. *Clinton Printing Co.* 169 Mass. 512, 513 (1897).

24

. . . Jurisdiction is not affected by a defendant's recalcitrance. *Crocker* v. *Cotting*, 170 Mass. 68, 71 (1898).

25

We think that the case at bar is not beyond our competence to decide. The greatest danger in attempting to do so is that of being misled by ready-made generalizations, and of thinking only in phrases to which as lawyers the judges have become accustomed, instead of looking straight at things and regarding the facts in all their concreteness as a jury would do. Too broadly generalized conceptions are a constant source of fallacy. Thus it is easy to say that the continuity of the sidewalk was an invitation, and then to discuss in universals the duty of one who invites the public upon his land. . . . *Lorenzo* v. *Wirth*, 170 Mass. 596, 600, 601 (1898).

26

. . . A man cannot shift his misfortunes to his neighbor's shoulders. . . . Ordinary street cars must be run with reference to ordinary susceptibilities, and the liability of their proprietors cannot be increased simply by a passenger's notifying the conductor that he has unstable nerves. *Spade* v. *Lynn & Boston Railroad Co.* 172 Mass. 488, 489, 491 (1899).

27

A trespasser is not *caput lupinum*. *Palmer* v. *Gordon,* 173 Mass. 410, 412 (1899).

28

The law does not trouble itself very much with such philosophic difficulties. The practical uncertainty arising from the ignorance of men is enough to be uncertainty in its eyes. . . . *Attorney General* v. *Equitable Accident Insurance Assoc'n,* 175 Mass. 196, 198 (1900).

29

A man cannot justify a libel by proving that he has contracted to libel. More specifically, a false statement of a kind manifestly hurtful to a man in his credit and business, and intended to be so, is not privileged because made in obedience to the requirements of a voluntary association got up for the purpose of compelling by a boycott the satisfaction of its members' claims to the exclusion of a resort to the courts. *Weston* v. *Barnicoat,* 175 Mass. 454, 458 (1900).

30

But every man of the world knows that the costumes worn upon the stage by dancing women vary so widely, not only in measure but in suggestion, that in this case a reference to what is usual would be wholly uninstructive. *Fay* v. *Harrington,* 176 Mass. 270, 275 (1900).

31

To defeat a man of a sufficiently certain gain is to inflict a loss which the law can recognize. *Emmonds* v. *Alvord,* 177 Mass. 466, 471 (1901).

32

Civil proceedings in court are not scientific investigations the end of which always must be objective truth. *Seaman* v. *Colley,* 178 Mass. 478, 481 (1901).

33

One interpretation is as idiomatic and natural as the other, and in our opinion that which we adopt is the only one consistent with justice and sense. *Boston & Maine Railroad* v. *Graham,* 179 Mass. 62, 68 (1901).

34

When we get close to the line of legal distinctions, technicalities often necessarily determine the precise place of division, although the general nature of the distinction depends upon larger considerations. Nevertheless it would be a matter for regret if a technicality having no relation to the policy of the law principally concerned should make the difference as to whether that law applied or not. *City National Bank* v. *Charles Baker Co.,* 180 Mass. 40, 42 (1901).

35

. . . If a single woman not otherwise distinguished should be minded to prolong the remembrance of her family name by a beautiful monument over her grave, we could not pronounce it unsuitable or improper as matter of law. *Davis* v. *Chase,* 181 Mass. 39, 41 (1902).

36

When the words in their literal sense have a plain meaning, courts must be very cautious in allowing their imagination to give them a different one. *Guild* v. *Walter,* 182 Mass. 225, 226 (1902).

37

. . . Upon questions of construction when no arbitrary rule is involved, it is always more important to consider the words and the circumstances than even strong analogies in earlier decisions. The successive neglect of a series of small distinctions, in the effort to follow precedent, is very liable to end in perverting instruments from their plain meaning. In no other branch of the law [trusts] is so much discretion required in dealing with authority. . . . There is a strong presumption in favor of giving words their natural meaning, and against reading them as if they said something else, which they are not fitted to express. *Merrill* v. *Preston,* 135 Mass. 451, 455 (1883).

38

This is an action against the owners and publishers of the Boston Herald for a libel printed in that newspaper. The alleged libel was a report of the contents of a petition for the removal of the plaintiff, an attorney at law, from the bar. The report was fair and correct, but the petition included allegations which would be actionable unless justified. In their answer the defendants rely upon privilege; and the main question raised by the plaintiff's exceptions is whether the publication was privileged, as ruled by the court below.

The petition had been presented to the clerk of the Supreme Judicial Court for the county of Middlesex in vacation, had been marked by him, "Filed February 23, 1883," and then or subsequently had been handed back to the petitioner, but it did not appear that it ever had been presented to the court or entered on the docket.

We are of opinion that the foregoing circumstances do not constitute a justification, and that the defendants do not bring themselves within the privilege admitted by the plaintiff to attach to fair reports of judicial proceedings, even if preliminary or *ex parte*.

No binding authority has been called to our attention which precisely determines this case, and we must be governed in our conclusion mainly by a consideration of the reasons upon which admitted principles have been established. . . . The chief advantage to the country which we can discern . . . is the security which publicity gives for the proper administration of justice. . . . It is desirable that the trial of causes should take place under the public eye, not because the controversies of one citizen with another are of public concern, but because it is of the highest moment that those who administer justice should always act under the sense of public responsibility, and that every citizen should be able to satisfy himself with his own eyes as to the mode in which a public duty is performed. . . . It would be carrying privilege farther than we feel prepared to carry it, to say that, by the easy means of entitling and filing it in a cause, a sufficient foundation may be laid for scattering any libel broadcast with impunity. *Cowley* v. *Pulsifer,* 137 Mass. 392–94 (1884).

39

The defendant has been found guilty of manslaughter, on evidence that he publicly practised as a physician, and, being called to attend a sick woman, caused her, with her consent, to be kept in flannels saturated with kerosene for three days, more or less, by reason of which she died. There was evidence that he had made similar applications with favorable results in other cases, but that in one the effect had been to blister and burn the flesh as in the present case. . . .

So far as civil liability is concerned, at least, it is very clear that what we have called the external standard would be applied, and that, if a man's conduct is such as would be reckless in a man of ordinary prudence, it is reckless in him. Unless he can bring himself within some broadly defined exception to general rules, the law deliberately leaves his idiosyncrasies out of account, and peremptorily assumes that he has as much capacity to judge and to foresee consequences as a man of ordinary prudence would have in the same situation . . . it is familiar law that an act causing death may be murder, manslaughter, or misadventure, according to the danger attending it. . . . We cannot recognize a privilege to do acts manifestly endangering human life, on the ground of good intentions alone. . . .

But if the dangers are characteristic of the class according to common experience, then he who uses an article of the class upon another cannot escape on the ground that he had less than the common experience. Common experience is necessary to the man of ordinary prudence, and a man who assumes to act as the defendant did must have it at his peril. . . . *Commonwealth* v. *Pierce,* 138 Mass. 165, 174, 176, 178, 179, 180 (1884).

40

. . . We cannot indulge in conjectures on the strength of seeming improbabilities, in the hope of doing substantial justice. . . . The standard of good faith required in sales is somewhat low, not only out of allowance for the weakness of human nature, but because it is not desirable to interfere too much for the purpose of helping men in their voluntary transactions more than they help themselves. . . . *Burns* v. *Lane,* 138 Mass. 350, 355, 356 (1885).

41

[The purchaser of a cemetery lot complained that the city had built a wall and terrace in front of his lot.] It has been said that rights of burial in public burial grounds are peculiar, and are not very dissimilar to rights in pews; that they are so far public that private interests in them are subject to the control of the public authorities having charge of police regulations . . . and when the master finds that the pecuniary loss to him is nothing, and that the injury or damage, if any, is "wholly one of sentiment and temper, of so slight a character as to be counted among the trifles which the law does not regard," and when it further appears that the plaintiff has lain by and taken no other action than to protest, while the city has "expended in the work in question a large sum of money manifestly to the general improvement and benefit of the cemetery, and the cost of removing or opening the wall and terrace across the avenue would largely exceed the amount or value of the plaintiff's individual interest in the premises," we are clearly of opinion that the plaintiff has no claim to equitable relief. *Perkins v. Lawrence,* 138 Mass. 361, 362 (1885).

42

A judgment *in rem* is an act of the sovereign power; and, as such, its effects cannot be disputed, at least within the jurisdiction. If a competent court declares a vessel forfeited, or orders it sold free of all claims, or divorces a couple, or establishes a will under statutes like [ours] a paramount title is passed, the couple is divorced, the will is established, as against all the world, whether parties or not, because the sovereign has said that it shall be so. . . . *Brigham* v. *Fayerweather,* 140 Mass. 411, 413 (1886).

43

The only question presented to us is whether the Public Statutes, c. 28, sec. 13 (St. 1861, c. 165,) can be interpreted to authorize a city to appropriate money for public concerts by a band. . . . The word "other" implies that the celebration of holidays is a public purpose within the meaning of the act, and indicates that purposes which are public only in that sense are included within its scope, although they look rather more obviously to increasing the picturesqueness and interest of life than to the satisfaction of rudimentary wants, which alone we generally recognize as necessary. We know of no simple and merely logical test by which the limit can be fixed. It must be determined by practical considerations. The question is one of degree. But in reply to the petitioners' argument, we may say that, if the purpose is within the act, we do not see why the city council may not create the occasion. Taking into account the history and language of the act, the safeguards attached to the exercise of the power, the smallness of the sum allowed to be expended, and the fact that it has long been assumed to be within the power of cities to give such concerts in the open air, we are not prepared to say that a case is presented for an injunction. *Hubbard* v. *Taunton* 140 Mass. 467–468 (1886).

44

. . . The existence of a corporation is a fiction, but the very meaning of that fiction is that the liability of its members shall be determined as if the fiction were the truth. That fiction or artificial creation is wholly within the power of its creator, and persons who deal with it must be taken to understand that it is so. . . . *E. Remington and Sons* v. *Samana Bay Co.*, 140 Mass. 494, 501 (1886).

45

. . . To cut the knot with a formula in the case I have supposed would be an unnecessary abandonment of the discriminations within our power, and, as a practical judgment, would be as likely to work injustice as justice. (dissent). *New England Trust Co.* v. *Eaton*, 140 Mass. 532, 546 (1886).

46

Fraud only becomes important, as such, when a sale or contract is complete in its formal elements, and therefore valid unless repudiated, but the right is claimed to rescind it. It goes to the motives for making the contract, not to its existence; as when a vendee expressly or impliedly represents that he is solvent and intends to pay for goods, when in fact he is insolvent, and has no reasonable expectation of paying for them; or, being identified by the senses and dealt with as the person so identified, says that he is A., when in fact he is B. . . . *Rodliff* v. *Dallinger,* 141 Mass. 1, 6 (1886).

47

If a man cannot complain when he knowingly walks through a door which he knows leads to a hole that may or may not be covered over . . . he cannot complain because a person, who has lawfully opened the hole and has also locked the door leading to it, has not put up a second less effectual barrier behind the door, unless that person has given him a right to expect it. . . . The extent of duty under such circumstances is a matter of expediency and degree, which different minds might fix at different points. *Kent* v. *Todd,* 144 Mass. 478, 490, 491 (1887).

48

. . . We cannot admit that a rule of construction, properly so called, not known to the law of the party's domicil when he made his will, is necessarily to be imported into it by reason of his dying domiciled elsewhere. For purposes of construction, it is always legitimate to consider the time when, and the circumstances in which, the will was made. . . . We are at a loss to see why his words should be held to acquire a new meaning upon his moving into a State where testamentary gifts are in lieu of dower unless shown to be in addition to it. *Staigg* v. *Atkinson,* 144 Mass. 564, 569 (1887).

49

... So far as the introduction of collateral issues goes, that objection is a purely practical one, a concession to the shortness of life. ... Filling teeth, however skilfully done, is generally unpleasant. ... People generally break off their dealings with those whom they find trying to cheat them. *Reeve* v. *Dennett,* 145 Mass. 23, 28, 30 (1887).

50

We think that courts should be slow to pronounce the Legislature to have been mistaken in its constantly manifested opinion upon a matter resting wholly within its will, when for so long a time everything has been conducted upon that footing. *Abbott* v. *New York & New England Railroad Co.* 145 Mass. 450, 459 (1888).

51

People do not generally try to drive across railway tracks when they know by the bell or whistle that a train is approaching; the jury therefore might find that the deceased would have stopped if the bell had been rung or the whistle sounded. *Doyle* v. *Boston & Albany Railroad Co.* 145 Mass. 386, 388 (1888).

52

To lead a person reasonably to suppose that you assent to an oral arrangement is to assent to it, wholly irrespective of fraud. Assent, in the sense of the law, is a matter of overt acts, not of inward unanimity in motives, design, or the interpretation of words. *O'Donnell* v. *Clinton,* 145 Mass. 461, 463 (1888).

53

Whatever practical uncertainty courts may have felt upon a subject [what constitutes promotion of a lottery] with which they are less well acquainted than some others of the community, in theory of law there is no uncertainty, and the sooner the question is relieved from doubt the better. *Commonwealth* v. *Sullivan,* 146 Mass. 142, 145 (1888).

54

It is contrary to first principles to allow a person whose overt acts have expressed assent to deny their effect on the ground of an undisclosed state of his mind for which no one else was responsible. *Rosenberg* v. *Doe,* 146 Mass. 191, 193 (1888).

55

. . . It must be remembered, whenever a new statute comes up for consideration, that although it may be found by construction to give what it gives as if in pursuance of a legal duty, there is no such legal duty in fact, and no antecedent right on the part of the persons who receive its benefits. It is only tautologous to say that the law knows nothing of moral rights unless they are also legal rights, and from before the days of Hobbes the argument has been public property that there is no such thing as a right created by law, as against the sovereign who makes the law by which the right is to be created. *Heard* v. *Sturgis,* 146 Mass. 545, 548 (1888).

56

It is true in most cases, that, when a fact in issue is to be inferred from facts proved, the court cannot instruct the jury as to probabilities or presumptions of fact, but can only determine that, if the jury draw the inference upon the presumptions which they have learned from their experience of life, they will be warranted so far as the court knows, and will not be making a mere guess without adequate data. . . . It does not appear that we have all the evidence before us. But it does appear that the room from which the cellar was entered was a bar-room, with a contrivance which might be used to prevent surprise, that the beer was concealed and in considerable quantity, and that there were drippings of spirituous liquors in half a barrel of empty bottles called smugglers. We cannot pronounce the inference that the beer was kept for sale so little warranted by the teachings of experience as to be but a mere guess. *Commonwealth* v. *Keenan,* 148 Mass. 470, 473 (1889).

57

Agreed facts are not to be dealt with on quite the same principles as contracts. *Richardson* v. *Boston,* 148 Mass. 508, 513 (1889).

58

[In a suit by one injured because his horse was frightened while driving along an adjoining street to the Boston Common, by reason of the firing of a cannon on the Common, Holmes said that the city was not liable.] The case, then, is simply that the city has failed to prohibit by legislation the firing of cannon in a public park, or has given its legislative sanction on certain conditions. It has no private interest in the matter, and there is no statute giving an action for such a cause. . . . Perhaps it will save future litigation if we go one step further, and intimate that, as the subject matter was within the city's authority to regulate by by-law, and as the by-law, so far as appears, is reasonable, those who act under it are justified in doing what we all know extra-judicially to have been done upon the Common time out of mind. *Lincoln* v. *Boston,* 148 Mass. 578, 581, 582 (1889).

59

[Query—whether a stone porch was a portico or a projection in the nature of a bay window, and therefore, restricted by deed.] Etymologically the words "porch" and "portico" are one. Formerly porch was used as synonymous with portico in its classic sense. "And he made a porch of pillars; the length thereof was fifty cubits." I Kings, vii. 6. The tendency in modern times, no doubt, has been to diminish "porch" to the shelter in front of the door of a building, and we are very willing to assume that, with the constant growth of distinctions and nice discriminations in the meaning of words, "portico" retains more of the original suggestion of length and of a roof supported by pillars, among architects and scholarly persons, and that porch is more specially appropriated to a smaller structure, generally with closed sides. But the distinction is not carefully preserved in common speech. With us portico, as well as porch, has shrunk, and usually means a shelter in front of a door. See Dyche and Pardon's Dict. 1754, also Imperial Dict. 1882, *Portico*. When porticos are cut down to the little structures which we all know, we think that special reference to the mode of support has vanished almost as completely as to the length. The parties to this deed did not mean by portico "a walk covered with a roof, supported by columns at least on one side." They meant the shelter to the door of a building, familiar to Massachusetts and to Boston. We are of opinion that they used it as a generic word, including a shelter with closed sides, as well as one with pillars. We agree that in determining the scope of the word we must look at the object of the restrictions and of the exceptions to it. But, as we have said, the permission extends to more serious structures, with closed sides, and therefore there is no reason for excluding porches. Indeed, a portico projecting not more than five feet would, or at least might, obstruct the view of a neighboring house with its pillars almost as completely as if its sides were closed. . . . *Attorney General* v. *Ayer,* 148 Mass. 584, 587 (1889).

60

This is a bill brought to restrain the defendant from filling up the plaintiff's mill-pond [and as a result of the solid matter from diminishing the water power.] The master reports that the defendant's land is on the slope of a hill running down to the pond, and that the only acts of the defendant tending to fill the pond have been those of cultivating and manuring his own soil in the ordinary way, for the purpose of raising garden vegetables. . . .

The respective rights and liabilities of adjoining landowners cannot be determined in advance by a mathematical line or a general formula, certainly not by the simple test of whether the obvious and necessary consequence of a given act by one is to damage the other. The fact that the damage is foreseen, or even intended, is not decisive apart from statute. Some damage a man must put up with, however plainly his neighbor foresees it before bringing it to pass. *Rideout* v. *Knox,* 148 Mass. 368. Liability depends upon the nature of the act, and the kind and degree of harm done, considered in the light of expediency and usage. For certain kinds there is no liability, no matter what the extent of the harm. A man may lose half the value of his house by the obstruction of his view, and yet be without remedy. In other cases his rights depend upon the degree of the damage, or rather of its cause. He must endure a certain amount of noise, smells, shaking, percolation, surface drainage, and so forth. If the amount is greater, he may be able to stop it, and to recover compensation. As in other matters of degree, a case which is near the line might be sent to a jury to determine what is reasonable. In a clear case it is the duty of the court to rule upon the parties' rights. . . .

We are of opinion that a man has a right to cultivate his land in the usual and reasonable way, as well upon a hill as in the plain, and that damage to the lower proprietor of the kind complained of is something that he must protect himself against as best he may. . . . *Middlesex Co.* v. *McCue,* 149 Mass. 103, 104, 105 (1889).

61

[Contract for purchase of system of heating to be paid for upon its "satisfactory completion."] In view of modern modes of business, it is not surprising that in some cases eager sellers or selling agents should be found taking that degree of risk with unwilling purchasers, especially where taste is involved. . . . We are of opinion that the satisfactoriness of the system and the risk taken by the plaintiff were to be determined by the mind of a reasonable man, and by the external measures set forth in the contract, not by the private taste or liking of the defendant. *Hawkins* v. *Graham,* 149 Mass. 284, 287, 289 (1889).

62

The exclusive right to particular combinations of words or figures, after they have been published, for purposes not less useful than advertising,—for poetry, or the communication of truths discovered for the first time by the writer,—for art or mechanical design,— now at least is a creature of statute, and is narrowly limited in time. When the common law developed the doctrine of trade-marks and trade names, it was not creating a property in advertisements more absolute than it would have allowed the author of Paradise Lost; but the meaning was to prevent one man from palming off his goods as another's, from getting another's business or injuring his reputation by unfair means, and, perhaps, from defrauding the public. . . . *Chadwick* v. *Covell,* 151 Mass. 190, 193 (1890).

63

If we were to depart from that rule, and to say that a man should have but one judgment, although he had different causes of action, when we thought he could get from a single judgment all the satisfaction he was likely to get, we should be legislating, instead of following the precedents, and legislating in very doubtful accord with the contracts of the parties. *Vanuxem* v. *Burr,* 151 Mass. 386, 390 (1890).

64

In these, as in many other instances, the law has to draw a line between conflicting interests, both intrinsically meritorious. When private inquiries are made about a private person, a servant, for example, it is often impossible to answer them properly without stating facts, and those who settled the law thought it more important to preserve a reasonable freedom in giving necessary information than to insure people against occasional unintended injustice, confined as it generally is to one or two persons. But what the interest of private citizens in public matters requires is freedom of discussion rather than of statement. Moreover, the statements about such matters which come before the courts are generally public statements, where the harm done by a falsehood is much greater than in the other case. If one private citizen wrote to another that a high official had taken a bribe, no one would think good faith a sufficient answer to an action. He stands no better, certainly, when he publishes his writing to the world through a newspaper, and the newspaper itself stands no better than the writer. . . . A person publishes libellous matter at his peril. *Burt* v. *Advertiser Newspaper Co.,* 154 Mass. 238, 243, 245 (1891).

65

If we were contriving a new code today, we might hesitate to say that a man could make himself a party to a bare tort, in any case, merely by assenting to it after it had been committed. But we are not at liberty to refuse to carry out to its consequences any principle which we believe to have been part of the common law, simply because the grounds of policy on which it must be justified seem to us to be hard to find, and probably to have belonged to a different state of society. *Dempsey* v. *Chambers,* 154 Mass. 330, 331 (1891).

66

[Can the county commissioners take a strip of land from a schoolhouse lot for a town way?] We must consider the relative importance and the necessities of the two uses generically, the extent of the harm to be done, accept any light that history may throw, and make up our minds under all the circumstances of the particular case as best we can; . . . there is a much greater freedom of choice as to where a schoolhouse shall be put than as to where roads shall run. *Easthampton* v. *County Commissioners,* 154 Mass. 424, 425, 426 (1891).

67

Of course it would be possible for an independent state to enforce all contracts made and to be performed within its territory, without regard to how much they might contravene the policy of its neighbors' laws. But in fact no state pursues such a course of barbarous isolation. *Graves* v. *Johnson,* 156 Mass. 211, 212 (1892).

68

Some rules and standards of conduct are plain enough for judges to be able to lay down without the aid of a jury. *Pinney* v. *Hall,* 156 Mass. 225, 226 (1892).

69

[Can a landowner recover damages, when a street is discontinued, thereby adversely affecting the value of his property and means of access?] It was intelligible for them to say that only the loss of access, the comparatively palpable injury, should be paid for, and not the advantage which the landowner had had the luck to enjoy of being where the crowd was; somewhat in the same way that the common law refuses to recognize the damage, often very great even measured in money, caused by cutting off a view. *Stanwood* v. *Malden,* 157 Mass. 17, 19 (1892).

70

The Legislature may think that a business like that of transmitting electricity through the streets of a city necessarily must be transacted by a regulated monopoly, and that a free competition between as many companies and persons as may be minded to put up wires in the streets and to try their luck is impracticable. Without wasting time upon useless generalities about the construction of statutes, it is enough to say that the statute before us had that consideration in view, and must be construed accordingly. *Attorney General* v. *Walworth Light Co.,* 157 Mass. 86, 87 (1892).

71

The explanation of the early law is a matter of antiquarianism, which would be out of place here. *Robinson* v. *Bird,* 158 Mass. 357, 360 (1893).

72

[A merchant enjoined a co-tenant from permitting sands and acids leaking through from the floor above and injuring his goods.] The only justification that could be urged would be that the interests of adjoining owners necessarily conflict, that they are both intrinsically meritorious, that the law has to adjust them by drawing a quasi physical line, and that the damage complained of was on the right side of that line and must be put up with by the plaintiff. . . . As any line of adjustment between conflicting rights must be drawn on practical grounds, there is no doubt that it may vary under different circumstances. . . . No doubt, when once it is decided that a certain liability or risk shall be attached to a voluntary relation, the party entering into that relation takes that risk. But what risks shall be attached to any relation is a pure question of policy. . . . *Boston Ferrule Co.* v. *Hills,* 159 Mass. 147, 149–150 (1893).

73

Presumptions of fact generally are questions of fact. They are merely the major premises of those inferences which juries are at liberty to draw, in the light of their experience as men of the world, from the facts directly proved. *Leighton* v. *Morrill,* 159 Mass. 271, 278 (1893).

74

. . . The statute of frauds may be made an instrument of fraud. But that always is true, whenever the law prescribes a form for an obligation. The very meaning of such a requirement is that a man relies at his peril on what purports to be such an obligation without that form. If the present case suggests the possibility that wrong may be accomplished through the forms of law, it equally suggests the danger which the statute was intended to meet. *Bourke* v. *Callanan,* 160 Mass. 195, 197 (1893).

75

A horse car cannot be handled like a rapier. Within the narrow limits of the possible, so far as the evidence shows, a prudent man had no reason to think one spot safer than another. *Hamilton* v. *West End Street Railway Co.* 163 Mass. 199, 200 (1895).

76

There are no sacramental words which must be used in a statutory power to take and hold lands in order to give a right to take the lands in fee. Any language in the statute which makes its meaning clear is sufficient. *Newton* v. *Perry,* 163 Mass. 319, 321 (1895).

77

If we are right in our understanding of the policy established by the Legislature, it is our duty to carry it out so far as we can do so without coming into conflict with paramount principles. *Emery* v. *Burbank,* 163 Mass. 326, 328 (1895).

78

I am unable to agree with the decision reached by a majority of the court on the first point discussed by them. I will not in this place go into any extended discussion of general principles. If I were making the law, I should not hold a man answerable for representations made in the common affairs of life without bad faith in some sense, if no consideration was given for them, although it would be hard to reconcile even that proposition with some of our cases. But the proposition, even if accepted, seems to me not to apply to this case. The proper meaning of the words used by the defendant has been settled by this court already. 159 Mass. 437. The representation was not made in casual talk, but in a business matter, for the very purpose of inducing others to lay out their money on the faith of it. When a man makes such a representation, he knows that others will understand his words according to their usual and proper meaning, and not by the accident of what he happens to have in his head, and it seems to me one of the first principles of social intercourse that he is bound at his peril to know what that meaning is. In this respect it seems to me that there is no difference between the law of fraud and that of other torts, or of contract or estoppel. If the language of fiction be preferred, a man is conclusively presumed in all parts of the law to contemplate the natural consequences of his act, as well in the conduct of others as in mechanical results. I can see no difference in principle between an invitation by words and an invitation by other acts, such as opening the gates of a railroad crossing (*Brow* v. *Boston & Albany Railroad,* 157 Mass. 399) or an intentional gesture, having as its manifest consequence, according to common experience, a start and a fall on the part of the person toward whom it is directed, in either of which cases I suppose no one would say that a defendant could get off by proving that he did not anticipate the natural interpretation of the sign. . . . I am of opinion, as I have stated, that in a case like the present a man takes the risk of the interpretation of his words as it may afterwards be settled by the court . . . [dissent in which C. J. Field agreed]. *Nash* v. *Minnesota Title Insurance and Trust Co.* 163 Mass. 574, 586, 587 (1895).

79

Presumptions of fact, or those general propositions of experience which form the major premises of particular conclusions of this sort, usually are for the jury. *Graham* v. *Badger,* 164 Mass. 42, 47 (1895).

80

[A man was indicted for mixing a dose "rough on rats" with tea with the intent of killing another.] . . . We assume that an act may be done which is expected and intended to accomplish a crime, which is not near enough to the result to constitute an attempt to commit it, as in the classic instance of shooting at a post supposed to be a man. As the aim of the law is not to punish sins, but is to prevent certain external results, the act done must come pretty near to accomplishing that result before the law will notice it. But, on the other hand, irrespective of the statute, it is not necessary that the act should be such as inevitably to accomplish the crime by the operation of natural forces, but for some casual and unexpected interference. It is none the less an attempt to shoot a man that the pistol which is fired at his head is not aimed straight, and therefore in the course of nature cannot hit him. Usually acts which are expected to bring about the end without further interference on the part of the criminal are near enough, unless the expectation is very absurd. . . . Intent imports contemplation, and more or less expectation, of the intended end as the result of the act alleged. *Commonwealth* v. *Kennedy,* 170 Mass. 18, 20, 21 (1897).

81

It is true that every one has notice of the force of gravitation, and therefore it would be possible logically to make owners absolutely liable if their buildings fall. . . . But it is for the public welfare that buildings be put up, and here as elsewhere policy and custom have to draw the line between opposing interests. . . . That line is the line between what could have been prevented by proper precautions and accident, meaning by accident that which could not have been foreseen and guarded against otherwise than by not building. For although all accidents could be prevented by not building, yet, as it is desirable that buildings and fences should be put up, the law of this Commonwealth does not throw the risk of that act any more than that of any other necessary conduct upon the actor, or make every owner of a structure insure against all that may happen, however little to be foreseen. *Quinn* v. *Crimmings,* 171 Mass. 255, 258 (1898).

82

. . . The meaning of the words cannot be shaken by putting cases where the difference between one claim and two becomes nice. Any distinction, no matter how sensible and how plain, leads at last to a line which is worked out by the contact of decisions clustering around the opposite poles, and which may seem arbitrary if we attend to it alone and not to the nature of the groups which it divides. *Smith* v. *American Linen Co.,* 172 Mass. 227, 229 (1898).

83

It used to be said in England, under the rule requiring notice of the habits of an animal, that every dog was entitled to one worry, but it is not universally true that every horse is entitled to one kick. In England, if the horse is a trespasser and kicks another, the kick will enhance the damages without proof that the animal was vicious and that the owner knew it. . . . In this Commonwealth, going further, it would seem, than the English law, a kick by a horse wrongfully at large upon the highway can be recovered for without proof that it was vicious. *Hardiman* v. *Wholley,* 172 Mass. 411, 412 (1899).

84

... To give evidence requiring words to receive an abnormal meaning is to contradict. It is settled that the normal meaning of language in a written instrument no more can be changed by construction than it can be contradicted directly by an avowedly inconsistent agreement, on the strength of the talk of the parties at the time when the instrument was signed. *Violette* v. *Rice,* 173 Mass. 82, 84 (1899).

85

[The American Waltham Watch Company sued to prevent another from marking its watches conspicuously as "Waltham Watches."] It is true that a man cannot appropriate a geographical name, but neither can he a color, or any part of the English language, or even a proper name to the exclusion of others whose names are like his. Yet a color connection with a sufficiently complex combination of other things may be recognized as saying so circumstantially that the defendant's goods are the plaintiff's as to pass the injunction line. ... So, the name of a person may become so associated with his goods that one of the same name coming into the business later will not be allowed to use even his own name without distinguishing his wares. ... Whatever might have been the doubts some years ago, we think that now it is pretty well settled that the plaintiff merely on the strength of having been first in the field may put later comers to the trouble of taking such reasonable precautions as are commercially practicable to prevent their lawful names and advertisements from deceitfully diverting the plaintiff's custom. *American Waltham Watch Co.* v. *United States Watch Co.,* 173 Mass. 85, 87 (1899).

86

We agree that if the sale was in the terms of the vote, and those terms were legal, it would be none the worse that the transaction came very near to illegality, and was framed so as to avoid it. One meaning of drawing a line between the lawful and the unlawful is that you have a right to get as near the line as you can if you do not cross it. *Clemens Electric Manufacturing Co.* v. *Walton,* 173 Mass. 286, 299 (1898).

87

. . . Generally speaking, when a statute requires the "fair cash value" of property on a certain day to be ascertained, Pub. Sts. c. 13, sec. 8, it refers to the actual judgment of the public as expressed in the price which someone will pay, not to what the court at a later time may think would have been a wiser opinion. It means the highest price that a normal purchaser, not under peculiar compulsion, will pay at that time to get that thing. . . . *National Bank of Commerce* v. *New Bedford,* 175 Mass. 257, 262 (1900).

88

The meaning of the words might vary according to circumstances, and the interpretation of them is a question for the instructed imagination, taking the facts just as they are. . . . We must decide, therefore, by drawing the line as we think most in accordance with the exact words used. . . . But we think that a line must be drawn somewhere, and that it falls most naturally where we have drawn it. . . . *Rotch v. French,* 176 Mass. 1, 3, 4, 5 (1900).

89

[Petition to set aside a decree of divorce after the death of the husband.] . . . The petitioner, relying on getting the advantages of a widow without any of the troubles which she found incident to being a wife, and thinking that she would be better able to prove her case if the opposition of her husband was removed, waited until his death before she took a step. Whether it be called laches or be given a harsher name, such a course put an end to any claim she ever may have had to be heard. *Brigham, Petitioner,* 176 Mass. 223, 228 (1900).

90

We agree that, in view of the great increase of actions for personal injuries, it may be desirable that the courts should have the power in dispute [to order medical examination of injured complainant]. We appreciate the ease with which, if we were careless or ignorant of precedent, we might deem it enlightened to assume that power. We do not forget the continuous process of developing the law that goes on through the courts, in the form of deduction, or deny that in a clear case it might be possible even to break away from a line of decisions in favor of some rule generally admitted to be based upon a deeper insight into the present wants of society. But the improvements made by the courts are made, almost invariably, by very slow degrees and by very short steps. Their general duty is not to change but to work out the principles already sanctioned by the practice of the past. No one supposes that a judge is at liberty to decide with sole reference even to his strongest convictions of policy and right. His duty in general is to develop the principles which he finds, with such consistency as he may be able to attain. No one supposes that this court might have anticipated the Legislature by declaring parties to be competent witnesses, any more than to-day it could abolish the requirement of consideration for a simple contract. In the present case we perceive no such pressing need of our anticipating the Legislature as to justify our departure from what we cannot doubt is the settled tradition of the common law to a point beyond that which we believe to have been reached by equity, and beyond any to which our statutes dealing with kindred subjects ever have seen fit to go. It will be seen that we put our decision not upon the impolicy of admitting such a power, but on the ground that it would be too great a step of judicial legislation to be justified by the necessities of the case. *Stack* v. *New York, New Haven, and Hartford Railroad,* 177 Mass. 155, 158–59 (1900).

91

The lines between liability and imunity are fixed, at least in part, by legislative considerations of policy. While it may not be a sufficient reason for making greater requirements of a defendant that the plaintiff was disabled by poverty from taking certain precautions, the circumstances and limited powers of a large part of the community may be taken into account in determining what persons who use or cross the highways must look out for, and what they shall be held entitled to expect from those whom they meet and may injure. The poor cannot always keep their children in the house or always see that they are attended when out of doors. In this case the evidence warranted a finding that the mother reasonably might expect her children to obey her, and that leaving them where she did for the short time that she left them there, occupied as they were, was not negligence, in view of the fact that one of them was nine . . . the case falls into that border region between two extremes which we leave to the jury. *Butler* v. *New York, New Haven and Hartford Railroad,* 177 Mass. 191, 193 (1900).

92

A decision could be made either way without contradicting the express words of the act, or, possibly, even any very clear implication. *Hooper* v. *Bradford,* 178 Mass. 95, 97 (1901).

93

There is a penumbra in which that identity [of husband and wife] although largely broken down by statute, still has a somewhat ghostly existence, and exactly where the line should be drawn is a point upon which people may differ. But there is no fiction of identity between mother and child. *Kerslake* v. *Cummings,* 180 Mass. 65, 68 (1901).

94

[Action for injuries caused by the plaintiff's horse taking fright at an electric car covered with white canvas and resting on a flat car which stood on the defendant's track near the highway.] As in many cases, perhaps it might be said in all, two principles or social desiderata present themselves, each of which it would be desirable to carry out but for the other, but which at this point come into conflict. It is desirable that as far as possible people should be able to drive in the streets without their horses being frightened. It also is desirable that the owners of land should be free to make profitable and otherwise innocent use of it. More specifically, it is desirable that a railroad company should be free to use its tracks in any otherwise lawful way for the carriage, incidental keeping and final delivery of any lawful freight. A line has to be drawn to separate the domains of the irreconcilable desires. Such a line cannot be drawn in general terms. We assume for the purposes of the argument that some uses of land might be imagined which would be held unlawful solely because of their tendency to frighten horses. . . . Others would be held lawful no matter how many horses they frightened. There is no doubt that an ordinary wooden building is lawful, even if painted white. Most of us are inclined to think, as at present advised, that a similar structure is equally privileged when it is on wheels, and that it is not less so when the whiteness is due to a wrapper which does not flap in the wind. Most of us regard the question as not too delicate to be within our competence to decide without the aid of a jury. *Patnoude* v. *New York, New Haven, and Hartford Railroad Co.*, 180 Mass. 119, 121, 122 (1901).

95

. . . Men are held liable every day in tort for the natural and proximate results of their wrongs, although the particular result could not have been foreseen specifically as necessary at the time of the act. *McNary* v. *Blackburn,* 180 Mass. 141, 143 (1901).

[319]

96

Of course the argument for the plaintiff is that his domicil is presumed to continue until it is proved to have been changed, that it could be changed only by his intent and overt act, and that he expressly denied the intent. The ambiguity is in the last proposition. . . . If a person is present with his family in a house in Brookline and intends to make his actual headquarters there for the rest of his life, and to live no more in the place of his former domicil, he cannot retain the old domicil by the simple means of intending, subject to his actual change, to retain advantages inconsistent with it. The proposition hardly needs illustration. When you intend the facts to which the law attaches a consequence, you must abide the consequence whether you intend it or not. *Dickinson* v. *Brookline,* 181 Mass. 195, 196 (1902).

PART III

APPENDICES

APPENDIX I

JUDGES OF THE MASSACHUSETTS SUPREME JUDICIAL COURT CONTEMPORARY WITH JUSTICE HOLMES

Name	Born	Appointed	Seated	Age	Previous Judicial Experience	Served Until	Years Served
MARCUS MORTON*	Apr. 8, 1819	Apr. 15, 1869	Apr. 19, 1869	50	11 yrs. Supr. Ct.	Aug. 27, 1890	21
WALBRIDGE A. FIELD*	Apr. 26, 1833	Feb. 21, 1881	Feb. 23, 1881	47	None	July 15, 1899	18
CHARLES DEVENS	Apr. 4, 1820	Oct. 3, 1873	Oct. 4, 1873	53	6 yrs. Supr. Ct.	Jan. 7, 1891	18
WILLIAM ALLEN	Mar. 31, 1822	Sept. 5, 1881	Sept. 13, 1881	59	None	June 4, 1891	10
CHARLES ALLEN	Apr. 17, 1827	Jan. 23, 1882	Jan. 24, 1882	54	None	Sept. 1, 1898	16
WALDO COLBURN	Nov. 13, 1824	Nov. 10, 1882	Nov. 14, 1882	58	7 yrs. Supr. Ct.	Sept. 26, 1885	3
OLIVER W. HOLMES*	Mar. 8, 1841	Dec. 15, 1882	Jan. 3, 1883	41	None	Dec. 8, 1902	20
WM. S. GARDNER	Oct. 1, 1827	Oct. 13, 1885	Oct. 20, 1885	51	10 yrs. Supr. Ct.	Sept. 7, 1887	2
MARCUS P. KNOWLTON	Feb. 3, 1839	Sept. 14, 1887	Sept. 20, 1887	48	6 yrs. Supr. Ct.	Sept. 7, 1911	24
JAMES M. MORTON	Sept. 5, 1837	Sept. 17, 1890	Sept. 23, 1890	53	None	Dec. 15, 1913	23
JOHN LATHROP	Feb. 8, 1835	Jan. 28, 1891	Feb. 2, 1891	55	3 yrs. Supr. Ct.	Sept. 11, 1906	16
JAMES M. BARKER	Oct. 23, 1839	June 18, 1891	June 26, 1891	51	10 yrs. Supr. Ct.	Oct. 3, 1905	14
JOHN W. HAMMOND	Dec. 6, 1837	Sept. 7, 1898	Sept. 13, 1898	60	12 yrs. Supr. Ct.	Dec. 1, 1914	16
WILLIAM C. LORING	Aug. 24, 1851	Sept. 7, 1899	Sept. 12, 1899	48	None	Sept. 16, 1919	20

* Judges who served as Chief Justices. Morton was Chief Justice from January 16, 1882 until August 27, 1890; Field from September 4, 1890 until July 15, 1899; and Holmes from August 2, 1899 until December 8, 1902.

[323]

APPENDIX II

TABLE SHOWING THE ANNUAL NUMBER OF OPINIONS WRITTEN BY HOLMES AS A MEMBER OF THE MASSACHUSETTS SUPREME JUDICIAL COURT

January 3, 1883 to December 8, 1902

1883	38	1893	72
1884	44	1894	46
1885	63	1895	59
1886	51	1896	63
1887	43	1897	73
1888	51	1898	61
1889	56	1899	100
1890	52	1900	80
1891	72	1901	105
1892	51	1902	111
	521		770

1883–1892	521	Opinions
1893–1902	770	"
	1,291	"

This Table includes his separate OPINIONS OF THE JUSTICES as well as those in which other members of the court concurred with him when he was the Chief Justice. It also includes his dissenting opinions, but not the PER CURIAM opinions rendered while he was Chief Justice, although many of these opinions were no doubt written by him.

APPENDIX III

TABLE SHOWING THE NUMBER OF DISSENTING OPINIONS OF THE INDIVIDUAL JUDGES OF THE MASSACHUSETTS SUPREME JUDICIAL COURT DURING JUSTICE HOLMES' TENURE OF OFFICE

	1883	1884	1885	1886	1887	1888	1889	1890	1891	1892	1893	1894	1895	1896	1897	1898	1899	1900	1901	1902	Total
Morton, M.	0	0	0	0	0	0	0	0	—	—	—	—	—	—	—	—	—	—	—	—	0
Field	1	0	0	1	0	3	1	1	2	0	3	0	2	2	2	3	0	—	—	—	21
Devens	1	0	0	1	0	0	0	0	1	—	—	—	—	—	—	—	—	—	—	—	3
Allen, W.	0	0	0	0	0	0	0	1	1	—	—	—	—	—	—	—	—	—	—	—	2
Allen, C.	1	0	0	0	0	0	0	0	0	1	0	0	0	0	1	0	—	—	—	—	3
Colburn, W.	0	0	0	—	—	—	—	—	—	—	—	—	—	—	—	—	—	—	—	—	0
Holmes	0	0	0	—	0	1	0	0	1	0	1	1	2	2	0	2	0	1	0	0	12
Gardner	0	0	0	0	0	0	0	—	—	—	—	—	—	—	—	—	—	—	—	—	0
Knowlton	—	—	—	—	0	1	0	2	0	4	3	2	2	3	1	4	0	0	2	1	25
Morton, J.	—	—	—	—	0	0	—	0	1	1	3	0	1	0	0	0	2	1	0	1	8
Lathrop	—	—	—	—	—	—	—	—	0	0	2	1	0	0	0	0	0	0	1	1	8
Barker	—	—	—	—	—	—	—	—	0	0	0	0	0	1	1	0	0	0	1	2	5
Hammond	—	—	—	—	—	—	—	—	—	—	—	—	—	—	—	—	0	0	0	0	0
Loring	—	—	—	—	—	—	—	—	—	—	—	—	—	—	—	—	0	1	0	1	2

[325]

APPENDIX IV

TABLE SHOWING THE NUMBER OF DISSENTING VOTES OF THE INDIVIDUAL JUDGES OF THE MASSACHUSETTS SUPREME JUDICIAL COURT DURING JUSTICE HOLMES' TENURE OF OFFICE

	1883	1884	1885	1886	1887	1888	1889	1890	1891	1892	1893	1894	1895	1896	1897	1898	1899	1900	1901	1902	Total
Morton	0	0	0	0	0	1	0	0	–	–	–	–	–	–	–	–	–	–	–	–	1
Field	1	0	0	0	0	0	0	1	1	2	3	2	1	3	1	1	0	–	–	–	16
Devens	0	0	0	0	0	1	1	2	0	–	–	–	–	–	–	–	–	–	–	–	4
Allen, W.	2	0	0	0	0	3	1	1	0	1	5	1	1	2	3	2	–	–	–	–	21
Allen, C.	0	0	0	1	0	2	0	1	2	2	–	1	1	2	–	–	–	–	–	–	21
Colburn, W.	0	0	0	0	–	–	–	–	–	–	–	–	–	–	–	–	–	–	–	–	0
Holmes	0	0	0	0	0	0	0	0	0	2	1	0	1	2	2	1	0	0	0	2	11
Gardner	0	0	0	0	0	–	–	–	–	–	–	–	–	–	–	–	–	–	–	–	0
Knowlton	–	–	–	–	0	1	0	0	1	5	5	1	2	3	2	1	0	1	0	0	22
Morton, J.	–	–	–	–	–	–	–	0	0	1	2	0	3	0	1	1	0	0	0	0	8
Lathrop	–	–	–	–	–	–	–	–	0	2	1	0	2	2	1	3	0	2	0	0	13
Barker	–	–	–	–	–	–	–	–	0	2	2	0	0	0	1	0	0	0	1	1	7
Hammond	–	–	–	–	–	–	–	–	–	–	–	–	–	–	–	0	0	0	1	2	3
Loring	–	–	–	–	–	–	–	–	–	–	–	–	–	–	–	–	0	0	0	1	1

[326]

APPENDIX V

CHRONOLOGICAL LIST OF CASES OF THE MASSACHUSETTS SUPREME JUDICIAL COURT IN WHICH JUSTICE HOLMES WROTE AN OPINION *

1883

Weber v. Couch, 134 Mass. 26
Langley v. Chapin, 134 Mass. 82
Byington v. Simpson, 134 Mass. 169
Commonwealth v. Fenno, 134 Mass. 217
Fisher v. Cushing, 134 Mass. 374
Stewart v. Griswold, 134 Mass. 391
Percy v. Bibber, 134 Mass. 404
Smith v. Moore, 134 Mass. 405
Williams v. Boston Water Power Co., 134 Mass. 406
Benjamin v. Dockham, 134 Mass. 418
Hemenway v. Hemenway, 134 Mass. 446
Guernsey v. Wilson, 134 Mass. 482
McCabe v. Cambridge, 134 Mass. 484
Murphy v. Manning, 134 Mass. 488
Jewett v. Brooks, 134 Mass. 505
Brown v. Eastern Slate Co. 134 Mass. 590
Hallgarten v. Oldham, 135 Mass. 1
Sloan v. Merrill, 135 Mass. 17
Brooks v. Boston and Maine Railroad, 135 Mass. 21
Oakes v. Manufacturers' Insurance Co., 135 Mass. 248
Davis v. German American Insurance Co., 135 Mass. 251
Chapin v. Chapin, 135 Mass. 393
Jones v. Ames, 135 Mass. 431
Brooke Iron Co. v. O'Brien, 135 Mass. 442
Batchelder v. Queen Insurance Co., 135 Mass. 449
Merrill v. Preston, 135 Mass. 451
Damon v. Bibber, 135 Mass. 458

---

* Dissenting Opinions are indicated in Italics.

Collins v. Sullivan, 135 Mass 461
Bates College v. Bates, 135 Mass. 487
Commonwealth v. Bacon, 135 Mass. 521
Commonwealth v. Goulding, 135 Mass. 552
Tyler v. Boyce, 135 Mass. 558
Eames v. Cushman, 135 Mass. 573
Brewster v. Warner, 136 Mass. 57
Case v. Baldwin, 136 Mass. 90
Foote v. Smith, 136 Mass. 92
Powers v. Guardian Insurance Co., 136 Mass. 108
Commonwealth v. Churchill, 136 Mass. 148

1884

Warfield v. Fisk, 136 Mass. 219
Goodnow v. Shattuck, 136 Mass. 223
Pratt v. Tuttle, 136 Mass. 233
Goddard v. Petersham, 136 Mass. 235
Cozzens v. Holt, 136 Mass. 237
Silva v. Wimpenney, 136 Mass. 253
Holcomb v. Weaver, 136 Mass. 265
Capron v. Anness, 136 Mass. 271
Nudd v. Powers, 136 Mass. 273
Ballou v. Billings, 136 Mass. 307
Wentworth v. Daly, 136 Mass. 423
Bassett v. Daniels, 136 Mass. 547
Fuller v. Somerville, 136 Mass. 556
Gertz v. Fitchburg Railroad, 137 Mass. 77
Decatur v. Walker, 137 Mass. 141
Storms v. Smith, 137 Mass. 201
McAvoy v. Wright, 137 Mass. 207
McMahon v. O'Connor, 137 Mass. 216
Damrell v. Hartt, 137 Mass. 218
Williams v. Churchill, 137 Mass. 243
Commonwealth v. Doherty, 137 Mass. 245
Commonwealth v. Wright, 137 Mass. 250
Brown v. New Bedford Institution for Savings, 137 Mass. 262
Commonwealth v. Scituate Savings Bank, 137 Mass. 301
Bacon v. Parker, 137 Mass. 309
Dexter v. Appleton, 137 Mass. 323
Gray v. Christian Society, 137 Mass. 329
Sears v. LeBetter, 137 Mass. 374
Gurney v. Waldron, 137 Mass. 376
Cowley v. Pulsifer, 137 Mass. 392
Bacon v. Abbott, 137 Mass. 397
Macaig's Case, 137 Mass. 467
Phillips v. Blatchford, 137 Mass. 510
Wheeler and Wilson Manufacturing Co. v. Burlingham, 137 Mass. 581

Purple v. Greenfield, 138 Mass. 1
New Salem v. Eagle Mill Co., 138 Mass. 8
Dietrich v. Northampton, 138 Mass. 14
Haydenville Savings Bank v. Parsons, 138 Mass. 53
Delano v. Trustees of Smith Charities, 138 Mass. 63
Ridley v. Knox, 138 Mass. 83
Mannville Co. v. Worcester, 138 Mass. 89
Miller's River National Bank v. Jefferson, 138 Mass. 111
Wood v. Cutter, 138 Mass. 149
Commonwealth v. Pierce, 138 Mass. 165

1885

Inhabitants of Granville v. Southampton, 138 Mass. 256
Inhabitants of Northborough v. County Commissioners, 138 Mass. 263
Woodcock v. Worcester, 138 Mass. 268
Manning v. Fitch, 138 Mass. 273
Worcester Gas Light Co. v. County Commissioners, 138 Mass. 289
City of Brockton v. Cross, 138 Mass. 297
West Bridgewater v. Wareham, 138 Mass. 305
Learoyd v. Godfrey, 138 Mass. 315
Tallman v. New Bedford Five Cents Savings Bank, 138 Mass. 330
Hurley v. Fall River Herald Publishing Co., 138 Mass. 334
Burns v. Lane, 138 Mass. 350
Osgood v. Kezar, 138 Mass. 357
Perkins v. Lawrence, 138 Mass. 361
Coombs v. Anderson, 138 Mass. 378
Kearns v. Cunniff, 138 Mass. 434
Baldwin v. Foster, 138 Mass. 449
Commonwealth v. Tabor, 138 Mass. 496
Commonwealth v. Patterson, 138 Mass. 498
Commonwealth v. Murray, 138 Mass. 508
Bigelow v. Norris, 139 Mass. 12
Boston v. Mount Washington, 139 Mass. 15
Hittinger v. Boston, 139 Mass. 17
Butler v. Stark, 139 Mass. 19
Low v. Welch, 139 Mass. 33
Thorne v. Brown, 139 Mass. 35
Cook v. Harrington, 139 Mass. 38
Daniels v. Lowell, 139 Mass. 56
Lynde v. Newark Insurance Co., 139 Mass. 57
Billings v. Fairbanks, 139 Mass. 66
Merriam v. Goss, 139 Mass. 77
Spurr v. Dean, 139 Mass. 84
Vinal v. Spofford, 139 Mass. 126
Burton v. Frye, 139 Mass. 131
Lowe v. Harwood, 139 Mass. 133
Allen v. Codman, 139 Mass. 136

Cook v. Merrifield, 139 Mass. 139
Williams v. Mercer, 139 Mass. 141
Paine v. Hollister, 139 Mass. 144
Mudge v. Parker, 139 Mass. 153
Para Rubber Shoe Co. v. Boston, 139 Mass. 155
Stone v. Houghton, 139 Mass. 175
Wright v. Wright, 139 Mass. 177
Commonwealth v. Perry, 139 Mass. 198
Hawks v. Locke, 139 Mass. 205
Dickinson v. Durfee, 139 Mass. 232
Merrill v. Eastern Railroad Co., 139 Mass. 238
Bartlett v. Raymond, 139 Mass. 275
Eastman v. Simpson, 139 Mass. 348
Whitehead and Atherton Machine Co. v. Ryder, 139 Mass. 366
White v. Duggan, 140 Mass. 18
Turnbull v. Pomeroy, 140 Mass. 117
Wright v. Dressel, 140 Mass. 147
Bassett v. Parsons, 140 Mass. 169
Smith v. Dickinson, 140 Mass. 171
Norcross v. James, 140 Mass. 188
Russell v. Tillotson, 140 Mass. 201
Richards v. Barlow, 140 Mass. 218
Grogan v. Worcester, 140 Mass. 227
Sawyer v. Orr, 140 Mass. 234
Hall v. Hall, 140 Mass. 267
Commonwealth v. Este, 140 Mass. 279
Dahill v. Booker, 140 Mass. 308
Attorney General v. Williams, 140 Mass 329, 335

1886

Phelon v. Granville, 140 Mass. 386
Worcester v. Northborough, 140 Mass. 397
Brigham v. Fayerweather, 140 Mass. 411
Carpenter v. Walker, 140 Mass. 416
Bigelow v. Sprague, 140 Mass. 425
Mount Hope Iron Co. v. Dearden, 140 Mass. 430
Commonwealth v. Parker, 140 Mass. 439
Commonwealth v. Barnes, 140 Mass. 447
Commonwealth v. Flaherty, 140 Mass. 454
Commonwealth v. Moinehan, 140 Mass. 463
Hubbard v. Taunton, 140 Mass. 467
Wilson v. Whitmore, 140 Mass. 469
Remington and Sons v. Samana Bay Co., 140 Mass. 494
Collins v. Collins, 140 Mass. 502
Boston and Maine Railroad v. Ordway, 140 Mass. 510
Gove v. Learoyd, 140 Mass. 524
New England Trust Co. v. Eaton, 140 Mass. 532, 544

Rodliff v. Dallinger, 141 Mass. 1
Flagg v. Mason, 141 Mass. 64
Jacobs v. Denison, 141 Mass. 117
Sturtevant v. Wallack, 141 Mass. 119
Frazer v. Bigelow Carpet Co., 141 Mass. 126
Cassidy v. Old Colony Railroad, 141 Mass. 174
Livermore v. Batchelder, 141 Mass. 179
Cowley v. McLaughlin, 141 Mass. 181
Foster v. Leland, 141 Mass. 187
Bragg v. Danielson, 141 Mass. 195
Clark v. Watson, 141 Mass. 248
Dove v. Johnson, 141 Mass. 287
Underwood v. Boston Five Cents Savings Bank, 141 Mass. 305
Commonwealth v. McCarty, 141 Mass. 420
Commonwealth v. Devlin, 141 Mass. 423
Blackinton v. Blackinton, 141 Mass. 432
Western Union Telegraph Co. v. Caldwell, 141 Mass. 489
W_____ v. W_____, 141 Mass. 495
Kennebec Framing Co. v. Pickering, 142 Mass. 80
Chapin v. Freeland, 142 Mass. 383
Norton v. Palmer, 142 Mass. 433
Peck v. Clark, 142 Mass. 436
Commonwealth v. Briant, 142 Mass. 463
Commonwealth v. Stevenson, 142 Mass. 466
Commonwealth v. Mandeville, 142 Mass. 469
Nott v. Sampson Manufacturing Company, 142 Mass. 479
Fortin v. Easthampton, 142 Mass. 486
O'Donnell v. Smith, 142 Mass. 505
Wells v. White, 142 Mass. 518
Stone v. Jenks, 142 Mass. 519
Northborough v. Wood, 142 Mass. 551
Beckwith v. Cheshire Railroad, 143 Mass. 68
Walpole v. Quirk, 143 Mass. 72
Commonwealth v. Lee, 143 Mass. 100

1887

Townsend v. Webster Five Cents Savings Bank, 143 Mass. 147
Morris v. Brightman, 143 Mass. 149
Eames v. Snell, 143 Mass. 165
Gibbs v. Taylor, 143 Mass. 187
New Bedford Railway v. Acushnet Railway, 143 Mass. 200
Stiff v. Keith, 143 Mass. 224
Marvel v. Babbitt, 143 Mass. 226
Krulevitz v. Eastern Railroad, 143 Mass. 228
Pierce v. Gould, 143 Mass. 234
Dole v. Keyes, 143 Mass. 237
Keith v. Keith, 143 Mass. 262

Weston v. Weston, 143 Mass. 274
Flynn v. Bourneuf, 143 Mass. 277
Batcheller v. Commercial Union Assurance Co., 143 Mass. 495
Abbott v. Cottage City, 143 Mass. 521
Hogan v. Barry, 143 Mass. 538
Ford v. Ford, 143 Mass. 577
Page v. O'Toole, 144 Mass. 303
Brown v. Ladd, 144 Mass. 310
Foley v. Haverhill, 144 Mass. 352
Hyde v. Mechanical Refrigerating Co., 144 Mass. 432
Packard v. Ryder, 144 Mass. 440
Delory v. Canny, 144 Mass. 445
Metcalf v. Williams, 144 Mass 452
Kenison v. Arlington, 144 Mass. 456
Doherty v. Hill, 144 Mass. 465
Sawyer v. Boston, 144 Mass. 470
Kent v. Todd, 144 Mass. 478
Welsh v. Woodbury, 144 Mass. 542
Staigg v. Atkinson, 144 Mass. 564
Reeve v. Dennett, 145 Mass. 23
Shepard v. Richardson, 145 Mass. 32
Bradford v. Brinley, 145 Mass. 81
Commonwealth v. Clifford, 145 Mass. 97
Fairbanks v. Snow, 145 Mass. 153
Brackenridge v. Fitchburg, 145 Mass. 160
Marshall v. Boston and Albany Railroad, 145 Mass. 164
Commonwealth v. Buckley, 145 Mass. 181
Commonwealth v. Clark, 145 Mass. 250
Bath v. Metcalf, 145 Mass. 274
O'Connell v. O'Leary, 145 Mass. 311
Langley v. Dauray, 145 Mass. 325
Wilson v. Winslow, 145 Mass. 339

1888

Doyle v. Boston and Albany Railroad, 145 Mass. 386
Commonwealth v. White, 145 Mass. 392
Commonwealth v. Locke, 145 Mass. 401
Commonwealth v. Carroll, 145 Mass. 403
Commonwealth v. McNeff, 145 Mass. 406
Ring v. Phoenix Assurance Co., 145 Mass. 426
Abbott v. New York and New England Railway, 145 Mass. 450
O'Donnell v. Clinton, 145 Mass. 461
Counsell v. Hall, 145 Mass. 468
Pickman v. Peabody, 145 Mass. 480
Eddy v. Adams, 145 Mass. 489
Woodbury v. Marblehead Water Company, 145 Mass. 509
Fogg v. Price, 145 Mass. 513

Brooks v. Brooks, 145 Mass. 574
Clifford v. Atlantic Cotton Mills, 146 Mass. 47
Moors v. Wyman, 146 Mass. 60
Newburyport v. Creedon, 146 Mass. 134
Commonwealth v. Sullivan, 146 Mass. 142
Donnelly v. Boston Catholic Cemetery, 146 Mass. 163
Rosenberg v. Doe, 146 Mass. 191
Brock v. Old Colony Railroad Co., 146 Mass. 194
Hunt v. Brown, 146 Mass. 253
Constantinides v. Walsh, 146 Mass. 281
Hoar v. Abbott, 146 Mass. 290
Pope v. Farnsworth, 146 Mass. 339
Whall v. Converse, 146 Mass. 345
Sturgis v. Paine, 146 Mass. 354
Clark v. Holbrook, 146 Mass. 366
Bridge v. Bridge, 146 Mass. 373
Boardman v. Boston Marine Insurance Co., 146 Mass. 442
Merrill v. Peaslee, 146 Mass. 460, 463
Heard v. Sturgis, 146 Mass. 545
Commonwealth v. Funai, 146 Mass. 570
Goreley v. Butler, 147 Mass. 8
Lombard v. Willis, 147 Mass. 13
Cummings v. Hodgdon, 147 Mass. 21
Commonwealth v. Purdy, 147 Mass. 29
Ayer v. R. W. Bell Manufacturing Co., 147 Mass. 46
Bradford v. Cunard Steamship Co., 147 Mass. 55
Brown v. Cunard Steamship Co., 147 Mass. 58
Sewall and Co. v. Boston Water Power Co., 147 Mass. 61
Metcalf v. Cunard Steamship Co., 147 Mass. 66
Peaslee v. Peaslee, 147 Mass. 171
Stone v. Wainwright, 147 Mass. 201
Mansfield v. Hodgdon, 147 Mass. 304
Dexter v. Inches, 147 Mass. 324
Minot v. Baker, 147 Mass. 348
Batchelder, Petitioner, 147 Mass. 465
Cutter v. Hamlen, 147 Mass. 471
Webster v. Ellsworth, 147 Mass. 602
Commonwealth v. McParland, 148 Mass. 127

1889

Conlon's Case, 148 Mass. 168
Commonwealth v. Bean, 148 Mass. 172
Savage v. Blanchard, 148 Mass. 348
Rideout v. Knox, 148 Mass. 368
Quincy v. Boston, 148 Mass. 389
Bartlett v. Stanchfield, 148 Mass. 394
Warner v. Bowdoin Square Baptist Society, 148 Mass. 400

Smith v. Morse, 148 Mass. 407
Hurley v. Hurley, 148 Mass. 444
Commonwealth v. Gavin, 148 Mass. 449
Ayer v. Kilner, 148 Mass. 468
Commonwealth v. Keenan, 148 Mass. 470
Littlejohn v. Fitchburg Railroad, 148 Mass. 478
Central National Bank v. Frye, 148 Mass. 498
Deming v. Darling, 148 Mass. 504
Richardson v. Boston, 148 Mass. 508
Plympton v. Dunn, 148 Mass. 523
Commonwealth v. Donahue, 148 Mass. 529
Rosenberg v. Doe, 148 Mass. 561
Emery v. Seavey, 148 Mass. 566
Starratt v. Mullen, 148 Mass. 570
Lincoln v. Boston, 148 Mass. 578
Attorney General v. Ayer, 148 Mass. 584
Stevenson v. Hano, 148 Mass. 616
Suffolk Savings Bank, Petitioner, 149 Mass. 1
Fearing v. Jones, 149 Mass. 12
Ogden v. Pattee, 149 Mass. 82
Atwood v. Wheeler, 149 Mass. 96
Frost v. Sumner, 149 Mass. 98
Middlesex Company v. Lane, 149 Mass. 101
Middlesex Company v. McCue, 149 Mass. 103
Downs v. Bowdoin Square Baptist Society, 149 Mass. 135
Cuniff v. Parker, 149 Mass. 152
Atwood v. Dumas, 149 Mass. 167
Goldthwait v. Day, 149 Mass. 185
Crossan v. New York and New Haven Railroad, 149 Mass. 196
Trecy v. Jefts, 149 Mass. 211
John Hancock Mutual Life Ins. Co. v. Worcester, etc., Railroad, 149 Mass. 214
Gilfillan v. Mawhinney, 149 Mass. 264
Reardon v. Thompson, 149 Mass. 267
Hawkins v. Graham, 149 Mass. 284
Woodman v. Metropolitan Railroad, 149 Mass. 335
May v. Skinner, 149 Mass. 375
New England Dredging Co. v. Rockport Granite Co. 149 Mass. 381
Eddy v. Coffin, 149 Mass. 463
Stratton v. Physio-Medical College, 149 Mass. 505
Middlesex Company v. Lowell, 149 Mass. 509
Commonwealth v. Freelove, 150 Mass. 66
Verran v. Baird, 150 Mass. 141
Ingram v. Cowles, 150 Mass. 155
Ryalls v. Mechanics' Mills, 150 Mass. 190
Mechanics' Savings Bank v. Waite, 150 Mass. 234
Slater v. Lamb, 150 Mass. 239

Johnson v. Knapp, 150 Mass. 267
Commonwealth v. McCormick, 150 Mass. 270
Commonwealth v. Sullivan, 150 Mass. 315

1890

Parsons, Petitioner, 150 Mass. 343
Mellor v. Merchants' Manufacturing Co., 150 Mass. 362
O'Rourke v. Beard, 151 Mass. 9
Clark v. Sawyer, 151 Mass. 64
Paige v. Barrett, 151 Mass. 67
Norwich and Worcester Railroad v. County Commissioners, 151 Mass. 69
Rawson v. Plaisted, 151 Mass. 71
Corcoran v. Snow Cattle Co., 151 Mass. 74
Harvard Unitarian Society v. Tufts, 151 Mass. 76
Pearson v. Allen, 151 Mass. 79
O'Connell v. O'Leary, 151 Mass. 83
Coullard v. Tecumseh Mills, 151 Mass. 85
Coughlin v. Boston Tow-Boat Co., 151 Mass. 92
Jefferds v. Alvard, 151 Mass. 94
Beard v. Boston, 151 Mass. 96
Barry v. Capen, 151 Mass. 99
Boyle v. New York and New England Railroad, 151 Mass. 102
Holden v. Metropolitan National Bank, 151 Mass. 112
Bates v. Westborough, 151 Mass. 174
Chadwick v. Covell, 151 Mass. 190
Collins v. Waltham, 151 Mass. 196
Gannon v. Ruffin, 151 Mass. 204
Donnelly v. Boston and Maine Railroad, 151 Mass. 210
Parkman v. Suffolk Savings Bank, 151 Mass. 218
Schwarz v. Boston, 151 Mass. 226
Boston and Maine Railroad v. Trafton, 151 Mass. 229
Day v. Worcester Railroad, 151 Mass. 302
Skillings v. Massachusetts Benefit Association, 151 Mass. 321
Cox v. Maxwell, 151 Mass. 336
Clark v. Merchants and Miners Transportation Co., 151 Mass. 352
Elmer v. Fessenden, 151 Mass. 359
Holbrook v. Payne, 151 Mass. 383
Vanuxem v. Burr, 151 Mass. 386
Baker v. Tompson, 151 Mass. 390
Commonwealth v. Gove, 151 Mass. 392
Commonwealth v. Oakes, 151 Mass. 394
Ashcroft v. Simmons, 151 Mass. 497
Harmon v. Osgood, 151 Mass. 501
Francis v. Rosa, 151 Mass. 532
Windram v. French, 151 Mass. 547
American Order Scottish Clans v. Merrill, 151 Mass. 558
Quincy v. Kennard, 151 Mass. 563

Ladd v. Boston, 151 Mass. 585
Phoenix National Bank v. Batcheller, 151 Mass. 589
Jepson v. Killian, 151 Mass. 593
Davis v. Jackson, 152 Mass. 58
Whiteside v. Brawley, 152 Mass. 133
May v. Skinner, 152 Mass. 328
Chase's Elevator Co. v. Boston Tow-Boat Co., 152 Mass. 428
Commonwealth v. Cleary, 152 Mass. 491
Commonwealth v. Mahoney, 152 Mass. 493
Desmond v. Fisher, 152 Mass. 521

1891

Miller v. Horton, 152 Mass. 540
Commonwealth v. Carney, 152 Mass. 566
Chase v. Thompson, 153 Mass. 14
Chase v. Phillips, 153 Mass. 17
Slater v. Cobb, 153 Mass. 22
Osgood v. Osgood, 153 Mass. 38
Johanson v. Boston and Maine Railroad, 153 Mass. 57
Roberts v. French, 153 Mass. 60
Bradbury v. Boston Canoe Club, 153 Mass. 77
June v. Boston and Albany Railroad, 153 Mass. 79
Lyon v. Royal Society of Good Fellows, 153 Mass. 83
Pierce v. Cunard Steamship Co., 153 Mass. 87
Tasker v. Stanley, 153 Mass. 148
Commonwealth v. Gay, 153 Mass. 211
Smith v. Bergengren, 153 Mass. 236
Peabody v. Knapp, 153 Mass. 242
Commonwealth v. Lannan, 153 Mass. 287
Odd Fellows Hall Assoc. v. McAllister, 153 Mass. 292
Coates v. Boston and Maine Railroad, 153 Mass. 297
Billings v. Marsh, 153 Mass. 311
Scott v. Donovan, 153 Mass. 378
BiSpool Sewing Machine Co. v. Acme Co., 153 Mass. 405
Calnan v. Stern, 153 Mass. 413
Killam v. Peirce, 153 Mass. 502
Cunningham v. Boston and Albany Railroad, 153 Mass. 506
Hayes v. Hyde Park, 153 Mass. 514
Troeder v. Hyams, 153 Mass. 536
Woods v. Doherty, 153 Mass. 558
Bullard v. Shirley, 153 Mass. 559
Goode v. Riley, 153 Mass. 585
Wellington v. Swasey, 154 Mass. 27
May v. Whittier Machine Co., 154 Mass. 29
McDonald v. Faulkner, 154 Mass. 34
Proctor v. Clark, 154 Mass. 45
Thomas v. Beals, 154 Mass. 51

Powers v. Boston, 154 Mass. 60
Tyndale v. Randall, 154 Mass. 103
Commonwealth v. Clancy, 154 Mass. 128
Commonwealth v. Watson, 154 Mass. 135
Lilienthal v. Suffolk Brewing Co., 154 Mass. 185
Merrigan v. Boston and Albany Railroad Co., 154 Mass. 189
Keen v. Sheehan, 154 Mass. 208
Burt v. Advertiser Newspaper Co., 154 Mass. 238
Bainard v. Newton, 154 Mass. 255
Macdonald v. Morrill, 154 Mass. 270
Adams v. Adams, 154 Mass. 290
Watuppa Reservoir Co. v. Fall River, 154 Mass. 305
Stratton v. Hernon, 154 Mass. 310
Dempsey v. Chambers, 154 Mass. 330
Hallowell v. Blackstone National Bank, 154 Mass. 359
Balch v. Pickering, 154 Mass. 363
Comstock v. Son, 154 Mass. 389
Debbins v. Old Colony Railroad, 154 Mass. 402
Commonwealth v. Ryan, 154 Mass. 422
Easthampton v. County Commissioners, 154 Mass. 424
Elmer v. Fessenden, 154 Mass. 427
Krell v. Codman, 154 Mass. 454
Bryant v. Peck and Whipple Co., 154 Mass. 460
Pomeroy v. Westfield, 154 Mass. 462
Dillon v. Connecticut River Railroad, 154 Mass. 478
Mason v. Pomeroy, 154 Mass. 481
Commonwealth v. Goodnow, 154 Mass. 487
Dana v. Dana, 154 Mass. 491
Howe v. Dickinson, 154 Mass. 494
Simonds v. Patridge, 154 Mass. 500
Wesson v. Washburn Car Wheel Co., 154 Mass. 514
Commonwealth v. Hyland, 155 Mass. 7
Commonwealth v. Marchand, 155 Mass. 8
Murchie v. Cornell, 155 Mass. 60
Buckley v. New Bedford, 155 Mass. 64
Commonwealth v. Perry, 155 Mass. 117, 123
Attorney General v. Algonquin Club, 155 Mass. 128

1892

Commonwealth v. Lannan, 155 Mass. 168
Nichols v. Ashton, 155 Mass. 205
McAuliffe v. New Bedford, 155 Mass. 216
Morse v. Sherman, 155 Mass. 222
Walker v. Winstanley, 155 Mass. 301
National Bank of Commerce v. New Bedford, 155 Mass. 313
Googins v. Boston and Albany Railroad, 155 Mass. 505
Standard Button Fastening Co. v. Harney, 155 Mass. 507

Bromley v. Mitchell, 155 Mass. 509
Commonwealth v. Ryan, 155 Mass. 523
Commonwealth v. Parks, 155 Mass. 531
Opinion of the Justices, 155 Mass. 598, 607 (separate opinion)
Brown v. Bradlee, 156 Mass. 28
Babbidge v. Vittum, 156 Mass. 38
Greeley v. Page, 156 Mass. 47
Copeland v. Sturtevant, 156 Mass. 114
Robinson v. Simmons, 156 Mass. 123
Chipman v. Manufacturers' National Bank, 156 Mass. 147
Atwood v. West Roxbury Co-operative Bank, 156 Mass. 166
Snow v. Alley, 156 Mass. 193
Billings v. Mann, 156 Mass. 203
Graves v. Johnson, 156 Mass. 211
Smith v. Edwards, 156 Mass. 221
Whitney v. Weed, 156 Mass. 224
Penney v. Hall, 156 Mass. 225
Commonwealth v. Dill, 156 Mass. 226
Commonwealth v. McNeese, 156 Mass. 231
Kinney v. Maher, 156 Mass. 252
Smith v. Spitz, 156 Mass. 319
Nonantum Worsted Co. v. North Adams Manufacturing Co., 156 Mass. 331
Perry v. Smith, 156 Mass. 340
Wellesley v. Washburn, 156 Mass. 359
Kingman, Petitioner, 156 Mass. 361
Powers v. Mann, 156 Mass. 375
Lord v. Advent Christian Society, 156 Mass. 387
Bourget v. Cambridge, 156 Mass. 391
Fogg v. Supreme Lodge of the Golden Lion, 156 Mass. 431
Commonwealth v. Ham, 156 Mass. 485
Brown v. Cotton and Woolen Manufacturers' Ins. Co., 156 Mass. 587
Kimball v. St. Louis and San Francisco Railway, 157 Mass. 7
Commonwealth v. Fletcher, 157 Mass. 14
Stanwood v. Malden, 157 Mass. 17
Ayer v. Philadelphia and Boston Face Brick Co., 157 Mass. 57
Attorney General v. Walworth Light and Power Co., 157 Mass. 86
Earle v. Angell, 157 Mass. 294
Alton v. First National Bank of Webster, 157 Mass. 341
Gould v. Camp, 157 Mass. 358
Young v. Douglas, 157 Mass. 383
Higgins v. Drennan, 157 Mass. 384
England v. Adams, 157 Mass. 449
Commonwealth v. Healey, 157 Mass. 455

1893

Commonwealth v. Poisson, 157 Mass. 510
Atlantic Works v. Tug Glide, 157 Mass. 525

Isham v. Burgett, 157 Mass. 546
Copeland v. Draper, 157 Mass. 558
Denning v. Gould, 157 Mass. 563
Connolly v. New York and New Haven Railroad, 158 Mass. 8
Liddle v. Old Lowell National Bank, 158 Mass. 15
Commonwealth v. Lowery, 158 Mass. 18
Abercrombie v. Spalding, 158 Mass. 32
Ela v. Ela, 158 Mass. 54
Noera v. Williams Manufacturing Co., 158 Mass. 110
Mead v. Phenix Insurance Co., 158 Mass. 124
Commonwealth v. Colligan, 158 Mass. 163
Commonwealth v. Bingham, 158 Mass. 169
Shepard v. Boston and Maine Railroad, 158 Mass. 174
Hobbs v. Massasoit Whip Co. 158 Mass. 194
Irwin v. Alley, 158 Mass. 249
Currier v. Hallowell, 158 Mass 254
Bill v. Boynton, 158 Mass. 274
Pelton v. Baker, 158 Mass. 349
Robinson v. Bird, 157 Mass. 357
Soper v. Manning, 158 Mass. 381
Lynch v. Union Institution for Savings, 158 Mass. 394
Abbott v. Hills, 158 Mass. 396
Sears v. Chapman, 158 Mass. 400
Bullard v. Moor, 158 Mass. 418
Vinton v. Greene, 158 Mass. 426
Taft v. Commonwealth, 158 Mass. 526
Boston Furnace Co. v. Dimock, 158 Mass. 552
Commonwealth v. Ellis, 158 Mass. 555
Commonwealth v. Gordon, 159 Mass. 8
Commonwealth v. Thompson, 159 Mass. 56
Atlantic Works v. Tug Glide and Owners, 159 Mass. 60
Ayer v. Philadelphia and Boston Face Brick Co., 159 Mass. 84
Mellen v. Wilson Sons Co., 159 Mass. 88
Harvard College v. Weld, 159 Mass. 114
Fletcher v. Stedman, 159 Mass. 124
Boston Ferrule Co. v. Hills, 159 Mass. 147
Moors v. Washburn, 159 Mass. 172
Dudley v. Sanborn, 159 Mass. 185
Clement v. Bullens, 159 Mass. 193
Leighton v. Morrill, 159 Mass. 271
Hanson v. Globe Newspaper, 159 Mass. 293, 299
Finnegan v. Fall River Gas Works Co., 159 Mass. 311
Lincoln v. Boston Marine Ins. Co., 159 Mass. 337
Keenan v. Edison Electric Illuminating Co., 159 Mass. 379
Bourget v. Cambridge, 159 Mass. 388
Swampscott Machine Co. v. Rice, 159 Mass. 404
Johnson v. Whiton, 159 Mass. 424

Hayes v. Jackson, 159 Mass. 451
Hickey v. Waltham, 159 Mass. 460
Greenfield v. Buckland, 159 Mass. 491
Davis v. New York, New Haven and Hartford Railroad, 159 Mass. 532
Lynch v. Boston and Albany Railroad, 159 Mass. 536
Knight v. Boston, 159 Mass. 551
Drummond v. Crane, 159 Mass. 577
Spaulding v. Flynt Granite Co., 159 Mass. 587
Taft v. Shaw, 159 Mass. 592
Commonwealth v. Shea, 160 Mass. 6
Saunders v. Bennett, 160 Mass. 48
Flynn v. Campbell, 160 Mass. 128
Veginan v. Morse, 160 Mass. 143
Carroll v. Western Union Telegraph Co., 160 Mass. 152
Lawton v. Fitchburg Savings Bank, 160 Mass. 154
Loftus v. North Adams, 160 Mass. 161
Roger Williams National Bank v. Hall, 160 Mass. 171
Commonwealth v. Lyons, 160 Mass. 174
Bourke v. Callanan, 160 Mass. 195
Chenery v. Fitchburg Railroad, 160 Mass. 211
Jackson v. Carson, 160 Mass. 215
Fitzsimmons v. Taunton, 160 Mass. 223
Engel v. New York, Providence and Boston Railroad, 160 Mass. 260

1894

Middlefield v. Church Mills Knitting Co., 160 Mass. 267
Commonwealth v. Goulet, 160 Mass. 276
Commonwealth v. Abbott, 160 Mass. 282
Blaney v. Salem, 160 Mass. 303
Lawrence v. Wilson, 160 Mass. 304
Commonwealth v. Melville, 160 Mass. 307
Bicknell v. Mellett, 160 Mass. 328
Riley v. Lissner, 160 Mass. 330
Commonwealth v. Swain, 160 Mass. 354
Freeman Manufacturing Co. v. National Bank, 160 Mass. 398
City of Quincy v. Attorney General, 160 Mass. 431
Hunting v. Damon, 160 Mass. 441
Slater v. Manchester, 160 Mass. 471
Keith v. Molineux, 160 Mass. 499
Commonwealth v. Gavin, 160 Mass. 523
Commonwealth v. McDonald, 160 Mass. 528
Dorr v. Clapp, 160 Mass. 538
Allen v. Smith Iron Co., 160 Mass. 557
Hyde v. Moxie Nerve Food Co., 160 Mass. 559
Folsom v. Ballou Banking Co., 160 Mass. 561
Connolly v. Eldredge, 160 Mass. 566
Walsh v. New York and New England Railroad, 160 Mass. 571

Opinions of the Justices, 160 Mass. 593 (Separate Opinion)
Cotton v. Boston, 161 Mass. 8.
Watson v. Wyman, 161 Mass. 96
Farrell v. Boston, 161 Mass. 106
Heavor v. Page, 161 Mass. 109
Lane v. Commonwealth, 161 Mass. 120
Sullivan v. Fitchburg Railroad, 161 Mass. 125
Hunnewell v. Bangs, 161 Mass. 132
Titus v. Boston, 161 Mass. 209
Rockport Water Co. v. Rockport, 161 Mass. 279
Sampson v. Boston, 161 Mass. 288
Dresser v. Cutter, 161 Mass. 301
Monaghan v. Putney, 161 Mass. 338
Thain v. Old Colony Railroad, 161 Mass. 353
Weber v. Bryant, 161 Mass. 400
McKim v. Glover, 161 Mass. 418
Kalleck v. Deering, 161 Mass. 469
Miller v. Hyde, 161 Mass. 472, 478
Bertie v. Flagg, 161 Mass. 504
Cahill v. Hall, 161 Mass. 512
Sawyer v. Freeman, 161 Mass. 543
Shaughnessey v. Leary, 162 Mass. 108
Commonwealth v. Skatt, 162 Mass. 219
Andrews v. Moen, 162 Mass. 294

1895

Barker v. Tibbetts, 162 Mass. 468
Cloutier v. Grafton and Upton Railroad, 162 Mass. 471
Commonwealth v. Davis, 162 Mass. 510
Commonwealth v. Loewe, 162 Mass. 518
Commonwealth v. Russell, 162 Mass. 520
Sullivan v. Lowell and Dracut Railway, 162 Mass. 536
Gray v. Parke, 162 Mass. 582
Cheney v. Cheney, 162 Mass. 591
Bowen v. Phinney, 162 Mass. 593
Moore v. Cushing, 162 Mass. 594
Usher v. Raymond Skate Co., 163 Mass. 1
Borden v. Mercer, 163 Mass. 7
Standard Button Fastening Co. v. Breed, 163 Mass. 10
Commonwealth v. Intoxicating Liquors, 163 Mass. 42
Connery v. Manning, 163 Mass. 44
Stratton v. Seaverns, 163 Mass. 73
Cunningham v. Merrimac Paper Co., 163 Mass. 89
Livermore v. Fitchburg Railroad, 163 Mass. 132
Holmes v. Jordan, 163 Mass. 147
Lyons v. Boston Towage Co., 163 Mass. 158
Tangney v. Sullivan, 163 Mass. 166

[341]

Commonwealth v. Kelley, 163 Mass. 169
Hamilton v. West End Street Railway, 163 Mass. 199.
Phillips v. Haddock, 163 Mass. 201
Robinson v. Way, 163 Mass. 212
Steel Edge Stamping and Retinning Co. v. Manchester Savings Bank, 163 Mass. 252
Lee v. Welch, 163 Mass. 312
Newton v. Perry, 163 Mass. 319
O'Brien v. Bailey, 163 Mass. 325
Emery v. Burbank, 163 Mass. 326
McCann v. Waltham, 163 Mass. 344
Palmer v. Jordan, 163 Mass. 350
Carr v. West End Street Railway, 163 Mass. 360
Atwell v. Jenkins, 163 Mass. 362
Commonwealth v. Welch, 163 Mass. 372
Order of the Golden Cross v. Merrick, 163 Mass. 374
Cloutman v. Concord, 163 Mass. 444
Martin v. Bowker, 163 Mass. 461
Jones v. Parker, 163 Mass. 564
Smith v. New York and New England Railroad, 163 Mass. 569
Nash v. Minnesota Title Insurance and Trust Co., 163 Mass. 574, 586
Lincoln v. Commonwealth, 164 Mass. 1
Commonwealth v. Quinn, 164 Mass. 11
Smith v. Butler, 164 Mass. 37
Graham v. Badger, 164 Mass. 42
Manning v. Reynolds, 164 Mass. 150
Hall v. Justices of the Municipal Court, 164 Mass. 155
Kenerson v. Colgan, 164 Mass. 166
Keene v. New England Accident Association, 164 Mass. 170
Roberts v. Cambridge, 164 Mass. 176
Nashua and Lowell Railroad Corp. v. Boston Railroad, 164 Mass. 222, 226
Chelsea Dye House Co. v. Commonwealth, 164 Mass. 350
Rand v. Boston, 164 Mass. 354
Lincoln v. Commonwealth, 164 Mass. 368
White v. Solomon, 164 Mass. 516
Commonwealth v. Gorman, 164 Mass. 549
Commonwealth v. Porter, 164 Mass. 576
Commonwealth v. Brewer, 164 Mass. 577
Smith v. Brown, 164 Mass. 584

1896

Tracy v. Wetherell, 165 Mass. 113
Flitner v. Butler, 165 Mass. 119
Almy v. Orne, 165 Mass. 126
Lee v. Gorham, 165 Mass. 130

Grover v. Smith, 165 Mass. 132
Commonwealth v. Meskill, 165 Mass. 144
Commonwealth v. Emerson, 165 Mass. 146
Commonwealth v. Bishop, 165 Mass. 148
Commonwealth v. Sullivan, 165 Mass. 183
Hollingsworth and Vose Co. v. Foxborough, 165 Mass. 186
Walsh v. Packard, 165 Mass. 189
Forest River Lead Co. v. Salem, 165 Mass. 193
Way v. Ryther, 165 Mass. 226
Dewing v. Dewing, 165 Mass. 230
Oxford v. Leathe, 165 Mass. 254
Oak Island Hotel v. Oak Island Grove Co., 165 Mass. 260
Margesson v. Massachusetts Benefit Association, 165 Mass. 262
Rose v. Fall River Five Cents Savings Bank, 165 Mass. 273
Smith v. Abington Savings Bank, 165 Mass. 285
Townsend v. Tyndale, 165 Mass. 293
Gutlon v. Marcus, 165 Mass. 335
Silvestri v. Missocchi, 165 Mass. 337
Driscoll v. Scanlon, 165 Mass. 348
Order of the Golden Cross v. Merrick, 165 Mass. 421
Commonwealth v. Rubin, 165 Mass. 453
Laplante v. Warren Cotton Mills, 165 Mass. 487
Bonnemort v. Gill, 165 Mass. 493
Hughes v. Gross, 166 Mass. 61
Parry v. Libbey, 166 Mass. 112
Emerson v. Somerville, 166 Mass. 115
Garfield and Proctor Coal Co. v. Fitchburg Railroad, 166 Mass. 119
Bennett v. Justices of Municipal Court, 166 Mass. 126
Van Ingen v. Justice of Municipal Court, 166 Mass. 128
McLauthlin v. Smith, 166 Mass. 131
Aldrich v. Adams, 166 Mass. 141
Palmer v. Evangelical Baptist Benevolent Society, 166 Mass. 143
Latham v. Aldrich, 166 Mass. 156
Brock v. Dore, 166 Mass. 161
Stevenson v. Dana, 166 Mass. 163
Crocker v. Cotting, 166 Mass. 183
Manning v. West End Street Railway, 166 Mass. 230
Corey v. Eastman, 166 Mass. 279
Mundo v. Shepard, 166 Mass. 323
Sweet v. Kimball, 166 Mass. 332
Commonwealth v. Smith, 166 Mass. 370
Sawyer v. Seaver, 166 Mass. 447
Williams v. United Reserve Fund Associates, 166 Mass. 450
Chase v. Henry, 166 Mass. 577, 581
Stalker, Petitioner, 167 Mass. 11
Commonwealth v. Fleckner, 167 Mass. 13
Allen v. Massachusetts Mutual Accident Association, 167 Mass. 18

McCann v. Kennedy, 167 Mass. 23
Bugbee v. Davis, 167 Mass. 33
Clare v. New York and New England Railroad Co., 167 Mass. 39
White v. Worcester Street Railway, 167 Mass. 43
Richardson v. White, 167 Mass. 58
Flaherty v. Powers, 167 Mass. 61
McKee v. Tourtellotte, 167 Mass. 69
Moore v. Edwards, 167 Mass. 74
Vegelahn v. Guntner, 167 Mass. 92, 104
Miller v. Wilkinson, 167 Mass. 136
Commonwealth v. Brown, 167 Mass. 144
Donaghy v. Macy, 167 Mass. 178

1897

Polson v. Stewart, 167 Mass. 211
Russia Cement Co. v. Le Page Co., 167 Mass. 222
Young v. Miller, 167 Mass. 224
Hogarth v. Pocasset Manufacturing Co., 167 Mass. 225
Otis v. Otis, 167 Mass. 245
Quincy v. Quincy, 167 Mass. 537
Murdock v. New York, 167 Mass. 549
Worcester v. County Commissioners, 167 Mass. 565
Durkin v. Langley, 167 Mass. 577
Whittaker v. Bent, 167 Mass. 588
Kenneson v. West End Street Railway Co., 168 Mass. 1
Horne v. Niver, 168 Mass. 4
Webster v. Melrose, 168 Mass. 5
Holbrook v. Aldrich, 168 Mass. 15
Burns v. Stuart, 168 Mass. 19
Braithwaite v. Hall, 168 Mass. 38
Willey v. Boston Electric Light Co., 168 Mass. 40
Municipal Signal Co. v. Holyoke, 168 Mass. 44
Robbins v. Atkins, 168 Mass. 45
Dixon v. National Life Ins. Co., 168 Mass. 48
Marcus v. Collamore, 168 Mass. 56
Demelman v. Hunt, 168 Mass. 102
Ford v. Davis, 168 Mass. 116
Swasey v. Emerson, 168 Mass. 118
Commonwealth v. Hunton, 168 Mass. 130
Wald v. Arnold, 168 Mass. 134
Gordon v. Albert, 168 Mass. 150
New England Awl Co. v. Marlborough Awl Co., 168 Mass. 154
Brauer v. Shaw, 168 Mass. 198
Smith v. Boston and Maine Railroad Relief Association, 168 Mass. 213
Ryan v. North End Savings Bank, 168 Mass. 215
Kanz v. Page, 168 Mass. 217
Luddington v. Goodnow, 168 Mass. 223

Ruffin, Petitioner, 168 Mass. 232
Mead v. Bowker, 168 Mass. 234
Hughes v. Malden and Melrose Gas Light Co., 168 Mass. 395.
Howe v. Berry, 168 Mass. 418
Paine v. Silva, 168 Mass. 432
Innes v. Boston, 168 Mass. 433
Bell v. New York, New Haven, and Hartford Railroad Co., 168 Mass. 443
Gilman v. Boston and Maine Railroad, 168 Mass. 454
Robinson v. Hodgkins, 168 Mass. 465
Commonwealth v. Abbott, 168 Mass. 471
Abbott v. Downs, 168 Mass. 481
Boston Marine Ins. Co. v. Proctor, 168 Mass. 498
Newburyport Water Co. v. Newburyport, 168 Mass. 541
Dobbins v. West End Street Railway, 168 Mass. 556
Andrews v. Keith, 168 Mass. 558
Whitcomb v. Dickinson, 169 Mass. 16
Attorney General v. Donahue, 169 Mass. 18
Wells v. Putnam, 169 Mass. 226
Lawrence v. Hull, 169 Mass. 250
Ryan v. New York, New Haven and Hartford Railroad, 169 Mass. 267
Tremblay v. Mapes-Reeve Construction Co., 169 Mass. 284
Studley v. Ballard, 169 Mass. 295
McCauley v. Springfield Street Railway, 169 Mass. 301
Lowcock v. Franklin Paper Co., 169 Mass. 313
Lamoureux v. New York, New Haven and Hartford Railroad, 169 Mass. 338
Maloney v. United States Rubber Co., 169 Mass. 347
Perry v. Potashinski, 169 Mass. 351
Thompson v. Norman Paper Co., 169 Mass. 416
French v. Hartford Life and Annuity Insurance Co., 169 Mass. 510
Haynes v. Clinton Printing Co., 169 Mass. 512
Mount Morris Bank v. Gorham, 169 Mass. 519
Roskee v. Mount Tom Sulphite Pulp Co., 169 Mass. 528
Whiting v. Price, 169 Mass. 576
Gallagher v. Hathaway Manufacturing Corporation, 169 Mass. 578
New York Life Ins. Co. v. Macomber, 169 Mass. 580
Iverson v. Swan, 169 Mass. 582
Commonwealth v. Hayes, 170 Mass. 16
Commonwealth v. Kennedy, 170 Mass. 18
Smith v. McEnany, 170 Mass. 26
Commonwealth v. Bond, 170 Mass. 41

1898

Crocker v. Cotting, 170 Mass. 68
Commonwealth v. Mulrey, 170 Mass. 103
Long v. Richards, 170 Mass. 120
Tracy v. Banker, 170 Mass. 266

[345]

Archambeau v. New York and New England Railroad, 170 Mass. 272
Winship v. New York, New Haven and Hartford Railroad, 170 Mass. 464
O'Malley v. Twenty-Five Associates, 170 Mass. 471, 478
Gray v. Standard Life and Accident Insurance Co., 170 Mass. 558
Stewart v. Thayer, 170 Mass. 560
Hopkins v. Reading, 170 Mass. 568
Lorenzo v. Wirth, 170 Mass. 596
Saunders v. Russell, 171 Mass. 74
Hamlen v. Keith, 171 Mass. 77
White v. Massachusetts Institute of Technology, 171 Mass. 84
Callamore v. Learned, 171 Mass. 99
Lockwood v. Roberts, 171 Mass. 109
Raphael v. Mullen, 171 Mass. 111
Bertha Mineral Co. v. Morrill, 171 Mass. 167
McIntire v. White, 171 Mass. 170
Sercombe-Bolte Mfg. Co. v. Lovell Arms Co., 171 Mass. 175
Smith v. Abington Savings Bank, 171 Mass. 178
Fleming v. Elston, 171 Mass. 187
Lewin v. Folsom, 171 Mass. 188
Judge v. Pfaff, 171 Mass. 195
Hamer v. Eldridge, 171 Mass. 250
Drury v. Moors, 171 Mass. 252
Quinn v. Crimmings, 171 Mass. 255
Allin v. Whittemore, 171 Mass. 259
Healey v. Lothrop, 171 Mass. 263
Spaulding v. Forbes Lithograph Manufacturing Co., 171 Mass. 271
Harris v. Hayes, 171 Mass. 275
Paine v. Silva, 171 Mass. 276
Thayer v. Badger, 171 Mass. 279
Lessard v. Revere, 171 Mass. 294
Sheehan v. Boston, 171 Mass. 296
Sewell v. New York, New Haven, and Hartford Railroad, 171 Mass. 302
Houghton v. Milford Pink Granite Co., 171 Mass. 354
Smith and Dove Manufacturing Co. v. Travelers Ins. Co., 171 Mass. 357
Lennox v. Murphy, 171 Mass. 370
Silsbee v. Webber, 171 Mass. 378
Loring v. Massachusetts Horticultural Society, 171 Mass. 401
Commonwealth v. Williams, 171 Mass. 461
Harris v. Quincy, 171 Mass. 472
Winslow v. Everett National Bank, 171 Mass. 534
Fox v. Rogers, 171 Mass. 546
May v. Wood, 172 Mass. 11, 14
Collins v. Greenfield, 172 Mass. 78
Beston v. Amadon, 172 Mass. 84
Pomeroy v. Boston and Maine Railroad, 172 Mass. 92
Morrissey v. Geisel, 172 Mass. 95
Hogg v. American Credit Indemnity Co., 172 Mass. 127

Ellsbury v. New York, New Haven and Hartford Railroad, 172 Mass. 130
Avery v. Monroe, 172 Mass. 132
Bergner and Engel Brewing Co. v. Arthur Dreyfus, 172 Mass. 154
Commonwealth v. Cleary, 172 Mass. 175
Mack v. New York, New Haven and Hartford Railroad, 172 Mass. 185
Brayden v. New York, New Haven and Hartford Railroad, 172 Mass. 225
Smith v. American Linen Co., 172 Mass. 227
Gallagher v. Hathaway Manufacturing Corporation, 172 Mass. 230
Whiting v. Price, 172 Mass. 240
Commonwealth v. O'Brien, 172 Mass. 248

1899

Vandercook v. O'Connor, 172 Mass. 301
Harrison v. Dolan, 172 Mass. 395
Johnson v. Kimball, 172 Mass. 398
Tilton v. Wenham, 172 Mass. 407
Hardiman v. Wholley, 172 Mass. 411
Honsucle v. Ruffin, 172 Mass. 420
Thomson v. Way, 172 Mass. 423
Commonwealth v. Lennon, 172 Mass. 434
Johnston v. Faxon, 172 Mass. 466
Spade v. Lynn and Boston Railroad, 172 Mass. 488
King v. Daly, 172 Mass. 492
Gates v. Johnston Lumber Co. 172 Mass. 495
Jewett v. Turner, 172 Mass. 496
Grafton National Bank v. Wing, 172 Mass. 513
Daley v. People's Building, Loan and Savings Association, 172 Mass. 533
Ford v. Mount Tom Sulphite Pulp Co., 172 Mass. 544
Edgar v. Breck and Sons Corporation, 172 Mass. 581
Orr v. Fuller, 172 Mass. 597
Globe Fire Ins. Co. v. Lexington, 173 Mass. 6
Betz v. McMorrow, 173 Mass. 8
Mugford v. Boston, 173 Mass. 10
Hall v. First National Bank, 173 Mass. 16
Lansky v. West End Street Railway, 173 Mass. 20
Allard v. Hildreth, 173 Mass. 26
Gannon v. New York, New Haven, and Hartford Railroad, 173 Mass. 40
Greve v. Wood-Harmon Company, 173 Mass. 45
Folsom v. County Commissioners, 173 Mass. 48
Dixon v. Williamson, 173 Mass. 50
Farrar v. Paine, 173 Mass. 58
Wineburgh v. United States Steam and Street Railway, 173 Mass. 60
Wilcox v. Forbes, 173 Mass. 63
Spaulding v. Jennings, 173 Mass. 65
Crocker v. Cotting, 173 Mass. 68
Weston v. Amesbury, 173 Mass. 81

Violette v. Rice, 173 Mass. 82
American Waltham Watch Co. v. United States Watch Co., 173 Mass. 85
Smith v. Howard, 173 Mass. 88
McCooe v. Dighton, Somerset, and Swansea Street Railway Co., 173 Mass. 117
Hilton v. McDonald, 173 Mass. 124
Osgood Co. v. Way, 173 Mass. 135
Stoughton v. Paul, 173 Mass. 148
Kimball v. Commonwealth Avenue Railway, 173 Mass. 152
Ward v. Venner, 173 Mass. 210
Henderson v. Boynton, 173 Mass. 217
Amherst College v. Amherst, 173 Mass. 232
Robinson v. Robinson, 173 Mass. 233
Archambeau v. Platt, 173 Mass. 249
Adams v. Batchelder, 173 Mass. 258
Brewster v. Seeger, 173 Mass. 281
Clemens Electrical Manufacturing Co. v. Walton, 173 Mass. 286, 297
Hilliard v. Weeks, 173 Mass. 304
Cusick v. Whitcomb, 173 Mass. 330
Richards v. O'Brien, 173 Mass. 332
Moore v. New York, New Haven, and Hartford Railroad, 173 Mass. 335
Williams Manufacturing Co. v. Standard Brass Co., 173 Mass. 356
Leary v Fitchburg Railroad, 173 Mass. 373
Moody v. Shaw, 173 Mass. 375
Parker v. Merrill, 173 Mass. 391
Appleton v. O'Donnell, 173 Mass. 398
Copithorne v. Hardy, 173 Mass. 400
Palmer v. Gordon, 173 Mass. 410
Derick v. Taylor, 173 Mass. 412
Coghlan v. Dana, 173 Mass. 421
Quigley v. Clough, 173 Mass. 429
Equitable Marine Insurance Co. v. Adams, 173 Mass. 436
Wood's Sons Company v. Schaefer, 173 Mass. 443
Parkinson v. West End Street Railway, 173 Mass. 446
Pead v. Trull, 173 Mass. 450
Dean v. Justices of the Municipal Court, 173 Mass. 453
Brennan v. McInnis, 173 Mass. 471
Parkman v. Bartlett, 173 Mass. 475
Lewis v. Shattuck, 173 Mass. 486
Harrington v. Baker, 173 Mass. 488
Bent v. Emery, 173 Mass. 495
Brown's Case, 173 Mass. 498
Cassidy v. Commonwealth, 173 Mass. 533
McCarvell v. Sawyer, 173 Mass. 540
Way v. Dennie, 174 Mass. 43
Boston Elevated Railway v. Presho, 174 Mass. 99
Fort Payne Rolling Mill v. Hill, 174 Mass. 224

Commonwealth v. Chance, 174 Mass. 245
Aslanian v. Dostumian, 174 Mass. 328
Harnois v. Cutting, 174 Mass. 398
Osborn v. Osborn, 174 Mass. 399
Viscardi v. Great Barrington, 174 Mass. 406
Brunham v. Upton, 174 Mass. 408
Holyoke v. Hadley Co., 174 Mass. 424
Hennebry v. Maynard, 174 Mass. 428
Robinska v. Lyman Mills, 174 Mass. 432
Clarke v. Warwick Cycle Manufacturing Co., 174 Mass. 434
Fitzpatrick v. Welch, 174 Mass. 486
Elastic Tip Co. v. Graham, 174 Mass. 507
Janvrin, Petitioner, 174 Mass. 514
Jager v. Vollinger, 174 Mass. 521
Hunnewell v. Haskell, 174 Mass. 557
Smith v. Postal Telegraph Cable Co., 174 Mass. 576
Trager v. Webster, 174 Mass. 580
Hill v. Pike, 174 Mass. 582
May v. Gloucester, 174 Mass. 583
Fitch v. Jefferson, 175 Mass. 56

1900

Welsh, Petitioner, 175 Mass. 68
Tyler v. Court of Registration, 175 Mass. 71
Brightman v. Bates, 175 Mass. 105
Bradley v. Hooker, 175 Mass. 142
Drysdale v. Wax, 175 Mass. 144
Quinn v. New York, New Haven, and Hartford Railroad, 175 Mass. 150
Commonwealth v. Nutting, 175 Mass. 154
Attorney General v. Oliver, 175 Mass. 163
Lowner v. New York, New Haven, and Hartford Railroad, 175 Mass. 166
Muto v. Smith, 175 Mass. 175
Gordon v. West End Street Railway, 175 Mass. 181
Campbell v. Dearborn, 175 Mass. 183
Wetherbee v. Partridge, 175 Mass. 185
Goodhue v. Hartford Fire Insurance Co., 175 Mass. 187
Forbes v. Douglass, 175 Mass. 191
Orne v. Barstrow, 175 Mass. 193
Attorney General v. Accident Insurance Association, 175 Mass. 196
Bennett v. Kimball, 175 Mass. 199
Callahan v. Boston, 175 Mass. 201
Freeman v. Boston, 175 Mass. 208
Gibbons v. British and North Atlantic Steam Navigation Co., 175 Mass. 212
Carson v. Brockton, 175 Mass. 242
National Bank of Commerce v. New Bedford, 175 Mass. 257
Aldrich v. Blatchford, 175 Mass. 369

American Mining Co. v. Converse, 175 Mass. 449
French v. Goodnow, 175 Mass. 451
Pratt v. Bidwell, 175 Mass. 453
Weston v. Barnicoat, 175 Mass. 454
Commonwealth v. Corkery, 175 Mass. 460
Glynn v. Central Railroad, 175 Mass. 510
Daniels v. Commonwealth Avenue Street Railway, 175 Mass. 518
Holt v. Roberts, 175 Mass. 558
Guerin v. Stacy, 175 Mass. 595
Opinion of the Justices, 175 Mass. 599
Rotch v. French, 176 Mass. 1
Browne v. Turner, 176 Mass. 9
Chick v. Nute, 176 Mass. 57
Andrews v. Andrews, 176 Mass. 92
Goodyear Shoe Machinery Co. v. Boston Terminal Co., 176 Mass. 115
National Construction Co. v. Travelers' Insurance Co., 176 Mass. 121
McCarty v. Nugent, 176 Mass. 124
Chisholm v. New England Telephone and Telegraph Co., 176 Mass. 125
Commonwealth v. Rozen, 176 Mass. 129
Commonwealth v. Mullen, 176 Mass. 132
Prouty v. Union Hardware Co., 176 Mass. 155
Bruce v. Anderson, 176 Mass. 161
Dudley v. Milton, 176 Mass. 167
Pearl v. West End Street Railway, 176 Mass. 177
Munroe v. Dewey, 176 Mass. 184
Hooper v. Shaw, 176 Mass. 190
Munroe v. Carlisle, 176 Mass. 199
Lincoln v. Street Commissioners, 176 Mass. 210
Marshall v. Mason, 176 Mass. 216
Brigham, Petitioner, 176 Mass. 223
McLean v. Wiley, 176 Mass. 233
Parke v. Mabee, 176 Mass. 236
Mulhall v. Fallon, 176 Mass. 266
Fay v. Harrington, 176 Mass. 270
Wentworth v. French, 176 Mass. 442
Weeks v. Edwards, 176 Mass. 453
Reed v. Deerfield, 176 Mass. 473
Plant v. Woods, 176 Mass. 492, 504
O'Brien v. Goodrich, 177 Mass. 32
Field v. Banks, 177 Mass. 36
Belding Brothers and Co. v. Northampton, 177 Mass. 39
Very v. Clarke, 177 Mass. 52
Ludlow Manufacturing Co. v. Indian Orchard Co., 177 Mass. 61
Commonwealth v. Ryberg, 177 Mass. 67
Garst v. Harris, 177 Mass. 72
Spillane v. Fitchburg, 177 Mass. 87
Kelley v. Calumet Woolen Co., 177 Mass. 128

Bond v. O'Gara, 177 Mass. 139
Lamson v. American Axe and Tool Co., 177 Mass. 144
Stack v. New York, New Haven, and Hartford Railroad, 177 Mass. 155
Riley v. Harris, 177 Mass. 163
Joseph v. George C. Whitney Co., 177 Mass. 176
Butler v. New York, New Haven and Hartford Railroad, 177 Mass. 191
Taber v. New Bedford, 177 Mass. 197
Nesbett v. Wilbur, 177 Mass. 200
Adams v. Pierce, 177 Mass. 206

1901

Golden Cross v. Stewart, 177 Mass. 235
Clarke v. Second National Bank of Springfield, 177 Mass. 257
Commonwealth v. Peaslee, 177 Mass. 267
Munroe v. Weir, 177 Mass. 301
Pearson v. Bailey, 177 Mass. 318
Graham v. Stanton, 177 Mass. 321
Bacon v. Hooker, 177 Mass. 335
Commonwealth v. Storti, 177 Mass. 339
Commonwealth v. Bow, 177 Mass. 347
Lincoln v. Burrage, 177 Mass. 378
Dedham National Bank v. Everett National Bank, 177 Mass. 392
Hall v. Rosenfeld, 177 Mass. 397
Miner Lithograph Co. v. Wagner, 177 Mass. 404
Cummings v. Perry, 177 Mass. 407
Hall v. Street Commissioners, 177 Mass. 434
Parke v. Murdock, 177 Mass. 453
Emmons v. Alvord, 177 Mass. 466
Moran v. Dunphy, 177 Mass. 485
O'Connell v. Mathews, 177 Mass. 518
Carpenter v. Fleming, 177 Mass. 525
Paul v. Costello, 177 Mass. 580
Daley v. People's Building, Loan and Savings Association, 178 Mass. 13
Corrigan v. People's Building, Loan, and Savings Association, 178 Mass. 40
Stark v. Mansfield, 178 Mass. 76
Flagg Manufacturing Co. v. Holway, 178 Mass. 83
Hooper v. Bradford, 178 Mass. 95
Hall v. Wakefield and Stoneham Street Railway, 178 Mass. 98
Elastic Tip Co. v. Arnold, Schwinn and Co., 178 Mass. 101
Emerson v. Gerber, 178 Mass. 130
Wheeler v. Klaholt, 178 Mass. 141
Healey v. Lothrop, 178 Mass. 151
Emery v. Boston Terminal Co., 178 Mass. 172
Parker v. Commonwealth, 178 Mass. 199
De Las Casas, Petitioner, 178 Mass. 213
Boston Woven Hose and Rubber Co. v. Kendall, 178 Mass. 232
Hoseason v. Keegen, 178 Mass. 247

Sawyer v. Metropolitan Water Board, 178 Mass. 267
Moors v. Ladenburg, 178 Mass. 272
Hill v. Marston, 178 Mass. 285
Scannell v. Hub Brewing Co., 178 Mass. 288
Cote v. Lawrence Manufacturing Co., 178 Mass. 295
Selectmen of Hadley, Petitioners, 178 Mass. 319
People's Savings Bank v. James, 178 Mass. 322
McNeil v. Boston, 178 Mass. 326
Crandall v. Colley, 178 Mass. 339
Morgan v. Wordell, 178 Mass. 350
Tremont and Suffolk Mills v. Lowell, 178 Mass. 469
Danforth v. Groton Water Co., 178 Mass. 472
Seaman v. Colley, 178 Mass. 478
Haskell v. Cape Ann Anchor Works, 178 Mass. 485
Lorden v. Coffey, 178 Mass. 489
Burt v. Tucker, 178 Mass. 493
Jordan v. Riley, 178 Mass. 524
Storti v. Commonwealth, 178 Mass. 549
O'Malley v. Twenty-Five Associates, 178 Mass. 555
Weatherbee v. New York Life Ins. Co., 178 Mass. 575
Commonwealth v. Sisson, 178 Mass. 578
P. P. Emory Manufacturing Co. v. Salomon, 178 Mass. 582
Opinion of the Justices, 178 Mass. 605
Williams v. Monk, 179 Mass. 22
Brummett v. Boston, 179 Mass. 26
D'Arcy v. Steuer, 179 Mass. 40
Goddard v. Boston and Maine Railroad, 179 Mass. 52
Graves v. Johnson, 179 Mass. 53
Hendrie v. Boston, 179 Mass. 59
Marlborough Association v. Peters, 179 Mass. 61
Boston and Maine Railroad v. Graham, 179 Mass. 62
Keohane, Petitioner, 179 Mass. 69
Amory v. Attorney General, 179 Mass. 89
Barry v. Lancy, 179 Mass. 112
Martin v. Meles, 179 Mass. 114
Haskell v. Merrill, 179 Mass. 120
Obery v. Lander, 179 Mass. 125
Bumpus v. French, 179 Mass. 131
Perry v. Lancy, 179 Mass. 183
Firth v. Rich, 179 Mass. 206
Irving v. Ford, 179 Mass. 216
Giles v. Royal Insurance Co., 179 Mass. 261
Wyman v. Whicher, 179 Mass. 276
Seaver v. Bradley, 179 Mass. 329
Scollans v. Rollins, 179 Mass. 346
Hall v. Grace, 179 Mass. 400
French v. Boston National Bank, 179 Mass. 404

Clark v. Boston, 179 Mass. 409
Sawin v. Cormier, 179 Mass. 420
Taunton Savings Bank v. Burrell, 179 Mass. 421
Newcomb v. Norfolk Western Street Railway, 179 Mass. 449
Commonwealth v. O'Brien, 179 Mass. 533
Kellogg v. Smith, 179 Mass. 595
Olds v. City Trust, Safe Deposit and Surety Co., 180 Mass. 1.
Moore v. Elmer, 180 Mass. 15
Walsh v. Loorem, 180 Mass. 18
Beston v. Amadon, 180 Mass. 23
Walton v. Ruggles, 180 Mass. 24
City National Bank v. Charles Baker Co., 180 Mass. 40
Robbins v. Brockton Street Railway, 180 Mass. 51
Storti's Case, 180 Mass. 57
Kerslake v. Cummings, 180 Mass. 65
Speirs v. Union Drop Forge Co., 180 Mass. 87
Vincent v. Norton and Taunton Street Railway, 180 Mass. 104
Patnoude v. New York, New Haven, and Hartford Railroad, 180 Mass. 119
Carpenter v. Pocasset Manufacturing Co., 180 Mass. 130
McNary v. Blackburn, 180 Mass. 141
Cotter v. Lynn and Boston Railroad, 180 Mass. 145
Murray v. Boston Ice Co., 180 Mass. 165

1902

O'Driscoll v. Lynn and Boston Railroad, 180 Mass. 187
Copeland v. Fifield, 180 Mass. 223
Pearson v. Bailey, 180 Mass. 229
Davis v. Rich, 180 Mass. 235
Cunningham v. Brackett, 180 Mass. 239
Fletcher v. Willis, 180 Mass. 243
Washburn Crosby Co. v. Boston and Albany Railroad, 180 Mass. 252
Sears v. Street Commissioners, 180 Mass. 274
Rutherford v. Paddock, 180 Mass. 289
Commonwealth v. Goldstein, 180 Mass. 374
Johnson v. Mutual Life Insurance Co., 180 Mass. 407
Homans v. Boston Elevated Railway, 180 Mass. 456
Chase v. Boston, 180 Mass. 458
Carson v. Canning, 180 Mass. 461
Russell v. American Bell Telephone Co., 180 Mass. 467
Whipple v. Rich, 180 Mass. 477
Morrissey v. Morrissey, 180 Mass. 480
Huebener v. Childs, 180 Mass. 483
Tirrell v. New York, New Haven, and Hartford Railroad Co., 180 Mass. 490
Commonwealth v. Best, 180 Mass. 492
Goff v. Hathaway, 180 Mass. 497

Train v. Marshall Paper Co., 180 Mass. 513
Heald v. Kennard, 180 Mass. 521
Commonwealth v. Duprey, 180 Mass. 523
Attorney General v. Goodell, 180 Mass. 538
Ferguson v. Jackson, 180 Mass. 557
Quinn v. Fire Association of Philadelphia, 180 Mass. 560
Earle v. Commonwealth, 180 Mass. 579
Bassett v. Harwich, 180 Mass. 585
Galvin v. Boston Elevated Railway, 180 Mass. 587
Woodward v. Central Vermont Railway, 180 Mass. 599
Thompson v. Cashman, 181 Mass. 36
Davis v. Chase, 181 Mass. 39
Brown v. Wentworth, 181 Mass. 49
Green v. Crapo, 181 Mass. 55
Haskell v. Avery, 181 Mass. 106
Brown v. Greene, 181 Mass. 109
Newhall v. American Legion of Honor, 181 Mass. 111
Plaisted v. Cooke, 181 Mass. 118
Tufts v. Waxman, 181 Mass. 120
Whitman v. Boston Elevated Railway, 181 Mass. 138
Commonwealth v. Rogers, 181 Mass. 184
Dickinson v. Brookline, 181 Mass. 195
National Machine Co. v. Standard Shoe Machinery Co., 181 Mass. 275
Gilchrist v. Cowley, 181 Mass. 290
Hayes v. Tidsbury, 181 Mass. 292
Forbes v. Appleyard, 181 Mass. 354
Norton v. Brookline, 181 Mass. 360
McGrath v. Watertown, 181 Mass. 380
Dunbar v. Boston and Providence Railroad Corporation, 181 Mass. 383
Driscoll v. Towle, 181 Mass. 416
Stoddard v. New York, New Haven, and Hartford Railroad, 181 Mass. 422
Meaney v. Kehoe, 181 Mass. 424
Dixon v. Amerman, 181 Mass. 430
Ward v. Newton, 181 Mass. 432
Lyman v. National Bank of the Republic, 181 Mass. 437
Stone v. Commonwealth, 181 Mass. 438
Leonard v. Leonard, 181 Mass. 458
Philadelphia and Reading Coal and Iron Co. v. Butler, 181 Mass. 468
Spencer v. Spencer, 181 Mass. 471
Barrett v. King, 181 Mass. 476
Roche v. Lowell Bleachery, 181 Mass. 480
French v. McKay, 181 Mass. 485
Priesing v. Crampton, 181 Mass. 492
Attorney General v. Vineyard Grove Co., 181 Mass. 507
Stratton v. Lowell, 181 Mass. 511
Attorney General v. Netherlands Fire Insurance Co., 181 Mass. 522

Nichols v. Rosenfield, 181 Mass. 525
Commonwealth v. Best, 181 Mass. 545
Hume v. Walker, 181 Mass. 546
Cambridge v. Trelegan, 181 Mass. 565
Nickerson, Appellant, 181 Mass. 571
Gould v. Gilligan, 181 Mass. 600
Gallagher v. Silberstein, 182 Mass. 20
Commonwealth v. Regan, 182 Mass. 22
Jackson v. Brockton, 182 Mass. 26
Plymouth Stove Foundry Co. v. Fee, 182 Mass. 31
Whitman v. Taylor, 182 Mass. 37
Oliver v. Gale, 182 Mass. 39
Curtis v. Curtis, 182 Mass. 104
Taft v. Decker, 182 Mass. 106
Cleveland v. Hampden Savings Bank, 182 Mass. 110
Tobin v. Brimfield, 182 Mass. 117
Squires v. Wason Manufacturing Co., 182 Mass. 137
Endicott v. University of Virginia, 182 Mass. 156
Holyoke Envelope Co. v. United States Envelope Co., 182 Mass. 171
Rogers v. Dutton, 182 Mass. 187
White v. Mott, 182 Mass. 195
O'Malley v. Commonwealth, 182 Mass. 196
Kane v. Worcester Consolidated Street Railway, 182 Mass. 201
Bartlett v. Slater, 182 Mass. 208
Guild v. Walter, 182 Mass. 225
Smith v. Mayor and Aldermen of Worcester, 182 Mass. 232
Sawyer v. Commonwealth, 182 Mass. 245
McCabe v. Maguire, 182 Mass. 255
Lemay v. Furtado, 182 Mass. 280
Cote v. New York, New Haven, and Hartford Railroad, 182 Mass. 290
Goff v. Britton, 182 Mass. 293
Brown v. Kellogg, 182 Mass. 297
Moore v. Mansfield, 182 Mass. 302
Cameron v. New England Telephone and Telegraph Co., 182 Mass. 310
Nason v. Tobey, 182 Mass. 314
Williams v. Clarke, 182 Mass. 316
Knowles v. Sullivan, 182 Mass. 318
Keith v. Marcus, 182 Mass. 320
Thompson v. Brady, 182 Mass. 321
Tileston v. Street Commissioners, 182 Mass. 325
Hardy v. American Express Co., 182 Mass. 328
Weatherbee v. New York Life Insurance Co., 182 Mass. 342
McKenna v. Eaton, 182 Mass. 346
Larabee v. New York, New Haven, and Hartford Railroad, 182 Mass. 348

INDEX TO CASES*

	PAGE
Abbott v. New York and New England Railroad	299
Adams v. Adams	140
Adams v. Batchelder	124
Aldrich v. Blatchford	254
American Waltham Watch Co. v. United States Watch Co.	315
Andrews v. Andrews	150
Attorney General v. Ayer	303
Attorney General v. Equitable Accident Insurance Ass'n	290
Attorney General v. Walworth Light Co.	308
Ayer v. Philadelphia and Boston Face Brick Co.	288
Barry v. Lancy	222
Beard v. Boston	287
Bent v. Emery	265
Bergner & Engel Brewing Co. v. Dreyfus	120
Blackinton v. Blackinton	159
Boston and Maine Railroad v. Graham	291
Boston and Maine Railroad v. Trafton	169
Boston Ferrule Co. v. Hills	309
Bourke v. Callanan	309
Braithwaite v. Hall	288
Brigham, Petitioner	316
Brigham v. Fayerweather	296
Brown v. Turner	28
Brown's Case	85
Bumpus v. French	103
Burt v. Advertising Newspaper Co.	306
Burns v. Lane	295
Butler v. New York, New Haven, and Hartford Railroad	318
Callahan v. Boston	195
Carpenter v. Walker	285
Carson v. Brockton	196
Chadwick v. Covell	305
Chase v. Henry	117
City National Bank v. Charles Baker Co.	291
Clemens Electrical Manufacturing Co. v. Walton	315
Commonwealth v. Brown	190
Commonwealth v. Davis	54
Commonwealth v. Ellis	184

* Complete opinions found in Part 1 are indicated in italics.

[357]

	PAGE
Commonwealth v. Freelove	81
Commonwealth v. Keenan	301
Commonwealth v. Kennedy	312
Commonwealth v. McParland	285
Commonwealth v. Nutting	19
Commonwealth v. Parks	181
Commonwealth v. Perry	59
Commonwealth v. Pierce	295
Commonwealth v. Sisson	220
Commonwealth v. Smith	186
Commonwealth v. Storti	89
Commonwealth v. Sullivan	300
Coughlin v. Boston Tow-Boat Co.	286
Cowley v. Pulsifer	294
Crocker v. Cotting	83
Crocker v. Cotting	289
Danforth v. Groton Water Co.	39
Davis v. Chase	292
Dempsey v. Chambers	306
Dickinson v. Brookline	320
Donaghy v. Macy	128
Doyle v. Boston and Albany Railroad	299
Dunbar v. Boston and Providence Railroad	44
Earle v. Commonwealth	274
Easthampton v. County Commissioners	307
Emery v. Burbank	310
Emmonds v. Alvord	291
Fay v. Harrington	291
Goode v. Riley	287
Graham v. Badger	311
Graves v. Johnson	307
Greenfield v. Buckland	288
Guild v. Walter	292
Hall v. Street Commissioners	212
Hamilton v. West End Street Railway	309
Hanson v. Globe Newspaper Co.	288
Hardiman v. Wholley	314
Hawkins v. Graham	305
Haynes v. Clinton Printing Co.	289
Heard v. Sturgis	300
Hooper v. Bradford	318
Hubbard v. Taunton	297
Janvrin, petitioner	10
Kent v. Todd	298
Kerslake v. Cummings	318
LaPlante v. Warren Cotton Mills	288

	PAGE
Leighton v. Morrill	309
Lincoln v. Boston	302
Lincoln v. Commonwealth	288
Lincoln v. Street Commissioners	200
Lorden v. Coffey	217
Lorenzo v. Wirth	289
McAuliffe v. New Bedford	51
McCauley v. Springfield Street Railway	289
McNary v. Blackburn	319
May v. Wood	70
Merrill v. Preston	292
Middlesex Co. v. McCue	304
Miller v. Horton	171
Moran v. Dunphy	76
Mulhall v. Fallon	207
Murphy v. Manning	109
Nash v. Minnesota Title Insurance and Trust Co.	311
National Bank of Commerce v. New Bedford	315
New England Trust Co. v. Eaton	297
Newton v. Perry	310
O'Donnell v. Clinton	299
Opinion of the Justices	5
Opinion of the Justices	6
Opinion of the Justices	23
Opinion of the Justices	33
Palmer v. Gordon	290
Parker v. Commonwealth	269
Patnoude v. New York, New Haven, and Hartford Railroad	319
Perkins v. Lawrence	296
Phoenix National Bank v. Batcheller	112
Pinney v. Hall	307
Plant v. Woods	73
Powers v. Boston	287
Quinn v. Crimmings	313
Reardon v. Thompson	286
Reeve v. Dennett	299
E. Remington and Sons v. Samana Bay Co.	297
Richards v. Barlow	133
Richardson v. Boston	301
Rideout v. Knox	162
Robinson v. Bird	308
Rodliff v. Dallinger	298
Rosenberg v. Doe	300
Rotch v. French	316
Ryalls v. Mechanics' Mills	286
Sawyer v. Boston	285

	PAGE
Sawyer v. Commonwealth	278
Seaman v. Colley	291
Sears v. Street Commissioners	224
Sewall and Co. v. Boston Water Power Co.	285
Smith v. American Linen Co.	313
Smith v. Dickinson	285
Smith v. Mayor and Alderman of Worcester	234
Smith v. Morse	167
Spade v. Lynn and Boston Railroad	290
Stack v. New York, New Haven, and Hartford Railroad	317
Staigg v. Atkinson	298
Stanwood v. Malden	308
Stone v. Wainwright	136
Storti v. Commonwealth	95
Storti's Case	99
Taft v. Commonwealth	288
Tasker v. Stanley	287
Tyler v. Court of Registration	241
Vanuxem v. Burr	305
Vegelahn v. Gunter and others	62
Violette v. Rice	314
Weston v. Barnicoat	290
White v. Duggan	285
Windram v. French	286
Woodward v. Central Vermont Railway	258